BI 3138426 9

KU-545-492

culture 63

39
35

168-70

PRINCIPLES OF SCHOOL LEADERSHIP

PRINCIPLES OF
SCHOOL LEADERSHIP

Edited by Mark Brundrett

Peter Francis Publishers

Peter Francis Publishers
The Old School House
Little Fransham
Dereham
Norfolk NR19 2JP
UK

© Mark Brundrett 1999

A CIP catalogue record for this book
is available from the British Library

ISBN 1-870167-33-3

UNIVERSITY OF
CENTRAL ENGLAND

Book no. 31384269

Subject no. 371.2 | Bru

INFORMATION SERVICES

Printed and bound in Great Britain by Biddles Ltd,
Guildford and King's Lynn.

Contents

Foreword   vii
by *Anthea Millett*

Introduction   xi

1. Education Management Training and Development: 1
    lessons from the past
    Mark Brundrett

2. School Effectiveness and Improvement   17
    Dianne Duncan

3. Strategic Leadership and Management in Schools   42
    Dominic Elliott

4. Managing Teaching and Learning   71
    Peter Silcock

5. Leading and Managing Staff   96
    Ian and Kath Terrell

6. The Efficient and Effective Deployment of Staff   122
    and Resources
    Neil Burton

7. Accountability   138
    Jan Wilson

8. Leadership   153
    Rob Bollington

    Contributors   184

    References   187

    Index   202

Foreword

All commentators seem to agree that the key to unlocking the full potential of pupils in our schools lies in the expertise of teachers and head-teachers. Equally, research and inspection evidence demonstrate the close correlation between the quality of teaching and the achievement of pupils and between the quality of leadership and the quality of teaching. It is these links which lie at the heart of the British Government's drive for school improvement. This was exemplified in the Green Paper *Teachers: Meeting the Challenge of Change,* (DfEE, 1998c) in the foreword to which the Prime Minister rightly stated that 'excellence should be seen as the norm' in our educational system.

The Green Paper also pointed out that 'all the evidence shows that heads are the key to a school's success'. In highly effective schools, as well as schools which have reversed the trend of poor performance and declining achievement, it is the headteacher who sets the pace, leading and motivating pupils and staff to perform to their highest potential. For these reasons the role of school leader is one that ought to be widely prized and aspired to and this has been one of the Government's key messages in striving to create a coherent, unique and world-class training strategy for headship.

It is a sad fact that, until recently, there was little being done at the national level to support headship training and development. With the honourable exception of the professional associations, little or nothing was being done to promote headship as a rewarding, if challenging, job and headteachers themselves traditionally put their needs last when in-service resources had to be shared out. It is small wonder HMI have been reporting for years that, while there have been improvements in leadership, headteachers still need to develop in core areas like communication, implementing a strategic vision for the school, and monitoring and evaluating the quality of teaching in the school.

That is why I am proud that, in association with LEAs, HEIs and others, the TTA has done so much to promote headship as a role to be prized, and as one for which people can be prepared through practical and professional training and development. Above all, we have advanced the idea of headship as a profession in its own right, especially to young graduates, trainee teachers and serving teachers. Seeing headship as a profession helps to establish the need for high quality training, flexible induction, and effective continuing professional development. Those three strands are the basis for the Government's national three-fold strategy for the training and development of headteachers. Each of the three strands is underpinned by the *National Standards for Headteachers*, which have been developed with the help of headteachers and many others, both inside and outside education. The National Professional Qualification for Headship (NPQH) provides high quality initial preparation for headship; the Headteachers' Leadership and Management Programme (HEADLAMP) enables flexible training during the induction phase of headship; whilst the Leadership Programme for Serving Headteachers (LPSH) is a leading-edge programme from which all experienced headteachers stand to gain a great deal. All of these programmes build on the considerable work already done in this area in schools, LEAs, higher education institutions, OFSTED, and, in Wales, OHMCI, and other agencies.

Throughout this work, there has been a keen attempt to close the gap between research and practice. The underpinning rationale for the Government's headship programmes owes much to the work of a generation of researchers who have told us a great deal about school effectiveness and improvement strategies. Much of this research has also begun to inform the content of the higher degree programmes offered by higher education institutions. For this reason the NPQH allows candidates to take account of their previous learning and experience, including work on recent and relevant higher degree programmes. It is also good to see that a number of higher education institutions are allowing reciprocal remission from the requirements of their courses for those who complete the NPQH.

Such partnerships, which encompass central government agencies, LEAs and higher education institutions, working within a framework established by a government highly committed to the modernisation of the education system, are vital if we are to provide the quality of leadership that our schools need and deserve. The aim must be to have school leaders who are not afraid to think ahead to future trends in teaching, training and school leadership. That is why the headship programmes have sought to juxtapose the best leadership and management practice from outside education with that from inside our schools in order to benefit pupils, teachers and society at large.

For too long the quality of headship training has been patchy and incoherent. The three Government headship programmes, developed in partnership with all those interested in the quality of our education system, are ensuring that we have world-class school leaders to guide schools in the key task of preparing our children for an exciting and challenging future in the Britain of the new millennium.

Anthea Millett,
Chief Executive, the Teacher Training Agency.

Introduction

Mark Brundrett

When, in 1995, it was announced that a new qualification for headship was to be developed under the aegis of the Teacher Training Agency (TTA), a stir was created throughout higher education institutions in England and Wales. Over a number of years a significant percentage of universities and colleges have been developing higher degree programmes designed to accommodate the management development needs of senior managers in schools. These degree programmes have sought to address the increasing demands on headteachers and others in senior roles in schools and have a strong basis in the growing research on school effectiveness and improvement which profoundly affected attitudes to the ways in which schools are managed.

It should be remembered, however, that the National Professional Qualification for Headship (NPQH) and its sister programmes the Headteachers' Leadership and Management Programme (HEADLAMP) and the Leadership Programme for Serving Headteachers (LPSH) are not wholly without antecedents. There has been a long involvement by government, both local and national, in supplying much-needed training to aspiring and serving headteachers and other senior staff in schools. Many headteachers and former headteachers, including this writer, are extremely grateful for the local education authority (LEA) courses which supported them in the early days of their management of a school. It is equally true that one may still hear colleagues speak very highly of the One Term Training Opportunities (OTTOs) which came into existence in the 1980s. What was new about the TTA initiatives was that, for the first time, a coherent 'ladder' of programmes of study and qualifications was set in place to support staff as they progressed through their careers.

We are thus living through an era when we are witnessing the emergence of two parallel sets of qualifications and courses. One set of such qualifications is provided by higher education institutions which offer long cherished awards such as MA, MEd, MSc and, more recently, MBA and even Doctor of Education; these courses seek to provide an *academic* grounding in the theoretical perspectives on education. The other group of qualifications is that same 'ladder' of programmes which has been provided under the aegis of the TTA (soon to be transferred to the National College for School Leadership), at least one of which (the NPQH) is likely to become a mandatory requirement for those seeking headship; these courses rightly pride themselves on their relevance to practical situations and to very real challenges and opportunities which school leaders may face.

It would be wrong however, to believe that these two sets of qualifications and courses are in some way *mutually exclusive* or at the opposite ends of some well defined polarities. Providers of higher degrees have worked hard in recent years in order to ensure that their courses are practical and relevant. Equally, TTA courses have been grounded in appropriate and relevant theoretical perspectives such as those which are steadily emerging from the school effectiveness and improvement networks. Moreover, on the very practical level, candidates for programmes such as the NPQH can, at the discretion of the relevant NPQH assessment centres, gain remission from the requirements of the qualification based on work which they have undertaken for higher degrees. Meanwhile several institutions of higher education have designed courses which specifically articulate with TTA qualifications, thus allowing reciprocal remission from their course requirements for those who complete the Agency's programmes. Those institutions which have not already redesigned courses in this way frequently offer Accreditation of Prior Learning which will, nonetheless, allow the possibility of using evidence of completion of TTA programmes to move through higher degrees more swiftly.

It is thus the central contention of this book that these two traditions should be viewed as *complementary* methods of gaining greater insight into the management of our schools. The authors are, therefore, drawn both from higher education and TTA training programme staff. Contributions are made both by university lecturers, and NPQH and LPSH trainers; a number of those contributing have also had extensive experience as headteachers, senior managers and school governors.

The first chapter offers an outline of the development of school management training and development up to and including the advent of the TTA-inspired leadership programmes. In the second chapter Dianne Duncan draws on both her extensive experience as a headteacher and upon her years as a lecturer in higher education to provide an overview of the now substantial literature on school effectiveness and improvement which has, as noted above, come to be so important in our attitudes to managing schools. The succeeding five chapters self-consciously concentrate on the 'key areas of headship' as defined by the *National Standards for Headteachers* developed by the TTA. Dominic Elliot brings his many years of work as a management consultant and lecturer in management to the issues of strategic leadership; Peter Silcock unpacks some of the complex background literature on teaching and learning; Ian and Kath Terrell, respectively a university lecturer and a serving headteacher, offer a discussion of the issues in leading and managing staff; Neil Burton discusses some of the highly technical aspects of the efficient and effective deployment of staff and resources; Jan Wilson, a highly experienced headteacher, lecturer and NPQH trainer, offers guidance on the vital topic of accountability. In the final chapter, Rob Bollington, who is a Centre Manager for NPQH Training and Development, returns to the topic of leadership which, although not a separate area in the national standards, is a subject which underpins almost all of the TTA management programmes.

These are exciting and challenging times in our schools. All the evidence suggests that good leadership and management offers one the central keys to enhancing the effectiveness of our work in order to offer increased opportunities for the pupils and students in our care. It is, therefore, vital that school leaders are provided with the best opportunities to enhance their knowledge and skills. This book applauds and supports both traditions in the development of management abilities and hopes to offer a resource to all of those interested in school leadership whether they be seeking higher degrees, national qualifications, or simply wish to find out more about a developing field of knowledge.

1. Education Management Training and Development: lessons from the past

Mark Brundrett

Introduction

Over the period of a generation a series of studies has emphasised the central role of the headteacher in enhancing school effectiveness. The work of Rutter *et al*. (1979), Mortimore *et al*. (1988) and Hopkins *et al*. (1994) all stand as testimony to major empirical studies which discovered and declaimed that the headteacher, as senior manager in the school, plays a pivotal role in the success or failure of educational institutions.

This chapter attempts to outline the development of school leadership and management training, beginning with the OTTOs of the 1980s, through the modern competence movement, and on to the more recent programmes of management training development under the aegis of the TTA as exemplified in the HEADLAMP, NPQH and LPSH initiatives. It is the central contention of this chapter that valuable lessons have been learned from the OTTO programme and the experience of the competence movement, and that the TTA initiatives have provided the basis for a coherent ladder of professional development.

One term training opportunities (OTTOs)

As early as 1967 the Plowden Report indicated the vital importance of high quality training for school leaders. Subsequently a number of studies testified to the complexity of the headteacher's role (see, for instance, Lyons, 1976; Nias, 1980; Lloyd, 1981; Gray, 1982). It is therefore not surprising that calls began to be made in the early 1980s for a more systematic form of management training for school leaders; indeed as early as 1982, Wood called for a 'training college' for headteachers.

In response to this mounting evidence Circular 3/83 (DES, 1983) produced by the DFE, promulgated by Sir Keith Joseph as Secretary of State for Education, proposed that extra grants should be made available for management training in schools. Such funding was to be used to establish a number of one term training opportunities (commonly referred to as OTTOs) which were to be targeted at headteachers and senior staff so that they would be better equipped for 'the increasingly difficult and complicated tasks of management'. Such courses included 'visits to schools and other institutions, seminars, private study and encounters with managers from other fields of education, commerce and industry'. Within six months of the DES initiative the National Development Centre (NDC) for school management training was established in Bristol. The original aim of the NDC was to improve the provision and effectiveness of management training for headteachers and senior staff in schools throughout England and Wales and to equip them with 'the practical skills, knowledge and attitudes needed to enable them to manage and develop their schools as effective institutions for pupils' learning' (Poster and Day, 1988). Later that brief was changed to one of promoting management development as well as training, since the NDC steering committee felt that training should not be isolated but form part of an overall LEA policy for the management development of the headteachers and senior members of staff. Since such policies frequently were not in existence then, the NDC acted as a clearing house for information, evaluation and provision of management development policies, courses and training for LEAs and training institutions throughout the country (Lund, 1990: 30).

The impact of such courses was summarised by Wallace (1988a) who noted that, during three initial years of OTTO and twenty day management courses, two thirds of participants came from the primary sector, that a total of 2,565 primary candidates were trained, and that this meant about one primary school in seven had been directly influenced. Wallace's survey also noted, however, that the initiative had only reached 4.5 per cent of those initially targeted and it was expected that 0.5 per cent of these would swiftly retire, therefore 96 per cent of those eligible did not receive training. The initiative had provided a significant response to the increased need for management training, but had not, largely through bad management (especially by LEAs), made the impact or been as effective as had initially been hoped (Lund, 1990: 30).

Hellawell (1988) interviewed the first group of six graduates, four of whom worked in primary schools, to see how they perceived the course had changed their managerial attitudes, behaviour and practice in school in the two years since the completion of the course. Hellawell's results showed the OTTO experience was perceived to be valuable by the head-teachers and their deputies or senior members of staff and was believed to have had a significant effect on management which had led to an improvement in relationships within the school. It was felt that OTTO courses provided the perfect opportunity for reflection on changes in management practice, something which was difficult to achieve later on shorter courses.

Criticisms of the OTTO scheme

Circular 3/83 was not, however, welcomed with the same enthusiasm by everyone. In fact it led to the publication of *Education plc* (Maw, 1984), the contributors to which made vigorous attacks on some of the proposals outlined in the circular. The main opposition was to the proposal that course members should meet with managers from commerce and industry to study their management practices and policies, since some of the authors felt it was wrong to equate education management with that of industrial or commercial management. A typical point of view, which summarised the theme of Maw's book, was expressed by Fielding (1984: 34): 'A commercially inspired managerial imperative is more likely to betray rather than enhance the specifically educational nature of our schools.'

Clearly many felt that central initiatives did little to reduce the burden on school managers and Dennison (1985) noted that the task of the head-teacher was 'if not impossible, … becoming increasingly more difficult'. Dennison went on to analyse the training introduced throughout DES Circular 3/83 (superseded by Circular 4/84) suggesting that a number of types of activity were promoted including the one term training opportunities for senior staff at specified centres (mainly in universities and polytechnics) and basic training courses of a minimum twenty days duration (usually for either primary or secondary headteachers). A National Development Centre (NDC) was also established collaboratively between Bristol University and Bristol Polytechnic.

Dennison pointed out that by 1984, two hundred and twenty staff had been released for one-term traineeships and a further five hundred and ninety would have attended 'basic training' courses. He, nonetheless, offered some biting criticisms of this training and noted that the project was 'loosely co-ordinated' and subject to comparatively 'little pre-planning' despite being the subject of rapid expansion. Dennison felt that the pace of the courses was 'frenetic' and that the individuals and higher education organisations leading the courses found themselves doing so without adequate time for preparation. He also went on to note that a 'substantial deficiency' of the initiative was that the objectives of the whole exercise were not clear cut and that 'as for many other education initiatives, a great deal of activity is generated but the underlying rationale and the overall intention seems uncertain'. Moreover with some 30,000 headteachers in schools in England and Wales the rate of provision would have had to have been much greater than the scheme allowed if sufficient training opportunities were to be provided. Dennison summed up his critique by raising a series of crucial questions including:

- What should be the essential elements of the initiative?
- How would achievement be assessed?
- What were the relative accountabilities of the DES, LEA providers, and headteachers?
- What time-scales were to be used in assessing achievement?

In the absence of answers to these questions Dennison bitingly observed that 'a management initiative ought to have management principles applied to it'.

Negative observations of the NDC courses were also made by Bolam (1984) and Ballinger (1985) who suggested that the course aims were often too limited and the selection of course content required more careful attention and planning. Equally, Evans (1986) compared the four task categories defined in the POST (Morgan *et al.*, 1983) project with the list of areas which OTTO training courses were expected to contain. He noted similarities but concluded that there were deficiencies in the latter model.

The central critique of the OTTO scheme can thus be defined as a set of concerns about (a) the methodology of the courses; (b) the coherence and relevance of curriculum content; (c) the consistency of delivery; and (d) the inadequacy of number of candidates trained.

The fragmentary nature of headteachers' work

In a very real sense lack of information about what school leaders *actually did* was one of the central problems which the planners of the OTTO courses faced in trying to help define an appropriate curriculum for school leadership. The important early work of Lyons (1976), Nias (1980), Lloyd (1981) and Gray (1982) has been mentioned earlier; attempts however continued to define the actual role and tasks of headteachers.

Clerkin (1985) attempted to discover 'what primary heads actually do all day' through a series of case studies lasting for a period of four weeks. He found the three case study headteachers spent much of their time working at 'high intensity tasks characterised by discontinuity and in some instances apparently non-essential commitments'. Stewart (1983) made a study of one hundred and sixty senior and middle managers in British organisations, excluding schools, over a period of four weeks. She found that the managers averaged 42 hours of work per week and 60 per cent of this time was spent in discussions. Fragmentation in work patterns was marked and in four weeks the managers averaged only nine periods of 30 minutes or more in a week without interruption.

In his research in 1985 on the Primary School Staff Relationship project (PSSR) Southworth (1988) had investigated staff relationships in six medium-sized primary schools in England. The project concluded that leadership was evident in all parts of the schools investigated and was not solely the function of the headteacher. Indeed evidence of the complex and fragmentary nature of the work of headteachers continued to be found in research. Hall *et al.* (1986) observed fifteen secondary headteachers for a single day and four out of this sample were observed regularly over period of one year. These headteachers were found to be 'at the mercy of events' having created few opportunities to think out and develop strategies to meet 'the complex demands on them for the development of school educational policy and classroom practice'. Similarly, Davies (1987) examined the nature and content of the work of primary headteachers in four schools of varying sizes and locations. Once again brevity, variety and fragmentation characterised activities, with a large number of short-term ones (about fifty per day), 60 per cent of which lasted less than 9 minutes and only 7 per cent lasted for longer than one hour – the average being just 13 minutes. Davies saw the primary headteachers at the centre of the 'information network of the school' and it was their 'people oriented' styles that enabled them to keep in touch with everything that went on in the school. The headteachers involved regarded themselves as the 'leading professionals' within their respective schools with most of their time spent in classrooms, either teaching or observing teaching.

Equally, a survey carried out by Hartle (NAHT, 1988) for the National Association of Head Teachers revealed that the headteacher's job embraced a wide range of management tasks including monitoring and controlling resources, budget preparation and control, staff management, setting objectives and goals, evaluating performance and providing leadership. Hartle found, amongst headteachers he surveyed, three distinct interpretations of their role. One group of headteachers felt that their central role was that of a teacher and that their credibility could only be maintained by demonstrating expertise in the classroom; a second group saw themselves as leaders of a team concerned with curriculum issues; the third group, in the minority, saw themselves as managers of resources.

In fact many of those findings were not surprising. Much of this work in schools re-affirmed the methodologically similar piece of work by Mintzberg (1973) who observed a group of managers from non-educational organisations and found that the activities of the managers were characterised by brevity, variety and fragmentation. The research did serve to highlight the complex nature of school leadership and management and under-scored the need for more systematic training of school leaders in what was already seen to be an increasingly complex role.

Concerns about the quality of leadership training

The importance of such research, and of finding some way of drawing upon it to improve further training and development initiatives, was highlighted by a startling report made by HMI (1985). The report found that in almost one-third of the schools visited poor leadership and management was adversely affecting the quality of work, the levels and deployment of resources and take-up of places on in-service courses for teachers. HMI identified poor management by headteachers in one quarter of British primary schools and the report stated that headteachers needed enhanced competence in tackling problems so that 'schools can become a more effective as well as more satisfying places in which to work'. The survey also showed that very little formal management training was taking place; where it had taken place and a headteacher had been 'exposed to some systematic management development, they were far more organised and articulate about their role and problems associated with it'.

Following publication of this report Everard (1986) interviewed head-teachers and senior post holders in twenty mixed comprehensive schools, one primary and three independent schools. The survey was intended to discover what management training had been received and how well it was felt such training had been delivered. He found that there had been a very low level of training in both quantity and quality and most head-teachers felt that they had learned management through an apprenticeship model. Everard's conclusion was that the situation left the development of education management skills purely to chance and proposed that, if training was to take place using an apprenticeship model, the headteachers who were acting as mentors should be given training in coaching skills. Everard identified twenty-two management training needs suggested by the respondents, to which he added a further six that he felt should be included on training courses. The comments he received from head-teachers about in-service management courses were discouraging, many respondents suggesting that courses which they had attended had been delivered by people who themselves had no management training.

In the same year as the influential HMI report outlined above, the importance of personal relationships in management training was identi-fied by Buckley (1985) who carried out a survey of seminars and confer-ences throughout Europe in which headteachers identified their training needs. The predominant needs identified were 'personal skills' and 'inter-action with other people', and a distinct antipathy was shown towards traditional management courses. The headteachers concerned also stated clear preferences for such school development to take place in practical situations and in their own school environment. Morris and Murgatroyd (1986) noted that management training should be based on communic-ation skills, social skills, group processes and human relations. They would also have liked to have seen the development of 'self insight and awareness on the part of the individual', 'team building' and 'relationships' through the use of counselling and 'family therapy techniques', and 'future analysis within the framework of school organisation'.

Questions were, of course, raised as to which organisations head-teachers might look towards to enhance their training, particularly in the light of the 'restricted' impact of OTTO courses already noted. Bailey (1986) emphasised the importance of involving LEA advisers and inspect-ors in management development policies. Wallace (1988b), who suggested that management development in schools needed co-operation and co-ordination between LEAs and schools, expressed a similar view. According to Wallace management needs arose naturally out of the performance of management tasks in schools, thus the role of the LEA should be one of careful observation and monitoring to identify the specific management development of individual headteachers in particular school contexts.

It was also in this period that some of the central developments in the school effectiveness movement began to impinge on notions of the importance of headteachers and began, at least, to shed light on the nature of headship. The highly influential School Matters project (Mortimore *et al.*, 1988) famously noted that, in the most effective schools observed in their survey, headteachers both involved and consulted staff in planning and decision-making. The importance of headteacher-staff relationships is a common theme amongst commentators and may be noted in the work of John (1980), Winkley (1983), Young (1984), Everard (1986), White (1987), Bell (1988) and Duignan (1988); all of whom emphasised the need for leadership on the part of the headteacher; a leadership which, they felt, should be characterised by a consultative management style.

The role of the headteacher

During a period when frequent comments about the uncertain nature of the role of the headteacher were discerned it does not seem entirely seren-dipitous that the statutory responsibilities of headteachers in England and Wales were set out in *The Education (School Teachers Pay and Conditions of Employment) Order 1987*. The document stated that the head-teacher 'shall be responsible for the internal organisation, management and control of the school'. The main roles delineated in this document included formulating overall aims and objectives of the school; participating in selection and appointment of staff; determining, organising and implementing an appropriate curriculum; reviewing the work and the organisation of the school; establishing and maintaining relationships with the governing body, local education authority, and parents and the community. The wide range of responsibilities, gaining official acceptance, is noticeable.

Having gained a re-affirmation in statute of the headteacher's role, Leithwood (1987) examined the training offered to school leaders in terms of its aims, content and evaluation. He recommended the importance of incorporating the individual's requirements into a course programme so that training was made relevant to personal needs and personal context. Leithwood also highlighted the importance of support and evaluation by course organisers after the training course which should, he felt, be provided for all school leaders including deputy headteachers and senior post holders. His work offered a comprehensive study of education management training, one pertinent observation being that school leaders were constantly 'responding to or catching up with the past' because of the large variety of government or local initiatives. In response to this 'change rich environment' Leithwood suggested that training should take place which aimed to provide leaders 'with the vision to shape the future'. Headteachers should, in Leithwood's view, be enabled to initiate their own policies for the future development of their schools based on their own philosophy and practice, into which government and LEA initiatives should be integrated.

In the same year that Leithwood made his observation, Squire (1987) argued strongly in favour of adapting industrial and commercial management theories to education since he felt that the education service was being managed by 'the largely managerially unaware who, it is fair to suggest, are unaware also of any pressing need to cure their unawareness'.

In 1988 several reports re-invigorated the debate. Southworth's (1988) work, which has been referred to earlier, recommended that headteachers should be helped to develop their 'conceptual skills' in order to keep them in touch with the needs and requirements of their schools. Southworth further recommended that headteachers should be selected with additional care and then supported and developed more extensively. Wallace (1988c) attempted in a survey to identify whether headteachers of small primary schools had distinctive management development needs and if so, how these might be met. The survey highlighted the need for management training especially in the first years after appointment. The headteachers in the survey had received 'no in-service management training at all and would have preferred guidance particularly in monitoring and evaluating school policies'. The survey carried out by Hartle, noted earlier, found that heads felt ill-prepared for their role and, indeed, all those surveyed accepted the need for more rigorous management training, especially for aspiring head-teachers. Moreover Day (1988) proposed a system of management training linked to certification, and suggested that such certification should be a pre-requisite of appointment to managerial positions in schools. Day summed up the situation as he saw it as one where there were 'few signs either nationally or locally of coherent strategies that take account of the needs of management education and training at all school levels'.

Such conclusions are not, of course, surprising but it is apposite to remember that they were made even before the advent of the major changes in governance brought about by the 1988 Education Reform Act. It has become a truism that challenges were seen to have increased exponentially after the dramatic change in the management of schools and colleges to increased emphasis on local management. There is evidence to suggest that, if anything, training needs have increased enormously in later years (Leithwood *et al.*, 1989; Leithwood *et al.*, 1992; Parkay and Hall, 1992; Bolam *et al.*, 1993; Webb and Vulliamy, 1995; Bolam, 1997).

The problems of conceptual confusion

Despite these exhortations for more systematic training, one of the central problems that faced course planners was, however, the conceptual confusion that continued to surround the very notion of education management. For instance Bush (1986) suggested that 'there is no single all embracing theory of educational management' since there was a 'diversity of educational institutions and constantly changing situations which occurred within them'. This notion was strongly supported by Hoyle (1986) who suggested that managers needed to study a variety of theories relating to educational policy, curriculum, organisation, management and change. Partly because of this conceptual plurality, training, he suggested, should emphasise the personal development of managers, rather than skills training, although the latter did have a place when offered in context. Hoyle continued: 'We should not assume that the major task involved in training managers is transmitting business skills, or even the skills of managing and motivating people.' He noted the importance for management training to provide ample scope for reflection and discussion about educational issues to make course members aware of their needs.

Towards the definition of management competences

Notwithstanding these theoretical complexities, there was agreement amongst those attempting to delineate the generic management tasks of headteachers; indeed there has been a long history of those who have identified task requirements as the key to enhanced training opportunities.

In fact Adams (1996) traced the development of competence-based education back to the 1920s when the drive for technical and rational management systems first came into focus, but located the beginning of the 'modern competency movement' in the late 1960s and early 1970s. He noted that the 'prime mover' in the establishment of this phenomenon was the seminal work of David McClelland, a Harvard psychology professor, founder of the consultancy firm McBer – later to evolve into the international management consultancy firm Hay-McBer.

Specifically in the field of education as early as 1981 Paisey referred to 'decision areas' in managing the school. Later in that same decade, Jones (1987) identified sixteen tasks for headteachers to perform and then sub-divided these into four main areas including 'leading', 'organising', 'human relations' and 'external relations'. 'Leading' referred to providing the leadership for the school to function through a framework of policies, aims and objectives, whilst at the same time enabling innovation and change to take place. 'Organising' was defined by reference to the structures for managing the curriculum, pastoral care, resources and administration. 'Human relations' was related to the tasks involved in managing personnel including both staff and pupils, whilst 'external relations' was defined as communication with governors, local education authority and the wider community. Wallace (1988c) defined, by contrast, eight areas of managerial responsibility and the NAHT (1988) identified a number of 'management tasks' including the management of 'people', 'time', 'resources and finances', 'administration', 'setting goals and targets', 'team building' and 'motivation', and 'curriculum development'.

McGill and Hendrey (1989: 14) carried this work forward by undertaking a questionnaire survey of two hundred and eighteen primary headteachers in the Grampian Region of Scotland in order to ascertain their perceptions of their management roles and training needs. Results showed that the training needs perceived as most crucial lay in the areas of curricular matters, administrative matters and personal time management.

We may, however, discern the influence of the competence movement writ large in the work of Hornby and Thomas (1989) who described the development of the national standards of managerial competence defined by the Management Charter Initiative (MCI) in the sphere of *general* management. MCI was given the responsibility of devising a set of generic standards or competence statements for managers and after extensive work first published a set of standards in 1988. Two sets of generic standards were produced – Management I, aimed at individuals taking up their first management position, and Management II for middle managers (Day, 1990; MCI, 1990). Cave and Wilkinson (1992) directed the debate on competence specifically to the field of education management. First they identified three constituents of 'education management capabilities' which they defined as knowledge relating to the school's 'context, functions and processes'; then they noted 'higher order capacities-generic cognitive abilities which determine appropriate action'. Four of the latter were identified as crucial: 'reading the situation', 'balanced judgement', 'intuition' and 'political acumen'.

Duignan and Macpherson (1992) also recognised the importance of cognitive factors, relating problem-solving to 'educative leadership' and defining the 'educative leader [as] a practically effective theorist'. Cognitive elements are central to the five components of problem-solving defined by Leithwood and Stager (1989) which include: interpretation of the particular nature of problems; identifying the implications of possible solutions for short-term goals and long-term aims or principles, constraints limiting courses of action; and the solution processes by which problems are addressed. They went on to distinguish between 'expert' and 'novice' problem-solvers and, later, Leithwood *et al*. (1992) suggested that new school leaders are often 'hostages to their existing knowledge'.

Earley (1991; 1992) noted that the School Management South project, like the work of MCI funded by the Employment Department's Occupational Standards Programme, was asked to devise a set of standards specifically for school management. Unlike most education development funded projects, however, it was not principally required to devise qualifications based on the developed standards and so was able to explore other issues, such as self-assessment, appraisal and institutional and team review. Powell (1992) outlined a School Management Task Force funded project on the development of self-support groups in the Yorkshire and Humberside Consortium which analysed the use of action learning sets as an example of a management development support group. Powell delineated a variety of benefits from this project, ranging from 'enhanced general communication and management' through 'reviewing practice', 'highlighting issues for development', 'better planning and organisation', 'developing and supporting others', 'the practical nature of the world', 'professional recognition', to 'personal benefits'.

Meanwhile Bowles (1992: 31-2) outlined the use of generic management standards based on the School Management South standards, which were, themselves, based on the MCI standards. Three LEAs in North West England were involved in the project. Responses from forty-one secondary schools were positive about the project and noted that the work was both 'valid and acceptable'. Recognition was given in the form of credit for 'what was already known', the framework was provided, there were 'individual and organisational links', and there was 'an aide to review and self-development'. Bowles noted, however, some concerns which took the form of problems of resource in terms of the short time-scale for the pilot in the West Midlands, the problems of providing an uninterrupted quality time for mentoring, and difficulties of working with standards under pressure of the normal working lives of the participants.

In an influential article Earley (1993) offered a critique of competence-based approaches to management development which was highly support-ive of the movement and which linked MCI and School Management South initiatives. Earley noted that there were other differences between the generic and school management standards in that the school manage-ment standards were derived from functional analysis workshops, where practitioners attempted to draw up a functional map of school manage-ment, and, therefore, did not produce the standards aimed at different levels of manager. Earley noted that the majority of the twenty-five parti-cipants from the seven pilot schools (three primary, three secondary and one special) reported that significant benefits had accrued from working with the standards and suggested similar benefits had been recorded by the School Management Task Force which undertook a follow-up project in the West Midlands Consortium, evaluated by Dudley (1992).

Equally influentially Jirasinghe and Lyons (1995; 1996) described the development of management competencies for headteachers in the main-tained sector through a job analysis involving two hundred and fifty-five headteachers. Acknowledging the work of MCI and NVQ the authors defined their approach to competencies as that 'which would tend to emanate from a personal-qualities framework … pioneered by Boyatzis and McBer'. They noted that no 'lead body' equivalent to MCI had yet been set up for education but that the School Management South project had already devised sector-specific standards for school management.

Criticisms of the competence movement

The 'competence movement', then, enjoyed a rapid, even dramatic, rise to eminence in the field of professional education and training. It has certainly not, however, been without its critics; indeed it has been subject to attack both in the wider literature and that specifically for education management. Cullen (1992) noted that competences tended to date quickly; both Vaill (1991) and Barth (1986) re-echoed the statements of a number of commentators who saw competences as atomistic and prone to list logic (for instance, Hager, 1995); others argued that competence-based education was conceptually flawed (Leat, 1993b) and based on behaviourist notions (Hyland, 1993a; 1993b; 1993c). Edwards (1993) suggested that competence systems re-asserted a modern certainty in a post-modern society whilst Chown (1994: 161) criticised what he saw as their 'static and partial models of teaching'. Ecclestone (1994) suggested competence systems undermined professional competence and emphasised bureaucratic surveillance, undermining democratic traditions in education.

Others accepted some elements of the competence movement but argued for broader systems of education and training which integrated competence into a wider framework of professional development. We may cite here, for instance, the 'capability' model (Stephenson, 1994), the 'lifeworld becoming' of Barnett (1994), the 'interactive model' of Burchell (1995) or the work of Kandola (1996) which sought to integrate the task-centred and person-centred elements of competence approaches.

TTA initiatives in management training and development

The TTA's first foray into education management training and development came in 1994 with the inception of HEADLAMP. The details of the scheme were published in May 1995 when it became clear that school governors would be offered the sum of £2,500 to spend on the training of newly appointed headteachers over a two-year period from the time of appointment. The TTA devised a scheme whereby providers of such training and development effectively held a franchise which in essence, required governors to spend the sum allocated on TTA-approved courses. In order to gain the status of TTA approval, HEADLAMP providers had to structure their programmes to focus on the generic needs of head-teachers as defined in a list of 'tasks and abilities' for headteachers devised by the TTA (1995); providers were, however, allowed to be flexible in responding to the needs of individual headteachers in the context of their schools (Busher and Paxton, 1997: 121). The HEADLAMP programme provided a considerable degree of flexibility for headteachers and governors in their choice of training and training-provider – over two hundred providers were registered by 1996. HEADLAMP pre-figured the NPQH scheme in that it was a centrally controlled initiative which was based on a set of generic standards that defined the required leadership and management capabilities of school leaders.

The importance of the arrival of the NPQH scheme should not be under-estimated since it marked a 'step-change' in management training and development. NPQH, which began full implementation in 1997, was noted as being a 'hugely ambitious programme' (Glatter, 1997: 191). For the first time an attempt was made (TTA, 1998a: 9) to offer management training to all prospective headteachers in England and Wales based on a set of defined national standards covering five 'key areas' of headship:

A. Strategic direction and development of the school
B. Teaching and learning
C. Leading and managing staff
D. Efficient and effective deployment of staff and resources
E. Accountability

By defining these key areas the TTA sought to avoid many of the pitfalls of the earlier OTTO experience in that the NPQH qualification had a clear basis in an agreed content which drew upon much of the research outlined in earlier sections of this chapter.

This same clarity of purpose and intent is evident in the LPSH, the writing of which was entrusted to the international management consultants Hay-McBer. This latter programme, whilst not a qualification, sought to offer a much-needed opportunity for experienced headteachers to reflect on their practice and to develop further their skills, knowledge and capabilities during the course of an intensive period of study away from the pressure of the exigencies of the workplace.

Naturally, these programmes have not been without their critics. One recurrent concern was the competence-based nature of all of the TTA management programmes (see, for instance, Lumby, 1995; Bazalgette, 1996). Other commentators have, however, pointed out that the TTA worked hard to ensure that the worst elements of the competence model were avoided (for instance, Glatter, 1997: 190). Indeed the TTA management programmes are a complex amalgam of teaching and learning methodologies, drawing not only on the best of the work in the general competence movement (for instance, Eraut, 1994) but also on the 'reflective practitioner' made famous in the work of Schon (1983; 1987); the development of specific school-management competences (Earley, 1991; 1992; 1993); and the assessment centre movement (see, for instance, Jirasinghe and Lyons, 1995; 1996).

The TTA programmes offered, for the first time, truly national courses of study based on the wide-ranging research which had taken place in the fields of school effectiveness and improvement and school leadership and management. To suggest that they would not be subject to change would be foolish in the extreme; but they provided the basis for a much-needed coherent and rational training system for school leaders.

Conclusions

The OTTO courses of the 1980s and the various competence-based initiatives of the early 1990s offered a much needed testing ground for nationally inspired management training. These initiatives contained within them a variety of inadequacies which were not surprising in that the course planners of that era initially lacked a coherent analysis of the work of headteachers on which to base the curriculum of such courses, whilst later schemes suffered from a somewhat reductivist notion of management development. Not only this but, in an era when the education system was far less used to centralised governmental intervention in education, the courses lacked coherence and consistency.

TTA leadership initiatives seem to have learned many of the lessons of the earlier OTTO and competence-based courses in having a curriculum based on a sound analysis of the work of headteachers which enjoyed broad consensus in the educational community. The TTA, understandably, insisted on a more consistent approach to the delivery of their courses to enable candidates in all parts of the country to feel confident that the course package is both relevant and congruous throughout the country.

2. School Effectiveness and Improvement

Dianne Duncan

The educational context has changed considerably since the first British research on school effects was carried out in secondary and junior schools (Rutter *et al.*, 1979 and Mortimore *et al.*, 1988). Both studies set out to examine whether there were differences in the effectiveness of schools serving similar socio-economic intakes in relation to the impact they had upon children's educational progress. With the emphasis on teacher and school accountability, the drive on the part of researchers in the early 1980s (see also Reynolds, 1982) to uncover the factors which accounted for the differences between schools with respect to educational outcomes, may seem unsurprising and scarcely worthy of note. But previous research had neglected the influence of the school on educational achievement largely because of the weight of social science evidence in Britain and the United States (Coleman, 1966; Plowden Report, 1967; Jencks *et al.*, 1972) which suggested that the differences between families, genetic and socio-economic circumstances far outweighed differences which might be explained by school variables. The effects of poverty, poor housing and inadequate diet have always had a depressing effect on children's educational achievement compared with their more economically advantaged counterparts. But what had not been possible until the Rutter and Mortimore studies, were research investigations which could, with more sophisticated statistical techniques, separate out the effects of families and socio-economic factors from the effects of schools. These were therefore pioneering studies and harbingers of a steady stream of longitudinal research studies in school settings which followed the progress of pupils over time in order to find out why some schools were more effective than others and what factors contributed to their success. There now exists a substantial body of international as well as British research which suggests that effective schools share many common features regardless of country, culture or administrative organisation.

By some twenty years after the publication of Rutter's (1979) work, education in England and Wales had undergone tumultuous change as a consequence of a substantial body of new educational legislation. The National Curriculum and increased budgetary powers under Local Management of Schools (LMS) had a powerful impact on the lives of pupils, teachers and schools which some thought was for the better; others for the worst. Part of a national drive to raise standards in pupil achievement was the introduction of the literacy and numeracy hours in order to boost the results of National Curriculum Tests in primary schools. Whilst not mandatory, many schools implemented them in the belief that not to do so might leave them vulnerable with respect to inter-school comparisons and national targets for improvement. The introduction by the Labour Government in 1998 of specific deadlines for higher levels of performance in literacy and numeracy signalled a new urgency in the drive to raise standards. School improvement, target setting and the overused terms, 'quality' and 'standards' grew high on the political agenda. Regardless of whether or not the notion of school improvement is politically driven, the need on the part of practitioners and policy makers for accessible and rigorously conducted research on how schools can become more effective and how teachers can improve their performance for the benefit of greater numbers of pupils, continues to be as relevant and timely, if not more so, than it was in 1979.

The purpose of this chapter is to overview some of the key findings of research on school effectiveness and show how it connects with later research on school improvement. Within the broader sweep of an examination of longitudinal research studies in Britain and the United States, some themes will be looked at more closely for their relevance to schools and teachers in the fast, tightly compressed, complex and uncertain world of the future. Among the most important of these is the impact of school culture in relation to effectiveness and changing concepts of leadership. Another recurring theme in the research is the importance of value-added factors to gain an accurate measure of school effectiveness. Rapid developments in statistical techniques and computer software packages made it possible to measure progress over time and to tease out intra-school differences in effectiveness between classes and departments across a range of subjects (Sammons *et al.*, 1997), but there were no quick fixes or blue-prints for schools in need of change and improvement.

Whilst the results of large-scale research projects yield invaluable insights and greater precision about what makes some schools more effective than others, a pressing concern for many teachers and headteachers has always been the vexed question of whether school improvement can overcome the effects of disadvantage (Mortimore and Whitty, 1997) and how far it is possible to reverse the downward spiral of ineffective schools (Gray and Wilcox, 1996). These latter concerns raise moral as well as pragmatic questions, suggesting that research on effectiveness and improvement is not neutral or value-free. Improvement for whom? More effective for whose benefit? For *all* children or certain groups of children? As Firestone (1991: 2) pointed out, 'defining the effectiveness of a particular school always requires choices among competing values'.

School effectiveness: key research findings

It is clearly not possible in one chapter to provide a comprehensive overview of *all* the research studies which mushroomed in the last quarter of the twentieth century. So the intention of this section is to highlight some of the salient features of the school effectiveness investigations in order to reveal the common themes and main developments in the field. For readers who want a more detailed research review in a concise and readable form, the report prepared for Ofsted by Sammons *et al.* (1995) is highly recommended. Before going on to discuss some of the research studies in detail, the concept 'effectiveness' needs unpacking in order to be clear about what precisely researchers were trying to measure and define. In Sammons *et al.* (1995: 3) we read that

> Mortimore (1991) has defined an effective school as one in which students progress further than might be expected from consideration of its intake. An effective school thus adds extra value to its students' outcomes in comparison with other schools serving similar intakes.

The concept 'effectiveness' therefore avoids the murky business of making judgements about 'good' and 'bad' schools by deliberately focusing on the concern of educational achievement as measured by student progress, attendance, truancy rates and attendance. Mindful of this definition, the promotion of progress is arguably the 'fundamental purpose' of schools.

One of the earliest studies of school effects was a meticulous study (Rutter *et al.*, 1979) of the progress of pupils in twelve secondary schools in inner London in which over two thousand pupils were followed through the whole of their schooling. The chief focus of the research was an examination of the patterns of school life and the kinds of learning environments experienced by pupils. The schools were situated in an area of extreme social disadvantage and yet some of the schools managed to exert a positive influence upon their pupils' development whilst others were far less successful in doing so. One of the most interesting features of the study was that in addition to a study of academic attainment by examination results, the affective factors of behaviour, attendance and what was then termed, 'delinquency', were also examined. The focus on pupil behaviour is not surprising given that Rutter was a child psychiatrist and two other members of the research team, including Mortimore, were psychologists. Indeed, Mortimore's presence on both the secondary and junior school studies may account for the continuity and points of similarity between the two studies. The investigation showed clearly that secondary schools varied considerably with respect to pupil behaviour, attendance and delinquency even when differences in intake had been taken into account. This was the first time a statistical analysis had been able to suggest causal links between the characteristics of schools as social institutions and outcomes. Perhaps the most important finding of the study was its ability to show *which* school variables were associated with good behaviour and attainments and which were not, for example:

- starting lessons on time;
- teachers who praised and rewarded pupils;
- the academic emphasis of lessons;
- regular and systematic use of homework to consolidate learning;
- good learning and leisure conditions for pupils;
- the extent to which pupils were able to take responsibility for their own learning and the life of the school as a whole.

All these variables were associated with positive outcomes. Conversely, the following all had negative effects on behaviour, attendance rates and academic achievement:

- starting late and finishing lessons early;

- an emphasis on punishment and discipline rather than academic content.

These factors all pointed to the implication that children's behaviour and attitudes are shaped by their experiences at school and are not solely the result of home and socio-economic influences. Another important feature of the study was that in addition to cognitive outcomes, it also examined social and affective factors. These less tangible, but equally important features of school behaviour are often neglected in large-scale studies of school effects. Rutter and his researchers were able to show that schools which did better than average in terms of children's behaviour in school also did better than average in examination success. Schools which were successful in academic achievement were also successful in promoting an ordered, well-disciplined school environment; thus the different forms of success were closely related. From this it is easy to see how schools with a low record of success in both pupil behaviour and examination results were often caught in a downward spiral of failure because of the impact negative outcomes had upon the climate of the school as a whole as well as on teacher morale and pupil self-esteem. Schools that become 'stuck' in this downward spiral often have great difficulty in pulling themselves out of trouble and generally need radical and planned change over a prolonged period of time before they begin to see a return for their efforts. The problem of how far ineffective schools can be moved out of decline is an important issue, not least for the lives of children and teachers who have to endure the unhappy experience of being part of a school which has been judged as unsuccessful.

Another interesting feature of the study was Rutter's assertion that academic emphasis, teacher actions, the use of rewards and praise, pupil conditions for learning, staff organisation and stability of friendship groups, all defined by Rutter as 'school processes', are less significant in their separate elements than in their overall contribution to the school's ethos, which he saw as a 'set of values, attitudes and behaviours which will become characteristic of the school as a whole'. This concept had not previously been explored in terms of its contribution to school effectiveness, but in a concluding comment Rutter suggested that pupils were influenced not only by the individual actions of teachers but also by a group influence emanating from the ethos of the school as a whole. He did not, however, comment on the impact which the school's ethos might have had upon teacher behaviour or state how a school came to develop its ethos in the first place, but he had uncovered what is considered to be a vital constituent in explanations of why schools differ so markedly in effectiveness. The impact of school ethos or culture on pupils' progress and teacher behaviour has recently begun to be systematically researched and it was mentioned in later research (see especially, Stoll and Fink, 1996) as a particularly powerful element in terms of its influence on school effectiveness. This will be discussed in greater detail later.

Rutter's study did not examine management and leadership styles in relation to school outcomes, nor did it explore the relationship between school processes and classroom teaching; but they were an important focus of a later study of London junior schools conducted by Mortimore and his research team in the early 1980s.

This study followed two thousand pupils through four years of classroom life in fifty randomly selected junior schools. Its key aim was to find out whether some schools were more effective than others in promoting pupils' learning once account had been taken of variations in pupil intake. The importance of this study in terms of its contribution to research on school effectiveness lay in the care that was taken to gain measures of individual family and social factors at the level of the individual child alongside initial attainment on entry to junior school. This provided the necessary baseline against which assessments of later progress in the junior school years could be made and which Mortimore (1988) argued was central to all studies of school effectiveness. Previous studies of school effects had been criticised because data had been collected at the level of the school rather than the individual, resulting in a failure to take properly into account, differences in intake. Mortimore's study closely followed the pattern of Rutter's research in several respects. For example, children's progress in both cognitive (mathematics, reading, writing and attainment in oracy) and non-cognitive (attendance, attitudes, behaviour and self-concept) areas were measured. Like Rutter, Mortimore and his colleagues found that schools *do* matter and can be a source of positive benefit, despite some examples of severe social disadvantage among individuals and the catchment area of the schools themselves. In reading and mathematics progress for example, the school was judged to be significantly more important in accounting for differences in pupil attainment than background factors. Wide variations were found between schools in children's attendance, behaviour, attitude and self-concept but there appeared to be a negligible relationship between cognitive and non-cognitive outcomes. For instance schools could be very effective in promoting social development but this did not mean that they were effective in the cognitive areas. This finding was paralleled in Rutter's study where a school's emphasis on pastoral care did not necessarily translate into gains in academic achievement. However a particularly interesting finding was a highly significant association between school effects on self-concept and progress in mathematics. One possible explanation of this relationship is that the combination of pupil success and teacher effectiveness positively feeds the self-concept of *both* parties in a self perpetuating cycle of the 'feel good' factor with respect to mathematics. What is less clear is why this was not also apparent in the other cognitive areas although schools which promoted good progress in mathematics also tended to do so in reading; which suggests the possibility that a positive self-concept in one area of the curriculum has a spin-off effect on others.

A further question examined in the junior schools' study was whether some schools were more effective for certain groups of children than others. Little difference was found in the size-of-school effects on the progress of children from different social and ethnic groups. Where schools were effective for one group they were also effective for the others. Effective schools drove up the progress of all pupils irrespective of background whilst ineffective schools usually depressed the performance of all pupils. There were two exceptions to this: firstly, girls had markedly higher attainments than boys in reading and writing and made slightly more progress than boys in mathematics. The findings in reading and writing attainments were broadly in line with those reported by Rutter *et al.* (1979) as well as those revealed by Ofsted reports and primary school National Curriculum test results for 1997. Secondly, Afro-Caribbean children were over-represented in schools which were ineffective in promoting reading and mathematics progress. In other words, Afro-Caribbean pupils appeared to be concentrated in the least effective group of schools in the study with the implication that had they attended one of the more effective schools, they might have fared better in their academic progress. Ending up in an effective or ineffective school in an area of social disadvantage seemed to be as much a factor of chance as being in the 'right' area for a hospital when a particular treatment or surgery is needed.

One of the most helpful findings of the junior school study was an analysis of the factors which were believed to have contributed to effective schooling. Twelve key factors (set out below in no particular order of significance) provided by Mortimore and his researchers (1988) is interesting for its consistency with later school effectiveness research (see especially Sammons *et al.*, 1995 and the survey on primary education in Leeds by Alexander, 1992):

- Purposeful leadership of the staff by the headteacher
- The involvement of the deputy head
- The involvement of teachers
- Consistency amongst teachers
- Structured sessions
- Intellectually challenging teaching
- The work-centred environment
- Limited focus within sessions
- Maximum communication between teachers and pupils
- Record keeping
- Parental involvement
- Positive climate

In almost all the school effectiveness studies, the leadership of the head-teacher is of paramount importance. Gray (1990) argued that 'the import-ance of the headteacher's leadership is one of the clearest messages from school effectiveness research'. Reviews by Purkey and Smith (1983) and the United States Department of Education (1987) concluded that leader-ship is necessary to kick start and maintain school improvement and that three characteristics, in particular, have been frequently associated with successful leadership: strength of purpose, involving other staff in decision-making, and professional authority in the process of teaching and learning. Five of the twelve factors which contributed to effective school-ing focused on classroom teaching which is an unsurprising finding given that junior school pupils spend most of their time in the classroom with the same teacher for at least one year of their schooling. However some of the observable features of classroom teaching presented in the study pointed to better learning outcomes when sessions were structured and had a limited curriculum focus. Positive learning outcomes were less likely to be associated with multiple curriculum *foci* or topic-centred forms of organisation. Mortimore's researchers found that in mixed curriculum sessions, the demands made upon the teacher's time, attention and energy could become too great for them to ensure effective learning for all groups. For these reasons, Mortimore (1988) urged the utmost caution over using a mixed curriculum methodology as a basis for teaching and learning.

It has to be remembered that this study was conducted prior to the introduction of the National Curriculum when schools had greater autonomy with respect to curriculum content. The messages of Mortimore's study on classroom learning will therefore have been welcomed by some and received critically by others. At the time, the teaching profession remained divided as to whether there should be more or less teacher direction, greater or less pupil-centred learning, greater or less pupil choice and whether a wide or limited range of curriculum activities were more positively associated with higher levels of pupil motivation and progress in learning. In 1988 the jury was still out on these pedagogical issues but a growing tide of research (see, for instance, Bennett, 1976; Galton and Simon 1980; Alexander, 1992) reported similar findings to those of Mortimore and his research team. As it turned out, events were largely overtaken by the introduction of the National Curriculum in 1988 and primary teachers had to adjust to a subject-centred curriculum.

Other characteristics which contributed to school effectiveness were the high expectations of children's learning, maximum communication between pupils and teachers and an emphasis on praise rather than criticism. The importance of a positive climate in a school where a tone is set which values learning and the achievement of pupils closely relates to Rutter's stress on the importance of shared values which are communicated to staff and pupils through the school's ethos.

One of the problems with school effectiveness research is that the findings are often rather obvious; to the extent that it has to be questioned whether the time, money and effort which goes into large-scale studies of schools is really worthwhile given that most practitioners would claim that they could have predicted many of the findings from their own stock of common sense and practical knowledge. There is probably more than a grain of truth in this viewpoint since research into schooling practices rarely comes up with unexpected findings (Rutter *et al.*, 1979). However, apart from the value inherent in knowing precisely which features of good practice are associated with successful learning outcomes, the most compelling feature of school effectiveness research is its remarkable consistency of findings over time and across different cultural contexts. For example, in one of the reviews of school effects research (Sammons *et al.*, 1995: 8), the key characteristics of effective schools cited by the authors are not only consistent across both secondary and primary schools but bear a very close resemblance to the list of junior school characteristics cited by Mortimore *et al.* in 1988. These key characteristics listed below are not intended to be seen as existing independently from one another but rather to be viewed in their relationship with school effectiveness.

- Professional leadership
- Shared vision and goals
- Concentration on teaching and learning
- Purposeful teaching
- High expectations
- Positive reinforcement
- Monitoring progress
- Pupil rights and responsibilities
- Home-school partnership
- A learning organisation

For a better understanding of the implications of this list it is worth reading the full discussion of each of these characteristics in the report prepared by Sammons *et al.* One or two of these characteristics will be highlighted here for discussion in order to show their consistency with findings over time and in countries other than Britain. For example, the quality of teaching is at the centre of effective schooling but, for a variety of reasons, high quality teachers do not necessarily bring about successful learning in their pupils. The kind of teaching most conducive to successful learning outcomes is what Sammons *et al.* call 'purposeful teaching' which involves four main elements: efficient organisation, clarity of purpose, structured lessons and adaptive practice. 'Adaptive practice' is associated with teaching which changes according to the context or particular form of learning in progress at the time and which is now often referred to as 'fitness for purpose'. Sammons *et al.*, summarising some North American research on structured lessons by Joyce and Showers (1988), stated that the more effective teachers:

- teach the classroom as a whole;
- present information or skills clearly and animatedly;
- keep the teaching sessions task-oriented;
- are non-evaluative and keep instruction relaxed;
- have high expectations for achievement (give more homework, pace lessons faster, create alertness);
- relate comfortably to the students, with the consequence that they have fewer behaviour problems.

Similarly, Schereens (1992) in his analysis of the international research on effective schools cited structured teaching as one of three factors consistently demonstrated to promote effectiveness. His understanding of what is meant by structured teaching differed slightly from other researchers in that it was probably more applicable to primary schools and basic skills teaching. Nonetheless it fitted closely with several research study findings on what is meant by effective teaching in Britain and the United States:

- making clear what has to be learnt;
- splitting teaching material into manageable units for pupils and offering these in a well-considered sequence;
- much exercise material in which pupils make use of 'hunches' and prompts;
- regular testing for progress with immediate feedback.

The research reviewed so far, has looked at studies of school effects in two early studies of London secondary and primary schools and a range of later findings drawn from British and North American research projects. Despite the shortcomings of effectiveness studies and their narrow focus on outcomes rather than the less observable, but some would argue more important, features of learning processes and pupil/teacher relationships, the findings showed a broad consistency of findings both before and after the 1988 Education Reform Act in England and Wales and within the international community of school effect researchers (see Scheerens, 1992 and van Velzen *et al.*, 1985). This is particularly important for schools having to make informed judgements about their short and long-term development strategies for Ofsted inspectors, set targets for improvement and keep the momentum of progress moving in a forward direction. Knowing what factors are most likely to work in the interests of pupil progress and national benchmarks of achievement like GCSE results as well as in the interests of teacher development and job satisfaction, provides an invaluable source of direction for discussion and strategic planning. Put another way, the consistency of findings in the school effects research provides practitioners with some well-defined foot-holds for future planning and whole school discussion.

Before we leave the field of school effectiveness research and move onto school improvement studies, some important questions need addressing and these will be examined over the course of the next three sections:

- Are the factors which account for effective schools simply the converse of factors which lead to ineffective schools?
- Can ineffective schools be lifted out of decline?
- How helpful are recent attempts to measure value-added features of school effectiveness, particularly at a time when the raw scores of league table results remain the main indicator by which the public judge schools to be 'good' or 'bad'?

Value-added

One of the developments in research on school effects (Sammons *et al.*, 1997) was a focus on the concept of 'value-added' as a means of measuring effectiveness. This arose out of a concern with the unjust and misleading use of raw scores in school performance tables, often referred to as 'league tables', as a method for comparing schools' performance. They argued that league tables are an invalid mechanism for judging accountability because they do not take into account differences in student intakes or show the progress a school may have made over time. One of the most serious flaws in the use of league tables as a means for judging schools' relative performance is that schools serving educationally advantaged areas may become complacent because their scores 'look good' in comparison with other schools. In reality, the progress of their students may be poorer than that of schools serving less advantaged catchments because whilst their examination results appear relatively good on the surface, they are actually lower than they might be when compared with previous years' performance and when intake predictions are taken into account. Conversely, students in schools located in socially and educationally disadvantaged areas may have made more progress than those in schools with advantaged intakes but, in terms of raw results, their true performance will be masked by a relatively poor showing in a league table. The implications of this method of differentiating the so-called 'good' from the 'bad' are that some schools do not see that improvement is necessary whilst others suffer negative public judgement when in fact, hard won progress has been made. The research added new insights and further weight to the case for the use of value-added factors since league tables were first introduced in 1991, although these approaches should not be seen as a panacea or an unproblematic 'solution' to the issues. Put simply, value-added approaches look at student progress over time, over a number of years in a primary school or from entry to public examinations in a secondary school. Value-added measures (Sammons *et al.*, 1997)

> separate the schools' contribution from that which relates to intake by controlling for prior attainment and other background factors. Such information shows whether students in a given school made more or less progress than similar students in other schools.

The need for value-added measures to supplement raw league tables was accepted and the School Curriculum and Assessment Authority (SCAA) published interim recommendations for a national value-added framework (Fitz-Gibbon, 1995). One of the problems of formulating a dependable national framework is the lack of reliable standardized assessments to measure the prior attainments of students at entry to school. At the time of writing, there are no national assessments for pupils entering primary schools and the National Curriculum results at the end Key Stages 1-3 may not show sufficient differentiation between pupils. What is needed (Sammons *et al.*, 1997) is a system which includes National Curriculum assessments in both statutory tests and teacher assessment alongside a baseline assessment which can be used for value-added measures. A very important point to bear in mind is that when using value-added measures for school evaluation purposes, they should not be viewed in isolation but as part of a whole and developing picture which should include student, teacher and parent viewpoints, school development plans, inspection evidence and community and regional contexts.

Linking school effectiveness with improvement

The use of a variety of value-added measures in a London research study marked an interesting development in the school effectiveness research. Building on the studies of Rutter *et al.* (1979) and Mortimore *et al.* (1988), Sammons *et al.* (1997) set out to shift the emphasis from comparisons of overall performance of students between schools to the comparison of students across different subject departments *within* schools. In an ambitious three-year project, they examined the GCSE examination results of ninety-four secondary schools in eight LEAs. Using a sophisticated statistical technique called 'multi-level analysis' (for a detailed explanation see Goldstein, 1995) the researchers were able to examine clusters of variables at the level of the individual, between departments and across schools. Multi-level analysis made it possible for the researchers to investigate three aspects of GCSE performance:

- consistency across subject departments;
- stability of results over three years (1990-1992);
- differential effects for different groups of students (such as high and low attainers).

In addition, the size of the data was sufficiently large (17,000 students) for the researchers to investigate evidence for differential effects with respect to ethnicity, gender and socio-economic disadvantage. One of the aims of the analysis was to test the differential school and departmental effects for the following student characteristics:

- prior attainment;
- gender;
- ethnicity;
- socio-economic status (students eligible for free school meals).

The authors presented both qualitative case study material and quantitative data to show the differences between schools and departments of total GCSE results and those of six specific subjects which included mathematics, English and science. When value-added measures are used rigorously and sensitively in the context of several different data sets, some illuminating findings are revealed. For example, it is possible for a school to have a good profile of academic results based on its total scores with widely differing performance of effectiveness at the departmental level. Indeed, the results showed that very few schools performed consistently across subjects and over time and those schools who did were at the extremes of the effectiveness range – strongly positive or strongly negative. This further confirms the limited value of trying to make judgements about schools' examination results in any one year based on one measure of outcome. By implication, this finding suggests the need for close monitoring of internal variations at subject and departmental levels.

A very important finding in the study was that schools achieve differing value-added results for different groups of children. Effective schools, for example, boosted the performance of *all* pupils but advantaged groups were likely to benefit most. By contrast, in less effective schools certain ethnic groups, particularly the Afro-Caribbean group, were most adversely affected whilst children of Asian descent in the same schools were least adversely affected. In terms of gender differences there were some differential subject effects: girls attained significantly higher scores than boys in English, English literature, history and French but significantly lower scores in mathematics and science once individual intake factors had been taken into account. These findings showed that in some schools certain groups of students had a less favourable experience of education than others. A knowledge of findings of this kind would make it possible for schools and/or departments to consider targeting these particular groups for extra teaching and resource provision to try and boost their performance in subsequent years.

Whilst international comparisons are problematic (Goldstein, 1996), reviews have suggested that the British education system did well for able students but had a much longer 'trailing edge' than evident in other countries (Sammons *et al.*, 1997). National figures suggested that 30 per cent of the British school population were relatively poorly served, within which certain groups of ethnic minority pupils were the worst affected.

The significance of this study of school and departmental effectiveness lay in its contribution to a more detailed and precise understanding of differential school and departmental effects with new insights drawn from the use of value-added measures. Sammons *et al.* (1997) also emphasised the key role which both school and departmental culture could play in fostering the academic effectiveness of secondary schools. Three features were highlighted for their positive impact upon a school's effectiveness:

- a culture which promotes a strongly student-focused approach;
- an academic focus;
- an orderly school climate where students' academic outcomes are perceived as the highest priority in classes, subject departments and at the school level.

This combination, the authors argued, had the best chance of fostering progress and giving a high value-added component to its students.

With respect to the impact of the headteacher on school effectiveness, clear and strong leadership remained an important feature, particularly in the establishment of a consistent vision, but the contribution of the senior management team (SMT) emerged as a crucial, additional element in providing a clear direction for the school. Findings from both qualitative and quantitative data indicated that the effectiveness of the headteacher as a key figure could be strengthened or weakened by the way in which the SMT operated. In the least academically effective schools, SMTs suffered from personality conflicts and individual divisions which negatively affected teamwork and consistency of approach. Effective SMTs promoted staff morale, high expectations, and set a good example with respect to teamwork. They also practised consistency in their approach to agreed policies for behaviour, rules and management, assessment and marking, homework and parental involvement. Consultation and collaboration about the former is practised at all levels from heads of departments to parents and students. Importantly, effective SMTs set the tone for a culture of continuous improvement in the school. As headteachers have moved into a more explicitly managerial role, the concept of leadership has shifted away from a concentration of power at the centre to a more devolved and layered form in which negotiation and agreement about a school's vision has become a wider responsibility. How the layers fuse together from middle management levels upwards, may be more important than the actions and behaviour of one man or woman at the top.

One of the strengths of this study of school and departmental effectiveness has been its concern to bring together teacher effectiveness, school improvement and school effects in a search for a more complex analysis of the interplay between school and departmental outcomes. These three inextricably linked constituents tended to be investigated and written up in separate or tenuously related research publications.

On the admission of several key researchers in the field, the theoretical bases of research on school effectiveness and improvement have always been weak. In recognition of this Sammons *et al.* (1997) formulated a model which showed how the contextual effects of individual students, teacher, school, department and classroom related to inputs (prior attainment, gender, socio-economic status). Inputs interacted with process (leadership of headteacher, the senior management team, heads of department, quality of teaching, and so on) which, in turn, affected outputs (student learning, motivation, behaviour, GCSE attainment, etc). This input-process-output model was set in the context of the national accountability framework and local/community influences (170). The model stressed the multi-level nature of school effects and the complexity of cross-level relationships from the school to department to classroom showing how they both mirrored and interacted with each other. The model provided a kind of diagrammatic map to show how the various levels fitted together in their respective contributions to academic effectiveness: at this level it is helpful but its explanatory power is less obvious. Its contribution towards a theory of effectiveness is also not clear. The model may well provide a useful reference point for school evaluation and critical reflection and whilst this has yet to be tested by practitioners and researchers, it undoubtedly marks an important first step in the search for a generic theory of school effectiveness.

Can ineffective schools be turned around?

Since the implementation of the four-year cycle of Ofsted inspections, schools have been under constant pressure to demonstrate evidence of progress and improvement across a range of indicators. Schools which are judged by inspectors to be ineffective have to show marked improvement within an agreed timescale. Failure to do so can result in the unthinkable – school closure. As Gray and Wilcox (1996: 90) rightly pointed out: 'Rarely can knowledge about how to improve have been at more of a premium.' Given the growing body of evidence which now exists on both sides of the Atlantic and Australia on school effectiveness, it might reasonably be assumed that researchers and practitioners could draw upon this stock of knowledge to help failing schools climb out of decline. However, this is not necessarily the case. Not only is there very little research on the actual process of bringing ineffective schools out of decline, but the assumption that the correlates of effectiveness are the same as the correlates of ineffectiveness, may be a false premise. The means by which an ineffective school can be improved may be quite different from the ways in which effective schools maintain their effectiveness.

Gray and Wilcox also argued that many case studies of improving schools showed an ill-founded optimism in their reports especially with respect to accounts of significant improvements over relatively short periods of time. They argued that not only does change take years rather than months to make a real difference but that the barriers to change are deeply embedded in the culture of the school and the psyche of the teachers who work within them. In an account of a project concerning an ineffective Welsh school, Reynolds (1991) wrote that the 'deep structures' of ineffective schools may have been overlooked. These were the long-held beliefs and prejudices which teachers use to rationalise a school's weaknesses. In this school, Reynolds observed that teachers projected their own deficiencies onto the children. They held on to past practices claiming that this was the way things had always been done and formed themselves into defensive sub-groups between which hostile relationships had developed. In this atmosphere it became difficult for the staff to move beyond a preoccupation with the personal problems of the pupils to a more open discussion about the educational problems facing the school. Only when the teachers were asked to shadow the pupils during the course of a morning or afternoon in an effort to help them understand the nature of the pupils' experience, did they begin to see for themselves the incompetence of some of their colleagues. Eventually, the school emerged as a more effective institution as the staff began to share and confront the school's internal difficulties in an attempt to find solutions and a more workable management structure; but one of the casualties of change was the headteacher who retired as a result of ill-health.

An essential component of change is the teachers' commitment and enthusiasm to suggested plans for improvement. Teachers also need to feel confident that the effort demanded in improvement projects will result in a pay-off for them, the pupils and the school as a whole. As Rosenholtz (1989) pointed out in her study, the business of mobilising teacher change may be more difficult in some cultures than others and she made a distinction between 'stuck' schools and 'moving' schools. In the former, 'few teachers seemed attached to anything or anybody, and they were more concerned with their own identity than a sense of shared community'. By contrast, 'in learning-enriched settings an abundant spirit of continuous improvement seemed to hover school-wide because no-one ever stopped learning to teach' (206-8). It would seem from this study that improvement projects which ignore the perceptions, opinions and potential gains for teachers are likely to risk early failure. Gray and Wilson (1996) referred to three main factors necessary to the change process and which survived context and circumstances across a number of studies. These were medium-to-long-term time scales, a staff consensus that there is a problem which needs tackling and an ability to prioritise. Whilst all three would appear to be self-evident, they had all, at times, challenged the most experienced school leaders.

From the early 1990s a number of LEA-initiated school improvement projects took place, all of which experienced limited to moderate success, which raises the question of how far the successes claimed by such projects are not 'just a more sophisticated version of the "Hawthorne" effect played out in educational settings' (Gray and Wilson, 1996: 102).

Ways of guarding against this possibility include closer, more critical scrutinies of the reviews which take serious account of insiders' views and perceptions of a school's problems. More information is also needed on how far change actually penetrated the classroom and influenced practice.

More research studies which focus primarily on the barriers to change which are specific to less effective schools, are urgently needed if greater numbers of schools are to be able to play a positive part in the current drive to raise standards of achievement. There is also another very serious impediment to change. In order to turn around an ineffective school, particularly in an area of social disadvantage, Sammons *et al.* (1997) pointed out that to make the crucial difference, teachers and school managers 'have to make *more* effort, give *more* commitment and be *more* resourceful and energetic' [original italics]. Such teachers are working against the odds and, as a consequence, have to exceed the efforts of their peers in more advantaged areas. Whether it is possible to sustain these levels of effort indefinitely is a question which has yet to be addressed. Furthermore, it can be argued that market-driven reforms exacerbate the problems of schools struggling to motivate 'hard to teach' pupils as popular schools increasingly cream off the balance in their intakes. In these circumstances, it is difficult to see how a worsening situation in terms of educational achievement and teacher morale could be averted.

School improvement studies

If school effectiveness research represents the *what* of change, school improvement is the *how* of change (Stoll and Fink, 1996). These two areas of research tended to follow diverging lines of enquiry. The gap between the two is now beginning to close and, increasingly, researchers are drawing on both fields of research for insights on how to help schools make desirable changes. Some of the links between the two have already been explored so the purpose of this section is to point up some of the key messages of school improvement research in terms of its implications for schools and practitioners. Fullan (1991) commented that not all change is improvement but all improvement leads to change. Embedded in this aphorism is the notion that change for the better is complex and problematic, seldom occurring without struggles or tensions. Readers in this field will find certain overused words are in the ascendancy – 'vision', 'collegiality', 'innovation' and 'empowerment', for example. Behind the improvement rhetoric, however, are some useful and illuminating insights. Firstly it is necessary to be clear about what defines school improvement. In 1985, the fourteen countries involved in an international school improvement project agreed the following definition:

> A systematic, sustained effort aimed at change in learning conditions and other related conditions in one or more schools with the ultimate aim of accomplishing educational goals more effectively. (van Velzen *et al.*, 1985: 34)

In a later research publication, Hopkins *et al.* (1994: 3) defined 'improvement' as 'a distinct approach to educational change that enhances student outcomes as well as strengthening the school's capacity for managing change'.

If these definitions are compared with those of school effectiveness discussed earlier on, some close similarities will be observed. However, the distinctive difference in the 'improvement' definitions lies in their emphasis on the relationship between *change* and educational outcomes. According to Hopkins *et al.* (1994) the stress is on the importance of assessing the outcomes of improvement for the pupils; so the aim here is to bring about a much closer link between the school and the classroom. Pupils and teachers must to be involved actively in school change.

It seems clear that there are no blue prints or short cuts to change. As indicated in the section on ineffective schools, change can trigger irrational and hostile reactions if teachers are locked into the culture of a 'stuck' school. Most of the research studies emphasise that things seldom go according to plan and in some circumstances the only way to get things moving is 'do and then plan' hoping that in the process, something will 'take root' (Louis and Miles, 1990: 204). Fullan (1992) took a similar view arguing that change was messy and seldom followed a logical and rationally planned sequence of events. His advice was to adopt a flexible and evolutionary approach to planning which allowed teachers to get started and modify as they go. In the Improving the Quality of Education for All (IQEA) project conducted by Hopkins *et al.* (1994), based on the experience of thirty British schools, the researchers found that school change brought with it a phase of de-stabilization or 'internal turbulence' which is predictable and uncomfortable. It would seem that schools have to learn to live with a period of turmoil, uncertainty and dis-equilibrium; without it, research studies suggest that successful, long-lasting change is unlikely to occur. It is at this point that most change hits a 'wall' of individual learning or institutional resistance. In order to survive this critical moment teachers need considerable support and guidance. Successful schools seem to recognise the need for this additional help whilst in less successful schools, change projects often founder at this point. Surviving or 'moving' schools get through this period by consciously or intuitively adapting the internal conditions of the school to meet the demands of the agreed change or priority. Schools then need to diagnose their internal conditions in relation to their route for change, before they begin developmental work. Once the 'wall' is successfully overcome through staff training days, classroom observation and devolved working groups, changes begin to occur in the culture of the school (Hopkins *et al.*, 1994). The researchers in this project emphasised the importance of horizontal, rather than top-down approaches to the management of change. Hierarchical structures simply reinforce the *status quo* and prevent wider 'ownership' of the commitment to change. Important too, is the creation of flexible working groups which give power and responsibility to individuals who are not necessarily senior members of staff or part of the management hierarchy. Effective working groups need to have a specific brief, a time-line and considerable authority and resource provision. Asking teachers to take on additional responsibility on the back of good will, without the necessary time to see development tasks through to successful conclusion, present another stumbling block to change. Even small amounts of time are precious and can encourage high levels of commitment. The availability of specific development funds can be equally valuable in stimulating enthusiasm and facilitating innovation.

A central messages in the school improvement research is that whilst there are some common themes to successful change there is no magic recipe which works for all schools. The particular context, history and prevailing circumstances of the school must be taken into account before any decisions can be made about what needs to be changed, how it should be set in motion and how far change can go before barriers and passive resistance slow the process down. According to MacGilchrist *et al.* (1997) schools seeking to change need to heed six key themes:

- change takes time;
- a school's capacity for change will vary;
- change is complex;
- change needs to be well led and managed;

- teachers need to be the main agents of change;
- the pupils need to be the main focus for change.

In 'intelligent' schools these interrelated themes become the guiding principles for change.

Changing cultures

Two elements which can either inhibit or promote success and positive change are the school culture and leadership. The significance of both these features is emphasised repeatedly in the research literature but few researchers have asked whether the changes which have swept through schools in England and Wales have so altered educational institutions that we need to re-define what is meant by leadership and culture. One study which brought some fresh thinking to bear on this issue was a fascinating and highly readable account of the relationship between school effectiveness and improvement (Stoll and Fink, 1996).

The concept of culture is not easy to capture because it lies hidden in the implicit meanings of the school and only its surface features are visible. Put simply, organisational culture can be defined as 'the way we do things around here' (Deal and Kennedy, 1983) but this homespun definition does not capture the complexity of the concept. What is meant by the culture of the school is defined as the routines, values, norms, procedures and expectations of the institution. This still falls short of an adequate definition largely because it ignores the crucial relationship existing between culture and structure. Culture is influenced by structure as structure is influenced by culture. This is best explained by an example (Hopkins *et al.*, 1994): 'the decline in religious beliefs (a change in culture) has led to a diminution of the role the Church plays in society and politics (a change in structure).' In other words, structure and culture are mutually reinforcing. Discussions of school cultures must take into account both external structures (for example, politics, market forces, changing economic needs) and internal structures (management and accountability frameworks). The defined roles and responsibilities within a particular school for example, combine elements of both structure and culture whilst ways of working are mainly cultural. Schein (1986: 6) argued that the term 'culture' should be reserved for the deeper level of *basic assumptions* and *beliefs* that are shared by members of an organisation, that operate un-consciously, and that define in a basic 'taken-for-granted' fashion an organisation's view of itself and its environment [original italics].

Traditional cultural patterns are no longer able to meet the myriad demands and challenges which face schools at the beginning of the twenty -first century. Rapid change has become a feature of educational life and 'moving' schools have to foster cultures which are dynamic and responsive to both internal and external structures. A model devised by Hopkins and colleagues (1994) has expanded Rosenholtz's (1989) dimensions of the 'stuck' and 'moving' school into four expressions of school culture which takes greater account of their shifting nature. Stoll and Fink (1996: 85) developed these ideas to show four main types of school culture which they called 'moving', 'struggling', 'cruising' and 'sinking' schools. In between these is a fifth type, the 'strolling' school which the authors characterised as 'moving towards some kind of school improvement but at an inadequate rate to cope with the pace of change which threatens to overrun their efforts' (86). Hargreaves (1994) stressed the importance of understanding the influence of teacher sub-cultures in the context of change and he proposed the concept of 'the moving mosaic' as the sub-culture most likely to be able to meet the needs of re-structured schools in a fast changing and some would argue, 'postmodern' world.

> Their [teachers] orientation is one of continuous learning and improvement. They are characterised by collaboration, opportunism, adaptable partnerships and alliances. Thus membership of groups overlaps and shifts over time to meet the needs of the circumstance and context. (MacGilchrist *et al.*, 1996: 88)

In their final chapter Stoll and Fink (1996) argued for the inclusion of a caring ethic in schools' cultural norms. Caring underlies all the constitu-ents of school effectiveness and improvement; their view of the school as a 'caring family' is founded upon a moral ethic in which improving schools

> have high expectations for all their members; they build on and recognise individual strengths while providing mutual support; they compensate and help individual weaknesses; and they behave in ways based on mutual trust, respect, optimism and intentionality. (192)

Leadership: a new conceptualisation

Stoll and Fink (1996) suggested that traditional conceptions of leadership which sort leaders into categories or typologies were inappropriate for today's schools. They proposed a re-definition of leadership stressing the humanistic face of education rather than one which focused on managerialism, individualism and a bureaucratic agenda. Their new-style leader was a more rounded and flexible professional who could be both leader and manager. Drawing on the perceptual tradition of psychology based on a view of human behaviour as the product of how individuals perceive the world, individuals could choose to act responsibly or irresponsibly. Essentially, we are accountable for our own behaviour and cannot blame others for our failures because we *choose* to behave in the way we do. Using the metaphor of 'an invitation or disinvitation' as a way of describing the positive and negative interactions which shape the self concept, Purkey and Novak (1990) suggested the notion of invitational leadership more readily aligned with the challenges facing schools at the beginning of the twenty-first century. Invitational leadership communicated messages to people which informed them that they are able, responsible and worthwhile. Disinvitations by contrast communicated messages which were uncaring, demeaning, devaluing, intolerant and hurtful. Invitational leaders worked from a clear set of principles which guided their choices.

> They operated from an invitational stance of optimism, respect, trust and intentionality. In effect, they might have behaved situationally as a manager, facilitator, counsellor or change agent depending on circumstances, but they remained steadfast in their stance with themselves and others. (Stoll and Fink, 1996)

Invitational leadership is a more inclusive concept than others suggested by previous research studies. It is more capable of being responsive to the changing and unstable social forces now shaping education.

The intelligent school

The research reviewed in this chapter has centred mainly on effectiveness and improvement. The missing link in the discussion is the connection between school improvement, school effects, and teaching and learning. To make clear the implications for classroom practice it is necessary to focus on how these four areas come together. MacGilchrist *et al.* (1997) showed how schools could become intelligent organisations by the way they made use of the now substantial body of knowledge, ideas and experience on improvement and effectiveness. Drawing on Gardner's (1993) notion of multiple intelligence the authors used the idea of intelligence to convey a new image. They conceptualised nine intelligences (112)

contextual	collegial
strategic	emotional
academic	spiritual
reflective	ethical intelligence
pedagogical	

which, when used in combination, could enable a school to achieve its goals through the use of its 'corporate intelligence'.

The *intelligent* school is characterised by its ability 'to apply the knowledge and skills it has to maximum effect in classrooms and across the school as a whole' (110). Many schools already use these intelligences but by increasing their understanding of them, they are in a better position to describe what is happening as well as what can be improved upon. Central to their idea of the intelligent school is the notion that teachers and heads have the power and ability to shape their own destiny. 'Empower' is frequently over-used in professional discourse but here it is used aptly to convey a new spirit of self-belief in our beleaguered profession. If teachers genuinely believe in their own ability and the goals of their schools many more pupils stand a chance of making progress and succeeding. In the words of one of the key researchers in the field:

If we, as a nation, are to improve learning and raise the average standards reached in schools and colleges we need well-informed, highly skilled practitioners ready and willing to champion the mission of their school. They must turn the public debate from one of shame and blame to one in which a self-critical but confident pride can play a part. (Mortimer, 1997)

3.   Strategic Leadership and Management in Schools

Dominic Elliott

Introduction

The importance of mastering the process of strategic management is shown by the hundreds of thousands of managers who have embarked on postgraduate courses such as the MBA. In response to this interest the study of strategy has grown at an exponential rate. Study of the processes and tools of strategic management is widely believed to have contributed to the success of many of the world's large and small businesses. In 1996 the then British shadow cabinet spent a number of days studying strategic management at Templeton College Oxford, as a part of their preparation for government. There is widely held confidence that management training will lead to improvements in organisational performance. Yet from another perspective successful entrepreneurs such as Bill Gates, Anita Roddick and Richard Branson have built global businesses without a formal management education. How can this be so?

The success of these three successful business people demonstrates the difference between strategic planning and strategic management. Strategic planning is a 'pseudo' science supported by many tools and techniques whilst strategic management is more akin to an art or craft and deals with the day-to-day control, direction and co-ordination of organisations and staff. The individual who can engender a sense of vision and shared values amongst those around them has a major advantage. Of course, formal training can sharpen these skills but the characteristics that make an individual an outstanding manager or leader cannot be taught in the class-room alone, hence the need for continuing professional development.

The broad aim of this chapter is to introduce and describe the process of strategic management by drawing upon a wide body of literature and examples from industry and commerce. Its emphasis on examples from non-educational establishments reflects the belief that by studying other people's problems and triumphs much can be learned and that the use of examples drawn from a range of industries encourages creative solutions. After reading through the many books, chapters and articles dealing with educational strategic management it became clear that such an approach was worthwhile and offered a real contribution to managers in schools.

The first section in this chapter examines the key debates within the field of strategic management over recent years, identifying the very different views concerning the nature of strategy. This is important because, whilst it is argued that, given the unpredictability of organis-ations and their environments, the pseudo-scientific approaches are funda-mentally flawed, such a process is outlined in this chapter as the basic framework for developing a strategic plan. The real trick, as Eisenhower noted, is to learn from the planning process and not to focus all our energies on rigidly implementing a plan that over time loses relevance.

Whittington (1993) chose to use *What is Strategy and Does it Matter?* as the title for his review of the different approaches to this subject. He concluded that it did matter; but a universally acceptable definition of what strategy is proved elusive. This difficulty is explained, in part, by the shift in emphasis for practitioners and researchers alike, from strategic planning to managing the whole strategy process from formulation to implementation. Thus the focus switched from tools for analysing the environment and organisation to issues of culture and later to stretching resources to improve effectiveness. The second section argues that under-standing and managing the strategy process does matter and may, if handled well, contribute to greater effectiveness.

What is strategy – and does it matter?

For the purpose of this chapter the term 'strategic management' will be used to refer to all elements of the strategy process, from implementation, analysis, planning, to setting the vision. The order of these elements is deliberate, to emphasise that it is not a linear process with a clear start and finish, but rather, that it is an iterative, complex process. With this important proviso stated, a linear model (see Figure 3.1 below) is suggested that describes an idealised view of the whole strategy process.

The relevance of strategic management to schools may seem limited; after all their regular day-to-day activities can proceed with little reference to plans or vision statements. Such a view misses the point of strategy which may be defined as the actual behaviour of organisations which often cannot be deciphered until after the event. For example, Mintzberg and Waters (1985) viewed strategy as 'a pattern in a stream of decisions … [and] strategies identified as patterns or consistencies in such streams'. Strategy is distinguished between those actions that were intended (planned) and those which emerged (realised). This distinction recognises that there is often a gap between what organisations do and what they say they are going to do (that is, what they planned to do). The future, after all, is uncertain and change is the only constant according to many observers. For plans to shape behaviour fully requires absolute certainty and does not allow for the bounded rationality of managers. In the face of

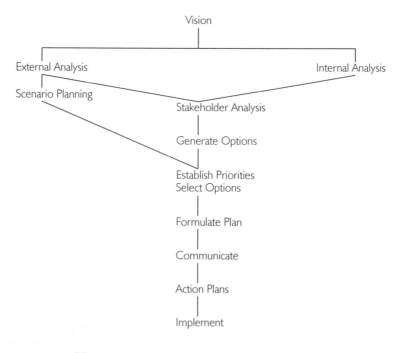

Figure 3.1:   The strategy process

such difficulties the temptation may arise to abandon thinking of strategic planning and simply to do the best we can as we encounter threats and opportunities. We must resist such a temptation because, despite its imperfect methodology, understanding the strategy process and using a few basic tools can enhance the ability of managers to deal with future uncertainty and move towards the vision that we have for our schools.

What is the relevance of strategic management to schools in the twenty-first century? In much of industry and in many local authorities strategic management is the process by which a strategy document is prepared, printed and distributed to key stakeholders. The plan is then filed until the next round of strategic management. The real aim of the process is to produce a plan which can then be forgotten whilst the managers and staff get on with the real day-to-day work of the business. In such organisations strategy is an inconvenience and with such an attitude it is not surprising that it is not treated seriously.

The strategy process – alternative perspectives

Whittington (1993) identified four approaches to the strategy question with the assumptions upon which each is based including the classical, the evolutionary, the systematic and the processual. For the purpose of our discussion we shall focus upon the two that have engendered the greatest debate in recent years (see for example, Mintzberg and Waters, 1985; Mintzberg, 1990, 1991; Ansoff, 1991; Egan, 1995), namely the classical and processual.

Whittington described the classical approach as the oldest and most widely accepted view of strategy. With its reliance upon logical, structured planning techniques and its assumption of rational decision-making it dominates traditional strategic management text books. Its influence can be clearly seen in the annual policy review processes of central government and local education authorities alike, where its relative transparency and logic made it particularly popular. The model was largely repeated in Weindling's (1997) process for strategic management in schools. In the 1960s, '70s and '80s the development of corporate planning in many of the world's largest businesses reflected the popularity of this view. Whilst the process has much to recommend it, its weakness lies in the assumptions that managers may infer about the nature of the whole process of strategic management. Its emphasis upon 'scientific' planning tools gives it a credibility that it does not fully warrant. As we shall see in the discussion of alternative views of the strategy process, such assumptions may hinder effective strategic management.

The classical approach sees strategy as formulated by specialist planners and senior executives, published and often circulated in glossy brochures before its implementation by the workers. Strategy is, therefore, deliberate. For the stereo-typical adherent of the classical approach strategy may be equated with the plan itself. The focus of strategic management is upon ensuring the formulation of the most suitable plan.

Where the classical approach emphasises the importance of planning, the processual school, as suggested by its title, is more concerned with managing the process of strategy from formulation to implementation. Strategy is viewed, not as a plan, but as a pattern amidst the myriad decisions made by an organisation over a period of time. A specific example concerns the importance of customer service to the success of Marks & Spencer. Whatever plans were made for personnel development, for training and induction and so on, the acid test of the success of Marks & Spencer's customer service strategy was the everyday interaction between customer and member of staff. How did an organisation such as Marks & Spencer maintain consistent standards of customer service? In our view the answer concerns the combination of a number of factors not easily separated from one another. At the heart was the corporate culture of Marks & Spencer which acted as a glue binding the many disparate decisions and actions that continued daily. That same cultural glue would influence relations with suppliers, colleagues, interest groups and other bodies. Supporting and reinforcing this culture was the company's style of leadership, staff treatment by the company and management in terms of communication, higher than industry-norm remuneration, superior fringe benefits and training. The issue of culture is explored further in the section dealing with implementation.

The example of Marks & Spencer reflects the key difference between the two approaches. Where the classical emphasises the planning or formulation of a strategic plan the processual is primarily concerned with implementation, arguing that it is often impossible to separate the two. The increasing rate of change, upon which so many authors agree, means that as soon as a plan is printed it is out of date. Are we to believe that organisations continue using a planned strategy that is obviously irrelevant to a new environment? The processual school is concerned, therefore, with understanding the nature of organisational culture, of internal and inter-agency politics. The strategy process is viewed, not as rational planning and implementation but as a messy process, often 'bodged', in which different stakeholder groups seek to exert influence to shift the direction of the organisation. In this type of scenario the role of the leader is not to sit in an ivory tower developing plans, although of course there will be a need to make use of the planning tools explained later in this chapter. The role of the leader is to share a vision of the future direction with other staff, to steer the organisation, to negotiate and seek to balance the needs of different stakeholder groups, to shape the organisational culture and, in the case of schools and colleges, keep within budget. Strategy is emergent in that the future cannot be fully predicted. The less precise the predictions the more emergent the strategy. Indeed Marks & Spencer used the customer confidence resulting from their consistently excellent good customer service reputation to enter new markets, to diversify into financial services, for example.

From a practical point of view, emergent strategy may appear to have little to commend it. It is emphasised here as a better descriptor of the strategy process in most organisations because it is vital to picture the complexity and difficulty of managing the whole process before proceeding to follow the classical model which forms the bulk of the rest of this chapter. The analysis and planning associated with the classical approach may be used to underpin the day-to-day steering of the strategy process, to aid managers to move towards their vision. The key contribution that an understanding of the emergent properties of strategy can offer is that managers must lead, must communicate and engender a common vision. It is, in real life, a messy process far removed from the sanitised view offered in many text books. A brief review of recent texts and articles dealing with strategic management in schools and colleges (for example, Preedy *et al.*, 1997; Middlewood and Lumby, 1998) makes no reference to the emergent nature of strategy and reprints the essentially classical model of strategy without warning.

Whittington's (1993) remaining two approaches are more appropriate to the private sector. The evolutionary approach is a philosophy of strategy which is Darwinian in nature. The fittest will survive and the market is the arbiter of natural selection. In this model strategy is seen as an expensive luxury because, it is held, the market will evolve more quickly than can the cumbersome political entities, that are organisations. Growth is achieved by pursuing many small initiatives, and giving full support to the successes whilst quickly killing off the apparent failures.

Whittington suggested that adherents of this approach advise that the best strategy is the one selected by the environment, not managers.

The systemic approach sees economic behaviour as embedded in the cultural, political and social peculiarities of particular national contexts. For example, the short termism of Anglo-American capitalism reflects the structure of capital in the United States and Britain. By contrast the preference of Japanese companies, reinforced by the ways in which business is financed, is to forego short-term profits in favour of longer-term market domination. For the British public sector the short-termist approach was reinforced by the Audit Commission's so-called 3 E's report in which efficiency and economy were emphasised to the detriment of effectiveness. Put simply, doing things cheaply was given a higher priority than doing the right things. In summary, each of Whittington's approaches appears plausible and the debate reflected in his typology reflects an important point; namely that strategy is not a uni-dimensional construct. As Egan (1995) noted: 'It has different connotations and characteristics depending upon different points of view and disparate interpretations of points of fact.'

An analytical approach – vision and mission

This section of the chapter outlines the rational model of the strategy process, and it is recommended for use as a framework for considering the formulation of strategy. The terms 'vision' and 'mission' are used in very different ways (compare, for example, Foreman, 1998 and Johnson and Scholes 1997), but here the terms are used interchangeably.

Developing a mission statement appears to have been one of the 'fads' schools and colleges have copied from private sector businesses. For the 'classical' school the mission is set by management and followed by everybody else. As Senge (1990) argued such 'imposed' visions 'at best, command compliance – not commitment'. Writers such as Mintzberg (1990) and Peters and Waterman (1982) advocated a shared vision or shared values, that is, a vision to which many people were committed. Developing a clear, shared vision is a constituent of the cultural glue that binds the decisions together. Whether explicit or implicit all successful organisations possess one.

Many successful organisations have a clearly expressed sense of vision. For Komatsu, the Japanese bulldozer manufacturer, the sense of vision was to encircle Caterpillar. Komatsu's strategy was to build market share slowly by targeting small groups of customers not fully satisfied by Caterpillar. For Microsoft 'Windows software on every desk' proved irresistible. Such simple statements offer a heuristic against which any manager or employee can check short or long-term decisions, asking whether it meets ultimate objectives? For Mintzberg and Waters (1985) the intended strategy by management combines with the emergent strategy of what the workforce really does to create actual behaviour. Thus the vision may be seen as setting the parameters for the stream of decisions in an emergent strategy. Both the intended and the emergent strategies represent ideal cases and the actual strategy of most organisations may be described as a mix of the two types. Each is an ideal case and the strategies of most organisations may be described as a mix of the two types. The nature of the industry, its environment and management style will determine its precise position. Deliberate strategies are favoured for stable environments and *visa versa*.

Whilst many mission statements do little more than adorn the front pages of the prospectus and annual report, a carefully constructed statement can help shape the values and expectations of all stakeholder groups. The process by which such statements are prepared can provide an opportunity for staff and governors to consider the aspirations of different stakeholder groups. Louis and Miles (1992) suggested a four-stage process arising from their study of United States high schools. First, visions are not fully articulated but are expected to evolve over the course of the planning process. Second, visions are developed collectively, through action and reflection, by all involved in the change process. Third, visions are not a simple, unified view of what this school might be, but are a complex braid of evolving key themes. Louis and Miles emphasised that visions are developed and reinforced from action. Fourth, the headteacher will play a significant role in spreading the vision to a broader group within and outside the school. Ideally the vision should be a long-term view of what the school is striving to achieve and the simpler the better as the earlier examples of Komatsu and Microsoft suggest.

A comparison of mission statements between Anglo-American and Japanese companies suggests that the latter take a much broader view of who their key stakeholders are. (There are a number of notable exceptions to this, for example, Marks & Spencer.) This difference is reflected in the actions of these companies. For example, a car component manufacturer supplied the same gear-box component to both Ford and Nissan. When a problem in this gear-box emerged the response of the two companies differed markedly. Ford's response was to despatch a senior executive who threatened the gearbox manufacturer with cancellation of the contract if the problem was not quickly resolved. Nissan, alternatively, despatched a team of engineers, in overalls, in a minibus to the gearbox factory site. Here they worked alongside the component manufacturer's staff until they had resolved the problem. Six years later the component manu-facturer had doubled in size, won international awards for quality and chosen not to supply Ford, but to work with Nissan and other Japanese manufacturers. Where Ford's mission statement omits any reference to suppliers but emphasises profitability, Nissan's refers to mutual benefit between itself and its suppliers. Whether their vision is reflected in practice or the other way around is difficult to discern. There is obviously a clear sense of shared values amongst its employees, values which have contributed to growth and profitability.

Weindling (1997) suggested a process by which staff and governors should be asked to write down what they like about a school as it is and how they would like it to be in three years time, using the headings of curriculum, physical structure and inter-relationships. A variant of this process might be to include other stakeholders such as pupils, parents and the local community or even parishes for voluntary-aided schools. The objective is not necessarily to incorporate the ideas of all groups but to ensure that an open mind is maintained. Clearly the management of ex-pectations needs to form a part of a wider consultation process. How open are schools, yours in particular, to the views of stakeholder groups?

There is some debate about the correct timing for developing a vision. The classical school suggested that it should be the first stage, Weindling (1997) that it should come later following the analytical stages. It seems with global companies such as Philips (consumer electronics) and IBM both views have merit. A strategy workshop is usually begun with the development of broad parameters for the vision so that a sense of direction is given to the analysis. Then the vision is re-visited at each stage of the process, refined, or even torn up, in the light of what analysis has shown.

In summary, vision statements can represent a powerful force, an aspiration around which a headteacher might seek to focus the energies of members of the school. Whilst aspirational, the vision will both reflect and shape the values of members of the school. A poorly prepared vision without accompanying symbols and action plans, generated without participation is likely to be treated with cynicism and thus fail to engender shared values. The last government's vision of 'back to basics' failed because of its incongruity with the actions of some of its members. In the case of Marks & Spencer a statement of vision, without supporting actions, would do little to incubate the desired levels of customer service.

Environmental analysis

The aim of environmental analysis is to develop a rich picture of what is going on outside your organisation. A simple, but powerful tool is the so-called PLESCT analysis (see Table 3.1). It provides a checklist to identify some of the major external forces and a useful framework for identifying key opportunities or threats. The matrix in Table 3.1 can be used to determine the potential impact and the likelihood of its occurring, providing the basis for prioritising action to deal with all eventualities. The headings should be used flexibly and adapted to your own circumstances. Some illustrations are included. Alternative scenarios can be developed from highly plausible, high impact opportunities or threats in the environment against which the efficacy of planned behaviour can be assessed.

For schools some key external factors might include local birth rates, possible political changes, the state of the economy, LEA re-organisations, new ideas in teaching and schools management. Given the apparent increasing rate of change it is impossible to predict with certainty what the future may hold. A tool widely used in industry is scenario planning, in which a number of alternative future scenarios are developed and considered against strategic options. Ideally a small number of plausible opportunities and threats are used to develop perhaps three or four scenarios, some positive, others negative. The purpose is to consider how your school would be able to overcome potential threats or exploit opportunities. For example, the change in government leading to increases or reductions in expenditure might offer one factor, or the use of information technology, which might become a core part of the curriculum in mathematics and English. How would existing staff adapt, what actions would need to be taken to ensure that those staff uncomfortable with new technology are trained and given the confidence to exploit it?

Another aspect of environmental analysis concerns a close understanding of immediate stakeholders. Misperceptions of the marketing discipline assume that it is rather cynical, concerned primarily with persuading us to become customers. Marketing in its fullest sense is much

Table 3.1: PLESCT analysis

	Plausibility[1]	Impact[2]
Political & Legal		
1. Standard Setting		
2. Literacy Hour		
3. Special Needs		
Economic		
1. Budgetary constraints or abundance		
2.		
3.		
Social & Cultural		
1. Gender performances differ		
2. Greater parental interest		
3. Increased social deprivation leads to behavioural difficulties and non-completion of homework		
Technological		
1. Demand for computer skills		
2. Internet services for education		
3.		

[1] 0 Implausible   5 Highly Plausible
[2] -5 High negative   +5 Highly Positive

broader than that. It refers to the process by which the needs and wants of people are identified and then satisfied. This requires a good understanding of customers and a real desire to meet their needs. Marks & Spencer's success was the result of both providing goods that people wanted to buy and doing it in a way that gave customers courtesy and the confidence that if they changed their minds then they could get a no-fuss refund. The range of goods provided has been copied by many other stores but the service culture has been more difficult to replicate.

The take it or leave it attitude of early industrialists, epitomised in

Henry Ford's words 'they can have any colour they want, so long as it's black' was possible in an economy where demand far exceeded supply. When General Motors offered 'any colour you want' Ford's dominant position was ended forever. The late twentieth century saw a shift in power towards consumers, and nowhere is this more true than in education. British consumers, in the form of parents, pupils and employers are now better informed, more willing to complain, have higher expectations and arguably, have a poorer perception of education than previous generations and some other countries. Social changes have altered the environment in which education is provided and effective schools must consider how this is to be dealt with as a part of their strategy.

James and Phillips (1997) suggested that the subject of marketing in education has increased in prominence because of attempts to introduce an educational market place; but marketing as 'the definition and satisfaction of people's wants and needs!' is a vital discipline in all sectors, regardless of whether they happen to be public or private. Responsiveness to parents' wishes need not be an inconvenience but understanding parental views, and those of other stakeholders, may provide the basis for improving schools or for communicating objectives. Thus marketing may mean shaping parental views through better communication as well as changing what schools and colleges do. At a micro, or more immediate level, a good understanding of what parents think, how they make decisions regarding schools and what they look for are keys to achieving and maintaining a successful school. Assessing parent attitudes can be done in many ways, monitoring complaints, recording and reviewing informal comments, questionnaire surveys, annual parent/governor meetings to name some of the more obvious. This is done easily with existing parents but Bagley *et al*. (1997: 261) reported that one school wrote to parents who had decided to send their children elsewhere: 'The previous headteacher wrote individually to catholic parents who had not chosen his school for their children and asked them why, and that elicited a number of very direct and frank answers.' Successful businesses welcome complaints; at worst they identify areas of poor service; at best they offer the opportunity to rectify a problem or provide evidence that expectations are not being managed. A good record for dealing with complaints must be a key performance indicator for excellent schools.

In selecting a school it is likely that parents will have a number of selection criteria, including past results, convenience, physical infrastructure, local reputation, evidence of creative work in classrooms. What are the important criteria? Do they remain stable? In marketing terminology such criteria are divided into a number of categories, core, expected and augmented criteria (see Figure 3.2). Returning to our retail example, both Sainsbury and Aldi have provided the same core benefit of providing a range of essential and luxury items for home consumption. This core benefit has been augmented by the way in which it has been provided and each store has carefully tailored its offering to its target customer groups as we shall see when we discuss internal resources. For schools the core benefit is education that meets legal requirements. The expected benefit concerns the standard of education parents expect a particular school to provide based on a combination of word of mouth and performance tables. This may be provided in a number of ways from traditional to 'trendy' approaches. Education may be augmented further by the moral ethos of the school, quality and content of picture displays, attitude of support staff and teachers to parents, extra curricular activities.

Success in business depends upon a good understanding of customers and then seeking to satisfy them. Trying to sell a product that no one wants is a short route to failure, as Clive Sinclair discovered when he

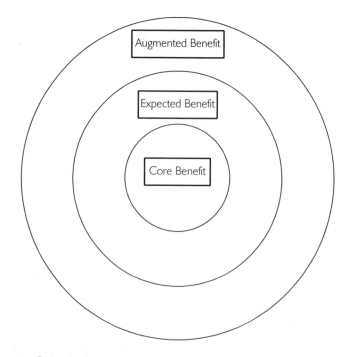

Figure 3.2: Criteria for selection of a school

launched his C5 invention during the 1980s. Market research, in the form of identifying the views of parents and other key groups, may highlight difficult problems or they may demonstrate that a school is not communicating effectively its strengths and achievements. The ubiquitous Windows software of Microsoft found that 99 per cent of the features requested by customers were already available. Microsoft had simply failed to tell the customers how to use the software properly. As Bagley *et al.* (1997) concluded, it is not simply a matter of using the right methods for data collection but having the desire to listen. Complaints should not be seen, necessarily, as a time-consuming nuisance, but as a valuable source of data regarding parental concerns. One school refused to publish a complaints procedure because it believed that to do so would be to encourage complaints. That school could not understand why it was suffering falling applications whilst other schools in its area were growing.

In summary, marketing should be concerned with identifying needs and wants before decisions are made regarding what products or services are required to meet them. That is, the process of business begins with the potential customer. It follows that successful businesses will be those which can supply goods and services that meet the needs of customers more fully than competitors. The use of a systematic process for collecting information related to parental views can provide a useful way of ensuring that school managers can avoid the dangers of merely responding to the demands of a small but vocal minority of parents who have the ability and confidence to put their ideas forward (Bagley *et al.*, 1997).

Marketing in the education sector has been receiving increasing attention (see for example, Bagley *et al.*, 1997; James and Philips, 1997; Gray, 1991; Barnes, 1993; Woods, 1993), but according to Whittaker (1993) there was little evidence that schools had taken on a market-oriented approach nor had they changed to make the adoption of such an orientation easier.

Stakeholders

An organisation's stakeholders comprise all groups who have a stake in it. Some groups may have an obvious and direct stake (staff, parents, pupils); others may be indirectly concerned (employers, local residents). Identifying these, their interests, aspirations and potential influence, is key to the strategy process. As Shell discovered when they sought to dispose of the Brent Spar oil rig in the North Sea, the least obvious stakeholder groups can exert tremendous power. Green Peace, through clever use of media images and an emotional argument forced the giant Shell and the British Government to back down over the issue of oil rig disposal. An environmental activist now advises Shell on such matters.

Internal analysis

As a first step the internal analysis might take the form of an audit of resources such as the staff-pupil ratio, number and quality of classrooms, the skills available on the teaching staff, finances and intangibles such as the presence of a supportive parent group. The audit need not be confined to those resources owned by a school in a legal sense but should include all those on which it can draw. It should identify not only the things that are done well but the things that are done badly.

Earlier in the twentieth century organisations were often structured according to the dictates of scientific management. There was a great belief in the division of labour to derive efficiencies by breaking complex tasks down into many small steps which the individual operator could master and repeat many hundred times a day. From the middle of the century there was an increased interest and concern with the motivation of staff resulting in job-enrichment programmes in which individuals and teams were given responsibility for complex tasks. The reductionist approach of 'scientific management' was challenged and replaced in many cases by a systems approach. For example, Porter's (1985) Value Chain model was developed to identify how manufacturing firms added value. His model distinguished between the support activities (for example, finance systems, quality control and personnel management) and primary activities concerned specifically with the task of bringing in raw materials, transforming these and selling them to customers. Support activities do not exist for themselves but for the satisfaction of customers and thus profit. Success depends upon managing linkages between primary and support activities. For example, the value chain for Aldi (see Figure 3.3a below), the discount supermarket, includes payment only in cash, limited range of items for sale, no branded goods, cardboard box displays and a minimalist head office, the whole constructed to provide basic goods at the lowest possible prices. In contrast, Sainsbury offers their customers choice of payment by cheque, credit card or cash; thousands of items for a high degree of choice; branded and own label goods; fancy displays with

Firm Infrastructure Small headquarters – maintain tight cost control				
Human Resource Management Recruitment and basic training of staff				
Technology Development				
Procurement Focus upon cheapest supplies				
Inbound Logistics	Operations	Outbound Logistics	Sales and Marketing	Service and after Sales
Cheapest supplies	Cardboard box displays	Customers pack own shopping	Local free newspaper advertising	Pay in cash only
Few lines	Inner city locations			Limited customer help inside store
No brands				
Cheap locations				

Figure 3.3a: Value chain 1 – Aldi

synthetic odours to make the shopping experience more pleasurable; coffee shops; parent and child parking spaces; and finally a large head office to deal with the range of suppliers that carrying many lines require and the specialists needed to design fancy displays (see Figure 3.3b below). Both Aldi and Sainsbury are successful companies. Both have designed and managed their value chains to meet the needs of specific customer groups. Success in both cases is dependent upon the way in which they manage the linkages between support and primary activities and their good understanding of who their customers are.

As the value chain was developed with the manufacturing sector in mind it is not easily applied to schools. As with all models, it needs to be adapted to meet the needs of a particular case. Figure 3.3c shows a possible value chain for a school. It highlights the support activities of planning, curriculum development, training, and so on, that go on behind the scenes but are vital to the success of any school. The primary activities are

Firm Infrastructure
Large planning division
Political lobbying

Human Resource Management
Recruitment and training, personnel presence in each store, extensive training for staff, customer service training

Technology Development
Investment in scanning technology for ease and speed of customer.
Sophisticated stock management and replenishment system

Procurement
Specialist buyers, focus upon value for money and managing large numbers of suppliers

Inbound Logistics	Operations	Outbound logistics	Sales and Marketing	Service and after Sales
Branded goods	Invest in lay out and displays	Assistance with packing	National media advertising	Coffee shops, toilets
Own label	Scanners for customer benefits	Money back banking service	Community – charity donations	Choice of pay method (cash, credit card, cheque)
Sophisticated warehouse systems	Range of trolleys for children of different ages /sizes		Loyalty cards	No fuss refund policy
Premium out of town shopping sites	Extensive product lines			Parent + child parking spots
Many suppliers	Specialist butchers, bakers, fishmongers in store			24 hour opening in some branches
				Customer queue management systems

Figure 3.3b: Value chain 2 – Sainsbury

arranged into a logical sequence. First there is the lesson preparation. What influence do the support activities have upon this important first stage? The quality and availability of supporting materials (videos, books, computers, equipment) will determine some of the options available to teachers, as will a carefully developed staff and school development plan. The sequence then progresses to the classroom and recreation time. Does the school make sufficient use of parent skills to enrich the learning experience or to provide reading support or offer extra curricular activities? School is not purely concerned with academic learning but with personal and social education. The careful recruitment of playtime supervisors is essential to maintaining the ethos of the school, yet how much time is given to ensuring that suitable staff are recruited, trained and monitored? Lack of space precludes a full discussion of the value chain. It is hoped

Management Infrastructure
Finance, planning, curriculum development, governors, community lliaison

School Infrastructure
Classrooms, sports fields, gym, play areas, links with other providers (swimming, music etc.)

Human Resource Management
Recruitment and training, appraisal and communication, LEA contact

Technology and Curriculum Development
IT infrastructure, lesson support materials including videos, computers, Internet, books etc.

Admissions
Governors, staff, promotional activity

Teaching Preparation	Lesson and Recreation	Marketing and Assessment	Staff-parent /pupil liaison	Service
Link with facilities (e.g. computers, lap tops	Link with facilities	Type of feedback	Parent evenings	Attitude of school to visitors
Time at school	Range of media for classroom support		Parent governor meetings	Complaints handling
Support at home	Lunchtime supervision		Home-school books	
Necessary materials	Extra curricular activities		Parental involvement	
			Extra curricular activities	

Figure 3.3c: Value chain for a school

that this short introduction provides some insight into a simple model that can assist school managers in understanding and linking the various activities which are performed within the school system.

Once the school's chain has been drawn the school management team should move on to consider areas of strength and weakness. The assessment of strengths and weaknesses may be, in part, an intuitive process but given the plethora of official studies, bench-marking reports or staff experience it should be possible to quantify or to develop proxy measures by which comparisons with other schools or establishments can be made. The performance and assessment data (PANDA) produced annually by the DfEE may provide one important source of comparative data with similar schools. While such data will inevitably be incomplete every effort should be made to use qualitative data, whether collected formally or informally, to complement official data.

In summary, the purpose of the internal analysis is to generate not only a list of available resources but to consider how the school uses those resources, how different activities are linked together, and, where possible, to identify key linkages that will support the movement of the school, its staff, pupils and other groups towards fulfilment of its vision.

Generating and selecting options

The key aim of strategic management is to achieve a fit between an organisation and its environment. The selected options should capitalise upon strengths, rectify weaknesses to exploit opportunities and overcome threats. By this stage in the strategy process schools should have a clear idea of key external trends and forces and a sense of how these may change in the future. Additionally, if the internal analysis has been conducted properly the school management team should have identified areas where there is a gap between current and desired performance. Bridging the gap sets the context for the development of strategic options. Typically the analytical stage of the strategy process identifies many issues. To cluster these and identify a small number of key issues is a useful step. These should then be prioritised and at this stage their impact upon the school development plan assessed. Not only should the resource implications of a particular course of action be considered but also the possible and probable responses of different stakeholder groups. For example, changes to the school day may be made for the best academic reasons but be interpreted by parents as teachers wanting a shorter day. What people perceive to be true is as important as what is true. Effective management of parents might be a key issue, with perhaps, their involvement in class, fund-raising, extra curricular activities, homework and communications.

The identification of a strategy will depend upon the quality of the analysis performed and the stakeholder views canvassed. The resource implications of alternative strategies should be readily identified and for this reason our section dealing with implementation focuses primarily upon the human issues.

Discussion of implementing a strategy has been avoided here because effective leadership and management of culture, two key issues, should provide an appropriate context. Without consideration of these two important issues the best laid plans are likely to founder.

Leadership

Leadership in management and particularly in education management has attracted the attention of many researchers. In the space available it is impossible to review this wide literature which encompasses many different approaches and perspectives. It is therefore, proposed to concentrate on a number of aspects of leadership and consider how these fit with the models of strategy outlined above.

Since written history began there has been an interest in the lives of great men and women. Often these writings have taken the form of hagiographies that emphasise the greatness of their subjects. Marx criticised the view that history was seen as the workings of great people and that the role of social and economic forces were largely ignored. In the classical view of strategy the leader is hero. The leader formulates a plan and leads the troops into battle. The role of the leader in the processual school is less glamorous and seems more concerned with the mundane negotiation with political forces and setting the context in which others produce the strategy. From a careful reading of recent literature concerning leadership in schools it is clear that many authors see this latter role as a key. For example, Beare *et al.* (1997) suggested that outstanding leaders not only have a vision for their organisation but secure commitment to it from their staff, they use participative forms of decision-making, they work with staff not above them, they implant the vision in the structures, norms and processes of their schools. In other words they view their role as one of influencing the strategy process and the climate in which it emerges rather than considering it to be of control and direction. Successful leadership will require that staff be treated according to their needs rather than the whim of the headteacher. Successful leadership requires delegating tasks to those best suited to them, so that the role of leadership is not necessarily confined to the headteacher but is a mantle assumed by those with the skills needed for a particular task or situation.

Contingency theory (Stacey, 1997) suggests that there is no one best way to lead in all situations but that some approaches may be more effective within a certain context. The zeal of entrepreneurs such as Branson and Roddick played a large part in publicising Virgin and The Body Shop and creating a sense of purpose amongst employees. Such a style may be appropriate to a new and rapidly growing business whilst the demands of managing an established organisation may require a more administrative style. This may explain the difficulties of the Body Shop and Virgin in recent years. Beare *et al.* (1997) used the examples of members of staff with different degrees of maturity, requiring different leadership styles.

In the early days of strategy the role of the leader was to set a personal mission statement and persuade, coerce or cajole staff to follow. As we have discussed the basis for this view of the strategy process is flawed and is not well suited to the complex and turbulent environment of schools. What then is the role of the headteacher in the strategy process? There are a number of dimensions to the role of headteacher and management team. First, there is the facilitating role of developing a shared sense of mission amongst all staff, governors and pupils. This must of course be effectively communicated to other stakeholders. The second is the more difficult task of acting as the guardian of this vision and leading from the front. At Coventry City Council in the mid 1980s the vision of the chief executive and elected members was that the authority vision should be focused upon a 'customer orientation'. Although widely publicised through various forms of communication the most significant symbol of this change was that the chief executive and chief officers spent one afternoon per week on inquiry desks. Not only did this bring them face to face with customers, dealing with every day problems, but it enabled them to learn directly from junior staff about operational problems and the types of complaint often encountered. In 1991 IBM made world record-breaking losses in excess of $5bn. The reason, arguably, was that IBM had become complacent and remote from customers. The turn-around under Lou Gerstner was achieved, in part, by the requirement that all senior executives,

Gerstner included, should spend 50 per cent of their time with customers. The speed and accuracy of customer feedback improved dramatically. In both cases senior managers led by example. Their efforts put their visions into practice, demonstrating to even the most hardened cynic that their vision and mission statements were not empty words.

In summary, for schools the task of leadership may be more difficult than in many larger organisations. The headteacher combines the leadership role with many executive tasks. Where many private sector firms can focus upon profit and other economic measures of performance the effectiveness of schools is more difficult to assess. In the capitalist world we accept the primacy of the shareholder as the main stakeholder, in schools the various government authorities hold legal power yet the objectives of the school must not give second place to the needs of pupils, parents, the local community and staff. The metaphor of a puppet on strings, pulled this way and that, may aptly describe the position of headteacher and management team. Good leadership is vital to a successful school, as Crawford (1997: 1) observed:

> Leadership and team working are at the core of managing people, the most important resource in the whole field of educational management or indeed any other sort of management … Proficient leading and team working is … central to effective performance within schools and colleges.

Culture

Torrington and Weightman (1993) criticised one school in which twenty-four out of forty-three staff had not worked elsewhere leading to the potential for 'professional narrowness, complacency and staleness'. The strong culture of the school was credited with this achievement, which stimulated much interest from companies seeking to reduce staff turnover.

Mitroff and Pauchant (1988) suggested that culture is to the organisation as personality is to the individual. Deal and Kennedy (1985) described it 'as the way we do things around here'. Most models of culture (see for example, Schein, 1985; Pauchant and Mitroff, 1989; Hofstede, 1991; Williams *et al.*, 1993) agreed that it may be thought of as combining a number of distinct layers, including individual beliefs and assumptions, coming together in the form of shared values and operating norms and ultimately, consistent patterns of behaviour. Bush (1998: 20) noted that:

> Every organisation has a formally instituted pattern of authority and
> an official body of rules and procedures which are intended to aid the
> achievement of those goals. However, alongside this formal aspect of
> the organisation are networks of informal relationships and unofficial
> norms which arise from the interaction of individuals and groups
> working within the formal structure.

The importance of culture was recognised by Hofstede (1991) who
asserted that it had achieved a status similar to that of structure in
organisational studies. As Bush (1998: 43-4) concluded, culture and
strategy are closely related:

> First, both are underpinned by values, leading to a clear vision the
> future of the school or college ... Secondly, culture is an important
> dimension of the context in which strategy operates ... Thirdly,
> culture need not be unitary as long as the subcultures do not come into
> direct conflict ... recognition of the value of alternative cultures may
> enrich the organisation.

Understanding the informal processes is clearly vital to managing the
strategy process, yet many authors agree that cultural change can only be
achieved in the long term. It is thus important to gain some insight into
the nature of culture within a particular organisation. One such model,
based upon a variety of anthropological and organisational studies is the
Cultural Web (Johnson and Scholes, 1997). An example of one for a new
university is shown in Figure 3.4. Such analysis, if it is to have any meaning, requires input from members of staff. A useful way of using the tool
is as the focus for discussion to examine differences and similarities in
perception.

The *stories* told in organisations help shape behaviour by communicating the unwritten values. An apocryphal story told at the Disney
Corporation is of a car park attendant who checks the temperatures of the
car engines of senior executives at 7.15 a.m. each day. If the engine is too
warm the executive is fired because it means that the executive has
recently arrived; the story is told to reinforce the view that to get on at
Disney you have to work hard and get in early. Staff at IBM claim that the
initials stand for 'I've been moved' or 'I've been married'; success at IBM

Stories
Win large research grants
VC communicates via video
Eccentric professional types
Symbols
Qualifications
Jargon
Car parking space
High powered computer/equipment
Rituals and Routines
Teaching comes first
Complicated bids
Work alone, little team spirit
Power Structures
Autocratic centre, administration 'tail wags the dog'
Technical support
Fierce interdepartmental infighting
Control and Reward Systems
Research sucess
Tight budgetary controls
Avoid complaints in teaching
Structures
Vertical hierarchy, little inter-school communication
Paradigm
Low cost educational provider at many sites
Maximise non-teaching income
Excellent programmes, poor internal ones

Figure 3.4:   Cultural web for a university

means giving your all to the company. *Symbols* are a powerful communications tool. The old Woolworth's company removed the pockets from staff
overalls to prevent pilfering. When Kingfisher bought the retailer the
pockets were sewn back on, a powerful symbol of trust. In many Japanese
companies all staff (including executives) wear the same type of overall to
symbolise the importance of team work. *Rituals and routines* provide a
powerful, socialising influence. Routines may include never leaving before
the boss; everything stopping for the doctors' walk around the ward in a
hospital. *Power* is located throughout the organisation. The lunch time
supervisor can go on strike; the aggrieved technician can sabotage essential
laboratory equipment; both can disrupt the smooth running of the school.
At the other extreme a displeased Ofsted inspector can bring in special
measures. Power is not always in the most obvious place. Few of us go to
work for altruistic purposes. Changes in the funding of universities led to
changes in *reward systems*. Where once administration was highly prized

and rewarded, research is, apparently the main objective. When rewards switched to researchers, academics paid less attention to administration (including course management and recruitment) to pursue research which would lead to promotion, leaving a gap in a key area of activity. Finally, *structure* may act as a facilitator or as a constraint. In hierarchical, tightly ordered organisations initiative may be stifled, new opportunities missed. Mintzberg (1983) argued that organisational success required a fit between structure and environment. Figure 3.5 shows the resulting matrix.

A simple and stable environment provides the right conditions for the extreme mechanisation of processes (machine bureaucracy) for lack of change and simplicity of environmental demands permits control through strict procedures. Organisational success follows the ruthless pursuit of efficiency. Examples include the large car plant of Henry Ford or IBM's focus upon sales in the 1980s. The selling task was tightly controlled, even down to the colour of the shirts of sales representatives. Arguably this mechanistic approach prevented IBM from noticing any change in the market place that favoured the rise of the personal computer. IBM sold

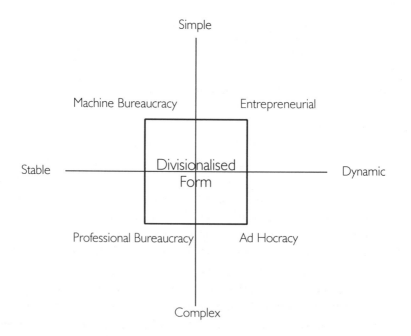

Figure 3.5:   Environment – Organisation Structure Fit
               (Source: Mintzberg, 1983)

mainframes for business and could not conceive, at that time, of the attractiveness of the small personal computer. In a simple and dynamic context, one mind is capable of understanding the environment. However, dynamism requires that decisions to change are made quickly, a characteristic alien to the machine bureaucracy. In this context the entrepreneur flourishes; with no need to consult others he or she can respond quickly to change. The professional bureaucracy occupies a stable environment but is expected to perform complex tasks. Hospitals, universities and schools provide examples of this. Professionals are employed to deal with the complexity of the task but do so within a relatively stable framework. Another structure, called the 'adhocracy', refers to small groups of highly trained individuals working together as in, for example, a research and development team of management consultancy. A collection of highly skilled brains enable it to deal with complexity, whilst its small size and network structure permit rapid decision-making to help it respond quickly to environmental change. The rise of Microsoft from an American garage to take on the multi-billion dollar IBM is one example of how, in the right environment, structure can become a major source of competitive success. The final pure structure is the 'divisionalised form' in which Mintzberg recognised that the large size of firms often meant that one company might incorporate a number of these. Of course each is a pure structure and in practice it is likely that an organisation will show a tendency towards a particular rather than a pure structure.

What is the relevance of structure to strategy? Structure will condition the types of response to the environment that an organisation can make. In times of rapid change, bureaucracy can stifle change, causing the structure to be out of fit with its environment and thereby limiting effectiveness. An extreme example concerns the fire service. In dealing with day-to-day crises and what we would consider to be the complexities and dynamism of house fires and road traffic accidents, the fire service developed a drilled response to such incidents. When it arrives at an incident each fire fighter knows exactly their specific task. Deviation from the drilled response requires authority from a supervising officer, who retains a note of all such deviations in order that the lives of other fire fighters are not placed in jeopardy. Put another way, the fire service operates in a very machine bureaucracy manner. For a large proportion of incidents such a style works well. However, when faced with a major incident that bears little resemblance to those practised, calls for deviation from the plan grow until the supervisor is overloaded with information and communications and is unable to cope. The emergency response is in danger of breakdown at this point as the structure fails to cope with the demands of the environment. Such a breakdown affected the police at Hillsborough in 1989 and was a key factor in that disaster (see Elliott and Smith, 1993). Structure provides the context in which strategy is implemented. If it does not fit with its environment then the strategy will at best be hindered, at worst fail. It might be likened to taking an electronic tool abroad and trying to use a three-pin plug in a two-pin socket.

Bush (1998) reviewing some research undertaken regarding the concept of culture in schools, reported that a number of different sub-cultures may exist within a school and that there may be difficulties in relationships with other groups whose behavioural norms are different. Wallace and Hall (1994) reported that senior management teams provide one example of a sub-group with a strong internal culture which often had weak connections to other groups. In the cultural web of the university the perceived remoteness of the vice chancellor and the belief that the 'administrative tail was wagging the dog' suggest that this may be a feature of educational groups of all kinds.

Achieving desired cultural change is a difficult and lengthy process. Kotter and Schlesinger (1979) advocated the use of education, communication and participation, elements reflected in the approaches recommended by Turner (1990) and Gorridge (1994). These included the development of a clear purpose or vision; communication of these and a published action plan; supporting and guiding people to build confidence; beginning with people in key positions (opinion formers); and finally by providing effective leadership. Symbolic actions such as that provided by Coventry's Chief Executive and the Head of IBM, described earlier, provide a powerful stimulus to change, provided they are not empty gestures.

Strategic management in schools

A review of the available literature showed a great emphasis upon classical approaches to strategy (see Cheng, 1996; Holmes, 1993). One notable exception to this was Middlewood's (1998) overview of strategic management in education. He recognised:

> Implementation cannot be separated from planning and the effective strategic manager remains alert to the constant linkage between what

is happening in the origination now and the trends, issues and consequent need for change.

Middlewood identified a hierarchy of strategic aspects and their relationship to the daily work of an organisation. At the uppermost levels are the semi-permanent elements of vision, mission and strategic plan. These may be usefully thought of as setting the parameters for the 'stream of decisions' which are formed by the more detailed school policies, development plans, personal and departmental action plans and so forth. These are more prone to change.

How well are schools coping with strategic planning was the question posed in a study conducted by Giles (1995: 5). The results suggested that in approximately 50 per cent of one hundred and six schools (from fifteen LEAs)

> Planning seemed *ad hoc*, with little whole-school strategic planning there appears to be little conscious link between the aims and objectives of the school identified in the strategic plan, and the use of resources to implement the priorities for change identified in the SDP [School Development Plan]. The SDP seemed isolated from a strategic plan, as well as from the action plans concerned with implementation in about two thirds of schools surveyed action plans were not complete enough to control implementation. As a result the SDP will, in effect, be a list of jobs to do, rather than agreed priorities which are being systematically resourced and implemented systematic evaluation of progress towards policy implementation is noticeably lacking.

At one level these findings suggest that strategic planning has not been effectively implemented by schools. This implies that the experiment of transferring strategic responsibility from LEAs to schools has failed. However, an alternative reading might challenge the research questions. Is assessment of the strategic plan a true indicator of effectiveness? Would better questions concern the appropriateness of the vision of a school and assess progress made in terms of the SDP, action plans and daily work schedules alongside a qualitative assessment of how far a school has progressed towards its stated objectives? The 'acid test', as Mintzberg and Waters (1985) recognised, lies in organisational behaviour, in what a school actually does, not necessarily what it says it will do. Surely an important indicator of performance concerns the movement of any school from its starting point towards its vision.

However, the research may indicate that the value of strategic planning has yet to be grasped within many schools. Planning may be seen as yet another required activity that brings little benefit. If this is the case then a sea-change in attitudes is required if the full benefits of strategic management in schools are to be achieved.

Conclusions

Although formal tools can play a vital role in devising a strategic plan, the strategy process is a non-linear process of some complexity. Organisational success requires the identification and communication of a clear sense of vision that can motivate staff. The emergent properties of strategy require that managers take care to develop a good understanding of their environments and to communicate with all stakeholder groups. Managing strategy should not be viewed as the development and execution of a plan but as a fluid, ongoing process of steering the stream of decisions and activities, on a day-to-day basis, towards a clearly articulated, jointly formulated and well-communicated vision. Attention needs to be focused upon the context in which such decisions and activities take place, the means of co-ordination through rules and structures, consideration of the vitally important informal norms and attitudes that give each organisation its distinctive character. Leadership in such a context is less concerned with the heroic charge from the front but more with a blend of nurturing, supporting, and cajoling where necessary. It must be recognised that realised strategy in a school is dependent upon the activities of all who participate in the system. The role of the leader is to bind the activities together, to facilitate others in their aspirations to achieve the vision, to draw together the disparate stakeholders and build excellent schools for those who work, study and benefit in other ways from them.

4. Managing Teaching and Learning

Peter Silcock

The relationships between learning and teaching

Learning and teaching are both inter-dependent and independent classroom processes. A teacher's purpose for teaching is to bring about learning and, broadly, any step taken to fulfil that purpose is called a 'teaching strategy'. Nevertheless, looked at socially, psychologically, and pragmatically, teaching and learning introduce very different studies. Anyone can learn without help, through a sensible application to the task; and teachers may waste enormous amounts of energy in a futile attempt to teach unreceptive pupils. Therefore teachers commonly set learning and teaching objectives separately, as part of their curricular planning. When Ofsted inspectors call on a school, they assess pupil-progress outside of any judgements they make about teaching skill.

The fact that classroom teaching and learning closely interrelate but are vulnerable to varying types of influence has a profound effect upon how they are treated in analysis. Putting forward proposals about the management of students' learning implies an intimately connected account of what will make for effective pedagogy: theories of human learning and development set up criteria which have to be met by theories of teaching. Effective teaching must, by definition, lead to effective learning. For that reason, when we study school processes, it would be surprising if constraints upon teaching performance did not figure somewhere in any list of circumstances affecting how well pupils cope with their lessons. Yet they might not. In other words, the relationship between the two kinds of process is asymmetric. Teaching exists to promote learning; but learning does not happen just to occupy teachers. And paying too close attention to the conventional ways teachers behave may distract us from a full realisation of what is really occupying learners at critical moments. Consequently, it is important to nail the conditions in which school pupils work best and how these conditions should be organised prior to any study of pedagogy. Only when we are sure about what is needed for pupils to make progress should we explore how teachers can plan their own actions to fulfil those conditions.

This chapter has two aims. It will spell out how teachers can manage each process, in its own terms, stressing their interrelationships; and, while doing so, it will raise the wider management issues which teachers should confront. A preliminary summarising of these issues will place them in their academic and historical contexts. Finally, during most of the first section, it is not intended to tackle the management of pupil learning and pupil cognitive development as distinct questions. Although, in school, teachers will work to enhance pupils' general intellectual progress and sometimes want to pass on facts and skills purely for their own sake, usually a teacher will want to achieve both together (see Halford, 1995, for a discussion of the relationships between learning and cognitive development). Given a concentration on teachers' management strategies, it is thought unnecessary to try to differentiate categories of outcome when, normally, it will be hard to separate these in any case.

The management of learning

There are three questions facing any teacher wanting to organise classrooms and curricula so that pupils learn effectively. Teachers have to know the *type* of learning they wish to promote, the *conditions* under which their pupils will learn in the ways specified, and the management *strategies* which are most likely to create these conditions. Answering the first two questions gives us theoretical grounds for answering the third.

In the past, fashions dictating how we studied learning and cognitive development reflected implicit self-pictures, models or 'meta-narratives', buried within the main psychological theories themselves. It was not so much a case of painstakingly discovering unvarnished truths about the way humans learn as that of realising how different sorts of learning require very different frameworks of explanation. Historically, the great divide in psychology marking the most decisive shift in our culturally accepted self-view opened up around the middle of the twentieth century, when a 'cognitive revolution' (Gardner, 1985) overturned our long-held behaviouristic assumptions about human learning (Atkinson *et al.*, 1990; Gardner, 1985; Gross, 1992; Sutherland, 1992; Walker, 1996). Because early pioneers of behaviourism such as John Watson, and later researchers such as B.F. Skinner, took it for granted that mental habits and behavioural routines were shaped according to laws applying to all animal behaviour, largely concerning the availability of rewards, they believed that a proper understanding of these laws would, in time, allow us to tailor our abilities to suit our ideals. Unfortunately, it turned out that some of the most typical human capabilities, such as our verbal behaviour (Chomsky, 1959), could not, without distortion, be regarded as wholly governed by the scheduling of rewards, or the withholding of rewards. Many psychologists became convinced that our mental powers set us apart from the rest of the animal kingdom.

This conviction mattered – not so much because the output from behaviourist research was suddenly noticed to be flawed or mistaken (largely, it was not), but because psychologists investigating perception, memory, thinking and problem-solving, realised that the new cognitive theories promised more for their research ambitions than did the older behaviourist programmes. If, for instance, minds could be assumed to have operations equivalent to those of computers, thought processes might, in some features, resemble software programmes run by the brain's hardware (Walker, 1996). Employing this assumption as a central analogy guiding their experimental research, information-processing theorists helped us grasp how facts could be communicated and organised in a meaningful way for ready retrieval and assimilated through rehearsal (Atkinson *et al.*, 1990; Gross, 1992). They sensitised us to key topics, such as knowledge-transfer and application (Salomon and Gibberson, 1987; Voss 1987), and the role of self-monitoring in the most efficient types of learning (Salomon and Gibberson; Adey and Shayer, 1994).

The cognitive revolution also overtook writers curious about the way human minds grow between infancy and adulthood. Developmental psychologists, such as Piaget (see Sutherland, 1992), contributed to the design of cognitive models by demonstrating how individuals are conscious agents for their own learning as well as adopting routine ways of coping with external pressures. This 'humanistic' tendency (in that it does not treat humans as something *other than* human beings), lends itself directly to teachers' work – partly because education systems are usually structured so as to enhance students' stage-related progress through time, but also because much developmental theorising overlaps with teachers' own intuitions and experiences. Psychologists exploring children's progress as thinkers and problem-solvers looked beyond maturational effects to the pervasive influence of a wider social context, just as many teachers have realised that the reasons for children's learning difficulties often lie somewhere within their immediate social environments.

Psychological theories of learning and cognitive development are not, always, correct or incorrect. Certainly, we have to decide which of them we can trust; but, more than that, we have to decide which best serve our educational purposes. Anyone desiring only that their students respond accurately to instructions may, still, use techniques inspired by behaviourists; if what we teach has to be memorised, applied and accessed in set ways, ideas taken from experimental research using computer-modelling meet our needs. Yet, in the third millennium, the fact of rapid alterations in what societies demand of citizens increasingly challenges our value judgements. A school's success is likely to be judged as much by how well it prepares its students for 'life-long learning' as by how satisfactorily it inculcates correct behaviour or improves examination performance (see, for example, Alexander, 1998). Such conclusions persuade modern teachers to value the sorts of qualitative gains in knowledge which developmentalists describe, and it is to these that we pay special attention when studying how teachers organise and manage what their pupils do.

How do children learn and progress in ways we most value?

Although all children have to attend school, no-one can force them to learn if they are unwilling to do so, or be sure that they will learn where they struggle with new ideas. Traditionally, teachers have believed that to stimulate pupils' interest is one way of shortening the odds in their own favour: any programme of study benefits from learner-enthusiasm. However, capturing their interest is no longer the guarantor of classroom contentment. For one thing, the implementing of a standard curriculum in England and Wales during the 1990s, structured as key stages, geared to chronological age rather than learners' experiences and preferences, meant that some programmes had to be tackled within a timetable where speed and efficiency of learning, not enjoyment, were priorities. This does not imply that imaginative teachers cannot arouse pupils' enthusiasm for National Curriculum subjects, simply that its progressive structure (topics cannot be left out because they seem unduly demanding) and the need to 'cover ground' adequately, makes engaging with some topics at more than a formal level of involvement that much more difficult.

A more basic argument is that if teachers were to pay heed to the intrinsic value of what is being learned, they would be likely to have broader aims than those of nurturing interests. Pupils can enjoy activities which actually serve their long-term aspirations in limited, possibly dubious ways, while they may find it hard to foster those vocationally-linked interests they need in order to earn for themselves prosperous and fulfilling life styles. Cognitive psychologists now look past traditional motivational factors in their search for the best ways to achieve that true conceptualising of knowledge called 'knowledge transfer', which, it seems, has become the educationists' 'holy grail' (Adey and Shayer, 1994; Desforges, 1997; also Salomon and Gibberson, 1987; Voss, 1987). It is the ability to *apply* what we learn to situations outside classrooms which signals in-depth understanding. Moreover, although interest will tend to colour any learning which leads to transfer, psychologists believe that it does not always, and it is not necessarily the best indicator. What matters is that learners oversee their own accomplishments so that, gradually, they are able to adapt and re-adapt themselves flexibly to whatever is asked of them. This capability is called 'metacognitive' ability (Adey and Shayer, 1994; Desforges, 1993; Salomon and Gibberson, 1987), and it is probably owed more to a staunch commitment to study than to interest.

When enquiring into what ensures a real conceptual understanding of school subjects, Desforges (1997) tagged 'personal commitment' as especially important. In one case study (1993) of a young girl he called Claire he noted her perseverance with story composition, and her refusal to give up on the most daunting of themes because writing stories was an activity to which she had committed herself. Her self-respect was wrapped around the talent she believed she had. Story-composition was not her only enthusiasm and she was able to apply herself intelligently enough to other subject areas; but it was in this particular enterprise that she had decided she would excel. Desforges predicted that, because of her commitment, Claire was likely to engross herself in literature and literary studies over the longer term, whereas other subjects in which she invested less of her own feelings of self-worth, would probably be discarded sooner or later as lifelong pursuits.

The work of teachers and psychologists shows us that there are factors 'internal' to pupils' attitudes to school subjects which not only ease pupils through sticky periods in their school careers but are needed for learning to happen at all in any long-lasting sense. There are different qualities and types of task-engagement, and if we care only about our pupils' surface compliance with tasks, we may be closing doors into subjects rather than opening them. So when teachers set learning objectives for a class they must have an eye on the sorts of organisation likely to encourage pupils' self-identification with what they do – which may tempt some personal investment in the academic enterprise. More practically, when the principle of direct pupil engagement with curricula generates a teacher's strategies to the organisation of learning, it is called 'constructivist' (see Pollard, 1990), since this term stresses that learning is something pupils have to *do* for themselves for their own reasons and in ways structurally affecting their own minds, rather than it being something which *is done* to them. The challenge for teachers at all levels is to manage activities in ways which increase the probability that learners will commit themselves to study – even the study of a standard curriculum.

It is interesting to see how strands of educational theory are often interwoven with political trends. Teachers being faced with obeying National Curriculum orders fairly strictly resulted in theories surfacing in academic texts which legitimised the newly-reformed systems. A few British educationists abandoned out-and-out learner-centred theories at pretty much the same time that politicians were asking whether such theories were responsible for assumed low educational standards which, in turn, might have some bearing on Britain's poor industrial showing in a world market. These theories were replaced by notions of how sophisti-cated societies such as our own expect citizens to exercise skills which do not develop naturally but have to be taught, sometimes in a fairly didactic or highly structured fashion (see for example, Galton's discussion of 'direct instruction' and 'factory models' of learning, 1989; or Reynolds and Farrell's promoting of 'whole-class' interactive teaching, 1996). In 1987, a twentieth anniversary evaluation of the *Plowden Report*, usually accepted as a beacon of primary-school child-centred education, was notable for contributions announcing the demise of the report's influence (Bennett, 1987; Halsey and da Sylva,1987).

In the area of educational/developmental psychology, which was earlier suggested as a prime theoretical resource for teachers, Piagetian ideas of intellectual development have been systematically undermined.

The hallowing of 'neo-Vygotskian' beliefs in cultural learning as guides for schoolwork persuaded a number of writers that 'social constructivism' can better explain the way individual minds grow. In some versions of social constructivism, human learning is treated as not only culturally influenced but to a high degree culturally determined, flourishing in social settings such as schools where the skills and ideas required for intellectual progress are most evidently communicated and shared (Liverta-Sempio and Marchetti, 1997 review some of these theories; see also Mercer, 1991; Wertsch, 1991; Lucariello, 1995 for a critique).

Referring to the most recent debates within the field of child psychology, it is possible to sketch a slightly different thesis. The Piagetian and Vygoskian images of children as learners compete as modes of explanation only if we work as researchers within one or other tradition, as developmental psychologists may have to do. For teachers, and indeed for some developmentalists who glimpse each tradition's strengths and weaknesses, the insights locked inside these two dominant schools of child psychology are complementary; (for relevant accounts see Adey and Shayer, 1994; Kitchener, 1996; Lucariello, 1995; Nelson *et al.*, 1998; Smith, 1996; Valsiner, 1992). Whereas Vygotsky (1962; 1978) taught us that growing minds must feed on socially given knowledge and skills, and that certain levels of understanding cannot be gained until this happens, Piaget (1978) explained the pro-active, constructivist processes which we assume whenever someone engages mentally with a task.

Terminologically, we can point to the connections being supposed between individual and society found in educationally meaningful acts of learning, by talking of 'co-construction' (Cole and Wertsch, 1996; Nelson *et al.*, 1998; Verba, 1994), where this concept implies that both poles of process are always involved when individuals are educated within institutions. In practice, teachers have little choice but to respect the discrete nature of the two elements found in important acts of learning – the subjective needs of students and the specific requirements of the learning task itself – whatever their theoretical inclinations might be. Janus-like, teachers face in two directions every time they begin a lesson. They struggle to meet the legitimate aspirations of learners as these are expressed in each pupil's relative degree of interest, commitment, attention-span and so forth; at the same time, they cannot ignore the pressing claims of social context, crystallised within the subject orders themselves, and monitored by politicians, parents, Ofsted inspectors and so on. Reconciling students' need for personal fulfilment with the priorities set by a modern society creates tensions within schools and classrooms that can make the business of teaching enormously arduous and difficult. If teachers had only to follow their pupils' inclinations, or simply 'deliver' a set programme of study, their job would at least be straightforward! Having to attain both goals together is the hard backbone of the job.

It is a challenge teachers can meet armed with insight as well as fortitude. Two research examples reinforce principles of curricular organisation on which practitioners might rely, when trying to teach in ways which combine the two research traditions discussed above. They are instances of action research: that is, the researchers taught a programme using methods teachers can simulate or sift through for points of contact with their own situations. Although, formally, these projects were organised within a 'neo-Piagetian' framework, they benefitted from Vygotskian insights, being attempts to show how bridging from individual interest to cultural demand is not only possible but can bring measurable rewards, where clear guidelines are closely followed. One project was organised at a secondary level (Adey and Shayer, 1992) teaching eleven to twelve-year-old learners; the other was American research carried out with children of younger primary school age (Resnick *et al.*, 1992). Each will be described, in turn (for a slightly different perspective on these sorts of project, see Silcock, 1999).

Adey and Shayer's teaching of science to eleven and twelve-year-olds proved so effective that it heralded, they suggested, a 'revolution in method'. As interventionists, they did not instruct a class group directly, preferring to elicit students' own ideas then challenge these with alternatives. The ensuing 'cognitive conflict' pushed students into attending harder to the scientific problems they faced, and, in that way, to learn. At the outset, researchers enabled those attending their programme to become familiar, through discussion, with the important characteristics of scientific problem-solving, including the specialised language they would need to make sense of it. Also, during the programme, they used a question-answer technique to lead young adolescents towards a 'mindful' overview of the principles underlying what they had achieved.

The golden rule of this constructivist approach is to maintain learners' sense of their own progress, and thus their conviction that they are in charge of events. For this reason, in the project described, learners' individual solutions to problems were scrutinised as stepping stones to final solutions: in no event were 'correct' solutions preferred in advance of learners' own problem-solving. Added to the psychological justifications for this strategy, its scientific merit was to make sure that students grasped the logical bond between problems and solutions (that is, they would know why a problem-solution worked). Adey and Shayer's meticulous attention to students' control of their own problem-solving is what shines through their methodology. It was not just that they learned science, through their school syllabus, they could also be shown to have acquired the 'higher order' thinking skills which advanced academic study requires and which Vygotsky pointed out (1978) do not develop naturally.

In Resnick *et al.*'s (1992) programme, young 'socially unfavoured' primary school pupils were taught arithmetic. Six rules of procedure were followed. First, children's own mathematical notions nurtured out of school were talked about in the classroom. Second, the children were not required to abandon these ideas, but (exactly as with Adey and Shayer's programme) were taught to trust and value them. Third, they were instructed in formal notation by linking this notation to pupils' familiar, though intuitive understandings. Fourth, core mathematical ideas were introduced rapidly, so that they could be applied to situations. Fifth, children were taught how to apply their new arithmetical knowledge in everyday problem-solving. Sixth, as part of this teaching, pupils were engaged in proper, mathematical discussion, that is, they did not simply work on written tasks. Like Adey and Shayer, Resnick *et al.* claimed to have achieved dramatic success, finding that their methods were 'effective for children of all ability levels' (223).

There are differences between these projects, but their stronger similarities derive from their both being grounded in comprehensible theory. What in both cognitive development and school learning seems to matter is a matching of new knowledge to existing cognitive structure such that learners can integrate the former into the latter. Learners' present knowledge is elicited to be shown as valuable and worthy of use, so that when new knowledge is introduced it is seen by learners as a means of making sense of what have become living issues. The new knowledge is not introduced as sets of ideas disembedded from the experiences they illuminate – which is a danger teachers can ignore when pressed for time. Maurice Galton (1998) noted that even science teaching had become a rather formal business, with teachers covering ground simply to fulfil their curricular duties. Constructivists assume that school pupils have to move fairly steadily from areas of confidence to areas of ignorance, and to try to short-cut this bridging from known to unknown is to broach failure.

The two studies in their different ways asserted that although there is always a duality at the heart of school learning, often creating tensions between individual ambition and social pressures, it is perfectly possible to reconcile one to the other. We have to refuse to dilute the essentials of each, that is, the learning needs of individual pupils and the structural and conceptual criteria built into valued knowledge. This is why we may speak of learners 'negotiating' meanings: they have starting assumptions about where a scheme of work is leading which they will negotiate around the topic or ideal being presented. Learning is never completely open-ended or freely chosen. As Eisner (1993) commented, 'knowledge is always constructed relative to a framework, to a form of representation, to a cultural code, (as well as) to a personal biography'. As we have to avoid the temptation of treating pupils' existing beliefs and attitudes as no more than an irritating barrier to their progress, so we have to resist the thought that new knowledge can be locked into an existing enthusiasm.

Such traps are more than hypothetical. In some constructivist paradigms, an individual learner's existing perspective so paramountly determines what happens that new ideas appear to be kept at arms length and only introduced to flesh out concepts which have already emerged. By contrast, in other approaches, individual pupils' schemas are considered likely to be 'incomplete, hazy or even plain wrong' (Bennett, 1992) so that school learning is 'believed to be optimised in settings where social interaction, particularly between a learner and more knowledgeable others, is encouraged' (12). Both these approaches might be called 'constructivist', and they differ mainly in stress; neither are altogether false. Only, when we try to tailor more complete accounts, each is found to benefit through accommodation to the other.

What characterises the job of organising school curricula seem to be two hard facts: that there is new knowledge to be gained, which may be well outside a learner's prior experience; and that this new knowledge has to be accessed through a learner's own voluntary actions, by a process of transforming the new ideas in terms of what is already known. Teachers have little choice but to 'bridge between paradigms' (Millar, 1989).

Learners as managers of their own learning

Learners have in some sense to manage their own learning. Such a realisation follows from our agreeing that learners construct their own minds through their own efforts, albeit within socially defined, publicly validated contexts. When teachers do accept such a principle, they acknowledge that learners must become aware not only of the specific requirements set by a classroom activity but of the factors which directly decide its nature, such as the reasons why it is worthy of our attention, and how it fits into an overall programme of work.

As a matter of policy, it is crucial that children properly perceive, at their personal level of comprehension, the reasons why they are being asked to follow a curricular project. After all, they can hardly commit themselves to a subject which has no apparent relevance to them; and some degree of commitment, as argued earlier, underwrites the in-depth cognitive structuring assumed by knowledge-transfer. Commitment transcends interest: pupils may not be immediately attracted to a school topic, but they can still admit its value *viz-a-viz* their own academic and/or professional futures. It is by no means out of the way to negotiate some form of 'contract' between teachers and otherwise reluctant learners, stipulating what each will contribute to guarantee that degree of task-'engagement' (Blyth, 1984; Wallace, 1996) the educational enterprise demands. This contract (notional or real), would be a first practical step in curricular management. Any amount of time spent explaining the value of a programme of study is justified if it is spent bringing learners into some form of teacher-learner partnership, since without it, any further action will do no more than mark time from the learners' point of view.

The validation of learners' existing knowledge, culture and language

All research using the constructivist model of learning takes as axiomatic the idea that learners' existing concepts must be elicited, validated through use, applied to real-life scenes, challenged and tested out as rigorously as possible. It may seem a tall order for teachers to expect learners to have already intuitions or views of any substance on topics which may by their nature hover well above a student's present intellectual horizons, but there will, actually, always be such views. Indeed, if there are not, this can be the tell-tale sign that the topic itself is unsuited to the age-group being taught. The puzzle is thought not to be that of eliciting views as that of teachers finding the time and opportunity to engage each individual pupil's contribution relevantly. In a sense, this is the nature of skilled teaching – manufacturing scenarios which maximise the opportunities for all learners to contribute to a common theme. The point of such scenarios is to create a discourse within which the relevant academic knowledge can function as gateways to problem-solutions, implying that the scenarios will throw up problems learners want to solve. Strategies which will optimise learning are those which best highlight the value of the new knowledge in answering questions already known to be topical.

Significantly, the principle of exploiting existing knowledge embraces not only the idea of individual preferences of viewpoint and opinion, but of cultural variabilities also. Whether cherished ideas stem from a culturally specific bias or an idiosyncratic experience makes no difference in so far as justifying their expression is concerned: and in certain contexts (such as moral and religious debate), it could well be that a personal view will be reinforced rather than modified by discussion. The point is that the effects of ensuring that pupils prefer their mental starting points are both cognitive and affective: teachers can judge what intellectual adjustments are needed to make progress, and can establish through the validating of that starting point learner self-esteem. The Resnick *et al.* (1992) study ingeniously demonstrated the wisdom of engaging pupils in discussion of newly introduced ideas using their existing language; they were actively obliged to use their existing intuitive categories to pin down what was novel. Bilingual and multilingual learners or children from working class homes studying (say) historical or geographical topics concerning some class-sensitive or ethnocentric themes might well have strong opinions grounded in their own cultures about the theme under consideration. Only in a secure context where it has been established unambiguously that such opinions can validly be stated might they surface.

Driver (1989) pointed out that there is a lot of research showing how childrens' prior conceptions can differ substantially from what has to be learned, and that therefore the business of enabling pupils to grasp what is new is at the heart of a teacher's job. She also reminded us (with Bell, 1986) that learners can make sense of an idea but not believe it; that is, teachers can succeed in teaching some fact or concept which learners nonetheless cannot see as relevant to anything else or contextualise within the actual worlds they inhabit. This chastening recognition underwrites the importance of teachers letting learners volunteer their own framework of meanings within which the new ideas can be shown to make sense. What is to be avoided (at all costs, really) is coercing students to acquire knowledge 'disembedded' from familiar contexts. We are back, if we do that, with mechanical learning for no other purpose than rote repro-duction. This can inhibit further progress by persuading students that it has no relevance to real life: it is not a means to a richer, fuller type of existence, but an end in itself, useful for party games, or a trivial pursuit.

Learning new ideas

Resnick *et al.* introduced a new mathematical language quickly. More usually, constructivists are cautious about introducing what is new except when they are sure it will be assimilated to what is already known. Introducing a new language as a potential form of discourse and as the sole medium in which a topic will be engaged must be differentiated.

Evidently, no learners can use familiar ideas to address what is novel unless novelty is already present. The rule is that one need not be wary of learners encountering subjects 'too quickly' (this is to disinter the 'readiness' fallacy), only of forcing on them the new language as preferable to their own from the start. There are many ways in which teachers can introduce new material rapidly and painlessly – through film, video, computer programmes, various visual and audio aids, books, posters, games etc. The value of introducing what is new, speedily, in a variety of ways, but without enforcing immediate usage, is partly that learners tend to employ different sorts of learning style and will learn anyhow at different rates and partly that the new ideas can remain semi-permanently fixed within an environment to be played with, exploited, dissected, syn-thesised, disputed, reflected on, rejected, replaced, and so on. When learners are invited to apply their own perspectives, they may uncover insights into the historical, geographical, scientific, and so on, concepts they are being asked to address, which catch others' imaginations also.

Resnick *et al.* went further. They scaffolded pupil discussions towards proper mathematical debates – in their project they mediated what was happening to guarantee it was mathematics which was being learned. This is to impose a 'top down' framework upon what is happening, and one can see that without this final step a curriculum might never escape from idio-syncratic problem-setting and unrealistic invention. A common criticism of the established idea of 'learning by discovery' is that it is fatuous to expect pupils to re-discover knowledge we have long been quite sure about, except in the sense that problem-solutions must be 'discovered' as relevant to real-life situations. This latter contextualising of knowledge is the constructivist principle, not the idea that, somehow, all knowledge must gradually emerge within self-generated environments.

Hypothesis testing

It is no accident that constructivists seem most at home in laboratories. It is part of the tradition of science teaching that method – the business of testing out hypotheses to check theories – is what reigns in science, not a set of known laws or rules. But all academic subjects, presumably, evolve through some type of hypothesis testing and if we wish our students to become in a nascent sense historians, geographers, musicians and so on, rather than simply knowledgeable in these subjects, they must learn to pursue the subjects independently of teachers. One might argue that indulging in hypothesis testing, which can be time-consuming, is best left to degree courses, rather than becoming integral to primary and secondary school work; or that hypothesising is appropriate for science studies but not literary studies or work in the humanities and the arts. Such an argument cannot be sustained. Given the cache these days accorded to experimentation in the arts, and the enormous variation in perspectives drawn from a world culture which informs the humanities, not only is hypothesis-testing a viable way of checking out all school subjects, it is the only sure way to prevent indoctrination or the early death of imaginative solutions to our severest social problems (for example, of pollution, racism, poverty) which sometimes seem universally endemic. Certain difficulties looming large now are unlikely to have gone away before our present students become adult. If we teach existing solutions as 'givens' without opening up subjects to innovation and radical exploration, we might be diverting some future world benefactors from their true vocation.

The difficulty of encouraging pupils to hypothesise in more 'practical' subject areas is another matter, although creative work, by its nature, is meant to invite openness and experimentation. It is quite possible for students to reject that invitation. When teaching art, for example, it has become common in primary school classrooms for children to copy work of famous artists such as Van Gogh, as a way into understanding the artist's work. Surely, there is more to be gained from, for example, pupils painting their own *Sunflowers* or *Pipe and Chair* or *Self Portrait* in order to compare these with Van Gogh's vision. Certainly, comparisons with valued models is necessary, but whereas the danger of art teaching was, once, that anything children produced was considered of value merely because it was fresh and seen with eyes unclouded by the adulterated experience of growing up, now we straightjacket imagination in the worn clothing of dead artists or the finished creations of musicians and dancers. We do not want the idea that there is no other way than the one presented by established artists, dancers, musicians.

Sharing meanings

In the educational literature, two models of learning are sometimes contrasted, that in which pupils are 'lone scientists' and that in which they are shown to be 'social beings' learning from others and from each other (Bennett 1992: 11), the latter being the 'correct' model. It is prudent to repeat: both are correct, depending on the perspective taken. All learners are alone in their musings and speculations, in the sense that their starting points will be uniquely determined (and will continue to be uniquely determined throughout life whenever they face new tasks), while their mental advances will be structured within culturally meaningful frame-works. This dual stipulation matters. The learning-potential bound up with it tells how pupils engaged in hypothesis-testing, in contexts where real-life problems are at issue, will devise unique solutions to those problems. This follows from first premises. Except regarding the very simplest forms of learning, we always interpret events and problem-solutions (even those passed on by the more knowledgeable) in terms of prior interpretations. Having made such interpretations, we will wish to share them, and in the sharing, come to negotiate, re-interpret, re-fashion and develop them further. As part of any curriculum project, learners should come together to talk about their own successes and hardships. This communal interplay of views stimulates motivation as well as providing venues for sharing insights.

It is as informed individuals that we best learn from (and teach, of course), members of groups. The extreme neo-Vygotskian idea that we can only learn properly through interaction with others is dangerous, because, if it were true, learners would always be swayed by the views of those in dominant social positions. Admittedly, it would be just as dangerous to assume the opposite, that individuals overcome obstacles only through personal effort and take nothing from group work apart from the learning of social skills. Both social interaction and individual hypothesis-testing are bedrocks of classroom learning. Successful education assumes the interaction between individual and social processes as much as between individuals within groups.

The management of teaching

Decisions taken about learning set up criteria for teaching. Whatever strategies teachers use, these must be geared somewhere to conditions we think enhance pupils' mental and behavioural improvement. That is why, historically, the nature of classroom teaching has altered in line with our altered views of learning. The behaviourist/cognitive divide mentioned earlier, which split apart our conceptions of human learning, also separated, loosely speaking, two phases of teaching. In the first phase, educationists believed, somewhat optimistically, that theoretical refinement and controlled experimentation would, one day, lead to a 'science' of pedagogy, whereby we would be able to engineer fairly precisely the sort of educated society we might set as our ideal. This optimism accompanied behaviourists' pretty exclusive reliance on the scheduling of rewards (and witholding rewards) as a discriminating factor in teaching success: by manipulating reward systems, teachers should have been able, eventually, to reach their various utopias. Lately, we have become less sanguine about what schools can achieve, sensing the limits set for any educative process by the effect prevailing cultural and socio-economic factors have upon individuals.

However, our beliefs about how to manage learning and cognitive development are not the only beliefs affecting professional teachers, although they are the ones which must always figure somewhere in a teacher's planning. We find when examining the peculiarities of teaching, or pedagogy, that added to the criterion set by learner needs are two very general sorts which qualify it. There are limitations owed to extrinsic circumstances (such as the accountability system operated by managers, Ofsted, politicians and parents, and requirements set by examinations and so forth); then, there are more intrinsic constraints born from teachers' own skill-resources, the limitations imposed by what they can put together from their own professional armoury. A useful way of describing this is to say that teaching, like learning, is structured in both 'top down' and 'bottom up' ways: when teachers take classroom decisions they will be working within limitations imposed by others and by their own skills.

Precisely how they cope with the two types of limitation depends on how these are conceived and how practically demanding they turn out to be. It also depends on how the constraints operate in classrooms *vis-à-vis* the particular needs of learners already discussed. It is not easy to weigh up how, at any one time, learner-demands, developed skills and externally devised frameworks differentially determine what teachers do; and to untangle the links between these influences we need, again, to turn to theoretical studies. Fortunately, there are, in the relevant literature, two dominant model-approaches to teaching which are helpful in guiding us towards a strategically balanced position regarding the various factors which impinge on teachers' work. These have been called 'technical rationality' and 'reflective practice' (for a comparison see Schon, 1983).

What is skilled teaching?

'Technical rationality' is a term suggesting how teachers can follow a publicly designed blue-print to resolve common teaching dilemmas. Whatever problems they face, there is somewhere a method or technique which can be selected, on rational grounds, to subdue these problems. By contrast, models of reflective practice suppose that teaching is such a complex business that practitioners have to rely for guidance on a set of mindful, practical coping-skills garnered from experience. They will not have the time, usually, to resort to textbook solutions or techniques which will, in any case, seldom fit the unique requirements of classrooms. For those who favour this second approach, teaching follows an intrinsic design: it corresponds to what good teachers do, because they have learned what does and does not work for them, professionally speaking.

Teachers must maintain a balance between the demands of technical rationality and the limitations set by their own reflective capabilities. Certainly, if we start by spelling out the former, teachers cannot avoid matching their work to those standards set by Ofsted (1995) and those researchers who have explored what makes for effective practice. In the light of empirical findings, we can be confident that the most effective teachers will benefit from firm, pro-active management, will share goals, teach purposefully, have high expectations of pupils, monitor and reward pupil progress (Sammons *et al.*, 1995). So, when Ofsted inspectors walk into a school they look, *inter alia*, for these things. Indeed, few teachers are likely to quarrel with researchers or inspectors about adopting such criteria. Strong leadership, workable communication systems and positive relationships, ordered classrooms and happy pupils are well-known foundations for good practice.

What effectiveness researchers typically omit from their studies are guidance on exactly how to design successful communication systems and professional rapport between staff, what types of expectations of pupil achievement teachers should have and what pupils should actually be rewarded for – they do not list the 'good' and 'bad' ways of attaining those desirable states which indisputably characterise successful schools. As an illustration: 'strong leadership' tops many lists of criteria determining good schools, but researchers (Sammons *et al.*, 1995) do not pre-determine how a 'strong' headteacher should or should not behave. This is not because they are unable to pigeonhole leadership qualities; it is because to do so would pre-empt other sorts of behaviour which might equally well fit the bill. Put simply: there is no *single* way to create harmony in class-rooms, communicate well, take strong decisions, maintain high staff morale and pupil self-esteem; and those who rely on technical rationality to post our way forward only state criteria so general and abstract that few teachers are ever likely to deny them, or even refer to them, except as items to be ticked off on a check list when preparing for a curriculum evaluation or school inspection. These criteria have value, for sake of accountability. But they leave the hardest teaching decisions virtually untouched.

When we suggest that teachers are reflective practitioners, we are accepting the weakness of technical rationality and validating the many and varied ways in which teachers sort out difficulties. It is teachers, themselves, in the special circumstances of their schools, faced by pupils of particular sorts, who have to contrive ways of resolving their own dilemmas. These ways cannot be prescribed in advance of our encounter-ing the dilemmas themselves, so it is sterile to try to list as 'competencies' the precise strategies which teachers habitually use. Yet, of course, some blue-print for good practice must exist: pragmatic skills alone cannot make for good teaching. Teachers who spend years refining their communica-tion and management skills may still not achieve satisfactory results, simply because there is more involved than behavioural expertise. Some-one who indoctrinates or terrorises pupils may have charisma and be extraordinarily skilled; someone who preaches drug-abuse or peddles ill-digested knowledge, may be pragmatically gifted. In other words, we can be reflective practitioners and still be abysmal teachers.

Such a conclusion is not lost on those who promote reflective practice, and many take pains to adapt the model as initially worked through by, for example, Schon (1983; 1987) so as to concede that thinking practitioners try consciously to use their undoubted skills in some ways rather than others. Carr (1995) insisted that teachers take a 'critical' perspective upon their own jobs, never allowing themselves to be wholly content with states of affairs decided by politicians, curricular specialists, and Ofsted inspectors. Other writers considered how they could help teachers unearth from their own experiences some built-in rationale, so as to prepare ground for improvement (Ferstenmacher, 1986; Pope, 1993). Confirming that professional teaching is too sophisticated an enterprise to be coped with purely pragmatically, Griffiths and Tann (1992) wrote that teachers should devise a variety of different forms of professional discourse, so as to take account of publicly validated, academic theories in helping them decide what is or is not good practice. Others, similarly, contrived ways of lifting teachers from a 'grounded' to a more sophisticated level of skill: the Pollard and Tann model (1992) of reflective teaching entailed practitioners assessing their performance in the light of publicly stated criteria and modifying skills as necessary. If reflective practice alone does not make for good teaching, but teachers must routinely assess their own success and adapt policies accordingly, then teaching is a form of 'action research', whereby teachers test out, term by term, year by year, different ways of achieving their aims, settling eventually on the most successful ways while knowing that these, too, may ultimately have to be discarded in the light of changing circumstances.

We return, better informed, to our earlier position of admitting that acceptable teaching must be built on the developed skills of practitioners but must follow routes determined by others; that is, it has to be both intrinsically and extrinsically founded. A brief critical review of the two model approaches not only exposes their built-in limitations but crystallises the relationship between them, introducing the further issues raised by our knowledge of pupil learning. Presumably, good teachers will always be reflective practitioners and skilled technicians, seeking to improve in those areas stipulated by Ofsted inspectors (among others) as important. If the two implied types of criteria were the only ones at issue, we might still wonder what precisely they meant for any one teacher seeking to ensure that pupils learn in worthwhile ways. General models do not in themselves prescribe behaviours: they simply provide further criteria by which professional behaviours can be judged. We can now clarify where the criteria worked out with regard to learning fit with the other two groups.

It is learner-specific conditions which fashion the direction in which a teacher's professional development must be *deployed*, both intrinsically (in terms of the development of special forms of skill) and extrinsically (providing precise goals to achieve). This is crucial. Studies of technical rationality and reflective practice show that teaching is directed within two interlocking contexts, that of public accountability and that owed to practitioners' available skills. But the point of teachers working within these two contexts is to guarantee that pupils learn, and any learner-specific factors we take into account must temper a teacher's regard for public expectation just as, during professional development, they will have helped forge pedagogic skill. This point is emphasised because teachers' responsibility to promote pupil learning is at the heart of the professional job and will, in the end, override other responsibilities and provoke whatever is needed in terms of practical strategy.

At the point of action, three interrelated pressures decide what teachers actually do. Two of these are very general, in that they set parameters rather than determine actions, the third points directly to the strategies needed to ensure that worthwhile pupil learning occurs. To be precise: when teachers plan lessons, initiate a teaching programme, select a resource, they will have the measure of their own capabilities and fallibilities, they will know what public bodies expect, they will have reasonably clear beliefs about how their own pupils learn. Each of these pressures lends its own discrete powers to a pedagogic decision, such that principles of practice are best described with regard to each one, while remembering that, in the end, they have to synthesise harmoniously.

Teaching as reflective practice

Teaching is a pragmatic business. Teachers have to meet practical dilemmas with practical solutions. One of Schon's (1983) most telling images is that of teachers' 'conversing with situations' to uncover what a particular environment demands of their judgements and resources. The nature of pragmatism is such that no solutions to problems are precluded on theoretical or ideological grounds. What works is what matters. Often enough, that is how it is in teaching. Pragmatism rules. There cannot be any 'no go' areas of teaching method, strategy or technique. Whole-class grouping, small group and individualistic teaching, the use of ICT and other forms of technology, hands-on experience, different forms of discussion, independently managed or negotiated learning, collaborations, co-operations, and so on, are all grist to any teacher's mill in terms of their potential for pragmatic problem-solving. Really knotty practical problems might be resolved by a teacher resorting to some singular, radical solution to which he or she never returns.

The detailing of this principle sounds like eclecticism ('pick and mix' according to situation), but it is not. Guiding criteria which will decide method are not, just, the practical nature of the problem itself and what might be thought pragmatically likely to work: there are (working beneath the surface of actions to much more virile effect) the aims to be achieved and values thereby fulfilled, which refer us back to the conditions required for pupil learning. Practical problem-solving has two poles: there are practicalities, and there are the reasons why the practicalities exist at all, that is, the aims of teaching. Once this is understood, pragmatism is seen to serve broader ends. The reflective practitioner becomes one whose action-research approach tests out all methods for their effectiveness in regulating the constructivist learning situations listed above. These need not be highly informal, despite the rather informal flavour of the con-structivist canon. As Millar reasoned (1989), constructivist (i.e. pupil-centred) learning does not necessarily imply constructivist teaching. What might make the difference to a teacher's opting for one technique or another are his or her existing strengths relative to the various types of constraints under which he or she works. Just as it makes sense for learners to move from areas of familiarity and confidence to areas of ignorance and weakness, so it makes sense for teachers to try out well rehearsed practices to fathom how far they work in achieving the learner commitment and mindful effort which have been pinned down as our main targets. Some teachers organise lessons very successfully in formal ways, some are expert story-tellers, and others set up co-operative tasks, experimental or play situations, with enormous dexterity. The funda-mental principle of method is the tie-up between what is expediently likely to work and the learner need.

Teachers as technological bureaucrats

Technical rationality is not the villain of teaching, as it is sometimes portrayed. Teachers have to be accountable to parents and to others, and this accountability is pre-decided as forms of report, National Curriculum assessments, forms of appraisal, league-tables of scores, Ofsted attainments, ethical and professional rules of conduct enforced by teacher-unions, peers and senior managers, and so forth. To fulfil their public obligations, it is necessary for teachers to grasp in fair detail the accountability systems which are operating; that is, they must know what form National Curriculum tests take, what the National Curriculum subject orders present, and what Ofsted inspectors look for. To say this is to say the obvious. But such obviousness is not always carried through in practice. Wilkinson and Howarth (1996) discovered that many teachers' understanding of what Ofsted inspectors looked for was based on hearsay and rumour rather than on a close study of the latest Ofsted framework. When researchers (Gray and Wilcox, 1995) followed up Ofsted's visits to schools, they found that a number of schools did not carry through the action plans they were obliged to draw up on the basis of the report. In other words, public accountability, conforming to external standards, may take second place to teachers' more pressing, parochial concerns.

Naturally, teachers' proper comprehension of the publicly devised framework in which they work is non-negotiable. This is not only because teachers are professionals who have to measure their actions against publicly-agreed criteria, but because the whole array of National Curricular legislation and further legislation flowing from the 1988 Education Reform Act transformed the bureaucratic peripheries of the job. New documents are published almost daily by government quangos such as the Qualifications and Curriculum Authority (QCA); and whereas it is unrealistic to expect teachers to be always up to date with these, some comprise such essential reading it is hard to see how teachers can carry out their jobs in ignorance of them. Teachers do not need reminding that their jobs have acquired a dimension of bureaucracy much vaster than the oldest teachers can ever have dreamed possible. The central control of education has spawned and continues to spawn written guidelines and directives (sometimes quite radical in what they imply for classroom action) which correspond to an ever-growing paper technology: in short, teachers as a daily part of their jobs apply systems dictated by someone else.

However, and this brings us back to the pivotal principle, whatever paper technologies are born from the fancies of politicians, their effectiveness depends on how far they promote pupil learning. Ofsted inspections have not always led to school improvement (Brimblecombe *et al.*, 1996; Gray and Wilcox, 1995) because their recommendations, which do not match teachers' own judgements about what will or will not work in classrooms, may well be ignored (Thomas, 1997). We have to see the point of this. No one else, other than teachers, can finally judge whether or not their teaching works: if it does not, there is absolutely no good reason for continuing with it, whatever an inspection report might advise. In general, this comment has to be made of any educational reform. A reason why the National Curriculum itself undergoes continuous revision is that it initi-ally made the business of teaching more time-consuming and pedagog-ically cumbersome than straightforward. It may have led indirectly to poor outcomes, as Galton suspected (1998). We cannot lose sight of the central purpose of teaching which is to promote the learning of pupils. A clean LEA bill of health, an excellent appraisal or Ofsted report, a happy senior management team, cannot stand in place of that. Obviously, one is not saying these sorts of evaluation are usually opposed to actual pupil attainments; that would represent an absurd idea. The bureaucracy of reporting and assessment, responding to evaluations and dictats from others, should be umbilically bound to the learning outcomes they are meant ultimately to reflect.

Teaching as ideology

Teachers are more than pragmatists and technologists. Tricks of practical problem-solving combined with a prudent attention to the guidelines worked out by others do not tell us how to teach in ways ensuring pupil commitment and quality learning. This is because our knowledge of key educational questions (concerning for example how to achieve knowledge transfer) is uncertain and in some areas scanty; and, as often as not, it waits upon more fundamental questions of value. Those systems of belief, related to personal and professional values, which give us answers to basic questions such as 'what is education for?' are called ideologies, and it is as imperative for teachers habitually to reflect upon their ideological com-mitments as it is for someone working in politics, religion, or philosophy. Theories which, here, underwrite accounts of learning and cognitive development (and therefore ultimately constrain how teachers should teach) have been called 'constructivist' or 'neo-Piagetian'. Such theories generate beliefs about appropriate ways to organise learning situations for pupils which, together with beliefs about what it is valuable for children to learn and the most appropriate way to guarantee their rights, combine ideologically. It is not essential that the theories of development outlined above should be believed – indeed, there are a number of 'neo-Piagetian' or 'post-Piagetian' positions which might be preferred (see Sutherland, 1992). But a commitment has to be made to some position or other. Otherwise, classroom decisions made will either lack consistency or will follow someone else's agendas.

Ideologies can give rise to dogma; they often polarise opinion unnecessarily and can generate rhetoric which proves unhelpful. For these reasons, many have sought to rid education of ideological discourse, and it is not as common as it once was to find ideological judgements made as a natural part of teaching. Occasionally, an educational break-through seems to herald an era when we will be able to rely on certain knowledge rather than a shakily held belief to show the way forward. The dawn of a computer age, for example, might seem such a break-through in teaching. Yet American research tells us that computers can be used well or badly in classrooms, and the 'hands-on' strategies, usually ideologically described (Luban, 1989; Weir, 1989), seem to make the difference.

The fact that value-soaked principles are thought politically inconvenient, or even damaging in their potential effects, does not mean that they should or can be ignored. It may be the very centrality of ideologies to the business of education that creates their power to distort our judgements. We have to be on our guard against bias and indoctrination, and seek regularly to justify our beliefs. But teachers cannot suppress their own values (for example, what they believe their fundamental purposes are as teachers). They can only act in the light of these, as well as in obedience to the pragmatics of classrooms and the dictates which will always shower from above. To recognise, review, act upon and defend a value-centred belief-system is part of being a professional educator, as much as it has to be part of the persona of a priest or a cabinet minister.

Conclusion

How teachers manage their curricula will be dictated by their awareness of their own skills within the bureaucratic context set by politicians and senior managers, but it will be most obedient to their professional beliefs – about themselves as people and as professionals, and about the nature of pupil learning and intellectual development. Issues connected with our best accounts of what happens when human beings learn, in ways thought likely to profit them over the long term, are at the heart of pedagogy. To manage both learning and teaching situations implies a sorting out of decisions in terms of the natural priorities born of the relationships between the processes as these have been described, then implementing these through appropriate school and classroom policies. Teaching is a complex business, affected by widely diverse matters originating in worlds as different as the economic, the technological and the psychological. But some of these matters will catch our attention more than others. If managing classrooms means managing priorities, teaching is about promoting those types of learning which substantially benefit pupils – that is its only priority of consequence.

5.   Leading and Managing Staff

Ian and Kath Terrell

Introduction

This chapter concentrates upon the issues and trends in leading and managing staff which emerged in the late twentieth century. The work is influenced by discussions with headteachers and teachers on a variety of professional development and training programmes during the 1990s. In addition, some of the work is based upon research, internal evaluation and consultancy activities not previously published. These varied activities include audits of schools for the *Investors in People* (IIP) standard, research conducted as part of the DES School Development Plan project, evaluation of TVEI (in two LEAs) and research on the impact of Ofsted inspection as a process of school improvement.

Leading and managing at a time of endemic change

The TTA (1998b) stated that headteachers should 'lead, motivate, support, challenge and develop staff to secure improvement'. These processes were further broken down into a range of activities (11):

- maximising the contribution of staff to improving the quality of education provided and standards achieved;
- ensuring constructive working relationships between staff and pupils;
- planning, allocating, supporting and evaluating work;

- managing performance, including through appraisal;
- motivating staff and ensuring they have high quality professional development;
- sustaining their own motivation;
- ensuring that all staff fulfil their duties as set out in the terms and conditions of service of teachers.

However many staff in schools have felt that they have been through a long period of improvement, or certainly change. The first issue in leading and managing staff is to be clear about the nature of change and improvement, its origins and our attitude to it, and the attitudes we wish to foster in our staff. At a time of multiple, rapid and continuous change, leading and managing staff has at its heart the ability to manage change in order to bring about higher standards of education. As it was stated in a Green Paper (DfEE, 1998c):

> In a world of rapid change, every pupil will need to be literate, numerate and prepared for the citizenship of tomorrow. They will need the self-esteem and confidence to learn throughout life, and to play an active part at work and in their community ... We need a new vision of a profession which offers better rewards and support in return for higher standards. Our aim is to strengthen school leadership, provide incentives for excellence, engender a strong culture of professional development, offer better support to teachers to focus on teaching in the classroom, and improve the image, morale and status of the profession.

We have known, perhaps for the past thirty years, that we have been in a time of rapid technological, political and social change. Certainly, since Toffler wrote *Futureshock* in 1971 we have experienced change that is endemic, constant, rapid and accelerating. A number of authors, (for example, Naisbitt and Aburdene, 1990; Caldwell and Spinks, 1992; and West-Burnham and O'Sullivan, 1998) identified what they saw as consistent, enduring and global forces or 'megatrends' that underpinned current changes. Such forces included:

- A technological revolution
- An information explosion
- Increased globalisation of the economic system

- Growing participation and equality for women in society and the economy
- Different patterns of relationships and family life
- Increased central control of education in terms of curriculum, quality control/inspection
- Decentralisation of the management of education to schools
- Transience

For those leading and managing staff, these factors provide a mixture of challenge and opportunity as they seek to create conditions in which children can be prepared to take their place in tomorrow's world.

We are, perhaps, too closely involved with these trends to say precisely where change will take us. We can look back at previous eras of change and name them by their key features. The Agricultural Revolution was based upon the movement from subsistence agriculture to mechanisation and a commercial approach. The Industrial Revolution created factories, industries, towns and cities based upon the power of steam and the fuel of coal. The revolution in our times is in information technology. So close and so ongoing are the attendant changes that it is hard to predict where they will lead us. There is a sense that we are only on the lowest slopes of the mountain of change being created by advances in information technology. What seems clear is that change is with us and will stay.

Education systems throughout the world are feeling the impact of these global trends. The demand for higher standards, the development of local management of schools and a concern for high quality teaching are not only to be found in the British system. They are trends which span continents, cultures and systems. Recent copies of education journals such as *School Effectiveness and School Improvement* provide testimony to this international dimension.

For school leaders and managers, these trends represent challenges that have not really been faced before. These can be expressed through the medium of a number of commonly heard statements:

'We don't know for sure what to expect next.'

'We cannot rely on the experience and expertise of the previous generation.'

'We have to be adaptable and flexible.'

'We have to cope with many different views.'

'We have to deal with the interests of many different "stakeholders" in our work including pupils, parents, the community, and business.'

'We would like schools to contribute to building a better society and way of life.'

Such perceptions and concerns have placed greater demands on schools. We are no longer satisfied with some 20 per cent of children in a limited number of selective schools succeeding in public examinations as was the case shortly after the 1944 Education Act. We are in an age of national targets for improving standards with the expectation that standards must improve. Our definition of what is of high quality and worth in schools has changed and will continue to change. Leaders must both expect this to happen during their leadership years and, furthermore, convince staff that they can continue to meet new demands.

How do leaders view these changes?

A key issue for leaders and managers is how they view change in education and how they encourage staff to view these changes. There are several attitudes towards change. Based on the ideas of Whitaker (1993) it is possible to see change in different ways:

The swing of the pendulum: 'If we wait long enough, the pendulum will swing back our way.'

Incremental: 'We just need to take one small, cautious step at a time.'

Doom: 'Whatever we do it will lead to disaster.'

Technological: 'All our problems will be solved by technological improvements.'

Victim: 'They will force us to change.'

Expert authority: 'An expert will be able to tell us what to do.'

Assertive: 'We will be able to take this opportunity to build a better school.'

Paradigm: 'We need to change our old ways of thinking.'

Back to basics: 'We need to concentrate on the basics.'

Taking control of pressures for change and not being a victim of them is central to schools that are 'moving', using the definition adopted by Hopkins *et al*. (1994). To achieve higher standards does not mean seeing all external pressures to change as irresistible. Hopkins used the term 'wandering' for those schools that adopt every new initiative and centrally imposed change, without any real impact being made. In such circumstances, a succession of staff, over a number of years, became fully committed to all manner of initiatives and changes. Most lasted for short periods of time before the next initiative took over. The school remained much as it did and key aspects of the culture of the school were unaffected. The key to raising standards lies in seizing the opportunities presented by change and working with staff to exploit the possibilities. Possibilities for change need to be evaluated in terms of their potential for achieving the underlying aims of the school and in terms of their ability to address individual and collective needs. The DfEE's (1998a) advice on school improvement was that:

The main responsibility for improving schools lies with the schools themselves.

The relationship between change and improvement

To most practitioners change is obviously not the same as improvement. Hopkins (1994: 3) saw school improvement in terms of 'enhancing student outcomes and strengthening the school's *capacity* for managing change' [our italics]. He gave a definition that defines school improvement as:

Raising student achievement through focusing on the teaching and learning process and the *conditions* which support it. It is about strategies for improving the school's *capacity* for providing quality education in times of change, rather than blindly accepting the edicts of centralised policies and striving to implement these directives uncritically [our italics].

Clearly the leader-manager must work on a notion of what improvement is. Student achievement is central in its broadest sense, not just in the sense of academic attainment. There is a call for recognition of the importance of the whole curriculum, of spiritual, moral and social education, of the development of social skills. Hopkins focused upon building the internal *conditions* and the *capacity* of the school to take on external pressures for change, and named:

- Leadership
- Staff development
- Reflection and enquiry
- Involvement
- Co-ordination
- Collaborative planning

These processes are best not viewed as merely acts of management or administration, but as avenues through which to create a culture of school improvement. They should be seen as some of the focal points. Another way of viewing the process of school improvement was provided by the DfEE's (1998a) five-stage cycle of school improvement. This cycle of school improvement illustrates the current context for leadership and management in a world where there is an emphasis on raising pupil achievement, calls for ever higher standards of professionalism and an increasing trend towards centrally mandated changes. But what is important is how such changes are mediated and led and how they are used to bring about school improvement.

Stage 1   The school analyses its current performance: 'How well are we doing?'   Looking critically at pupils' current achievements is an essential first step towards improvement.

Stage 2	Compares its results with those of similar schools: 'How do we compare with similar schools?'	By comparing current and previous results, and those from similar schools, a school can better judge performance.
Stage 3	Sets itself clear and measurable targets: 'What more should we aim to achieve this year?'	With good information, a school can set itself realistic and challenging targets for improvement.
Stage 4	Revises its development plan to highlight action to achieve the targets: 'What must we do to make it happen?'	Once it has set its targets, the school must take de-termined action to improve.
Stage 5	Takes action, reviews success, and starts the cycle again.	A school must monitor and evaluate its actions in terms of improved pupil performance.

Complexities of school management and leadership

As a consequence of external pressures for change, the 1980s and 1990s saw an explosion of school management, and leadership as a field of activity, legislation, research, literature, advice and guidance. Let us list some of the areas of educational management that have developed:

- school development planning;
- local management of schools;
- staff development supported by targeted funding;
- teacher and headteacher appraisal;
- target setting;
- school self evaluation;
- development of the role of governors.

As in any explosion, a small core of matter grew in volume and became disconnected. Hence, the document *From Targets to Action* (DfEE, 1997) repeated some of the language of school development in the earlier document *Planning for School Development* (DES, 1989) without any reference to it, as though they were disconnected.

The key issue at all levels has been to make links and connections between what can appear as disparate initiatives into practical focused and solid strategies for school improvement. As the headteacher and senior management team struggle with this problem there is the danger of not doing anything, or of putting the wrong bits back together and creating something that was neither intended or will not work.

In the late 1980s, school development planning research suggested that schools faced the difficulty of linking school development and financial planning. In the late 1990s research for *Investors in People* (IIP) audits revealed the difficulties that schools were still facing in linking financial plans for development to staff and school development plans.

The managers of the twenty-first century need to have the capacity to draw all aspects of management together within a clearly focused set of aims. Making the connections between vision, mission statements, strategic plans, and short-term school plans is one thing. Linking to financial plans and staff development plans, while incorporating school and individual targets and Ofsted inspection action plans adds to the complexity. Indeed, this can be even more difficult when each of these areas is in the hands of a different senior manager, emphasising the need for greater co-ordination, a team approach and involvement.

In larger schools and particularly those with strong subject departments, leadership and management is made more difficult by the possibility of tension between whole school development and the development of individual department areas. The flavour of the document, *Planning School Development* (DES, 1989) was of a whole school plan focusing on between three and five priorities. Throughout the 1990s some schools retained a school plan as a compilation of department plans, while others moved towards a whole school plan, without much reference to individual departments. Clearly some tension would remain between whole school and departmental plans unless there were effective communication and clarity about aims and strategy.

There is a real problem in deciding which management activities and strategies are vital to the well-being of the school and its improvement and which are fashionable but not particularly essential. For instance, *building* mission statements can be very effective in:

- creating a team approach;
- focusing on key issues and values;
- guiding strategic development;
- creating consensus.

However, the leader-manager must decide whether mission statement building is necessary. What if the school built a mission statement a few years ago with the previous headteacher? What if there are some more pressing things to be addressed more urgently? What if the goals of creating a mission statement can be achieved by, for instance, developing a teaching and learning policy through collaborative teams? The idea of having a mission statement should not become a *mantra*, or an item on a checklist of effective practice. As Bowman and Asch (1996) pointed out:

> Most mission statements can be located in this cell (of impoverished strategy), particularly if they contain pious platitudes that no one really believes. Unfortunately mission statements have been devalued as a strategy device because they have been used indiscriminately and have been thrust into organisations in inappropriate ways. This is the mission statement as a fashion item (everyone else has one, so perhaps we should have one too?). This is unfortunate because a well-crafted mission statement can be a powerful working document. But it must be preceded by a thorough analysis of the organisation's situation.

As Fullan (1991: 138-53) stated: 'serious reform is not implementing single innovations. It is changing the culture and structure of the school.' Goddard and Leask (1992) outlined the need to manage multiple innovations and coping with 'initiative overload' through mapping the key characteristics of the initiatives, analysing and developing core values and planning implementation strategically. A school with a clear and shared vision and set of aims is best placed to make the links between the many initiatives and concerns it has to deal with.

Balance between leadership and management

Defining and distinguishing between leadership and management is useful and important. Leadership and management are not interchangeable concepts (Foster, 1989). Many texts have noted the differences. West-

Burnham (1997) for instance described 'leadership' as concerned with vision, strategic issues, transformation, ends, people and doing the right things. He contrasted this with 'managing', which is to do with implementation, operational issues, transactions, concern for means, systems and doing things right.

However, the problem for headteachers, teachers and, indeed, other managers is that they need to be both leaders and managers. Leadership and management are not enough on their own, particularly perhaps in small schools where other roles such as that of classroom teacher must also be undertaken. As Duignan (1989) illustrated: 'Leaders, as culture builders, work through daily management structures and routines to achieve purposes and end values. Daily management transactions are not ends in themselves, but means to higher ends.' Duignan went on to describe the way the culture of the organisation is questioned, developed and articulated through the daily routines.

Some leadership activities, for example, the creation of vision and mission statements, strategic plans and so on, can be interpreted wrongly as one-off events. Problems can arise if such activities are seen as once-and-for-all events as opposed to ongoing and developing processes. Leadership needs to be displayed through the day-to-day management of the school. The classic case would be the school with a written vision and mission statement, which the staff regarded as a sham in the every day working of the school. The challenge is how to get both vision and mission statement into the day-to-day leadership and management of the school. Having grand visions without doing so leaves one open to the accusation of being a 'dreamer'.

Working with people is inevitably about managing, debating, and conducting transactions. The daily transactions of a manager need to be permeated by the leadership qualities of vision and concern for ends. This means using management meetings, conversations and all the other varied 'transactions' of the school day. Occasions for articulating the vision or 'walking the talk' as a leader arise in the myriad exchanges of the daily life of a school. Most leadership needs to be conducted through the management of the school. There is the case for *showing leadership through management* rather than distinguishing between the two. A key illustration of this leader-manager role is explored in the TTA's (1998) document which defines subject leadership as being effective when, for example, there are:

- teachers who work well together as a team;

- parents who are well informed about their child's achievements;
- senior managers who understand the needs of the subject.

Leadership and management activities are suggested; yet, importantly, leadership through management activities, such as team meetings, is implied.

Being strategic

Much of what is written about management and planning assumes that schools are rational organisations where what are planned as actions will end in a set of pre-determined consequences, outcomes or the meeting of pre-determined success criteria. Decision-making is on the basis of perfect knowledge, and perfect decisions can be made by a skilled decision-maker acting on free will. Weindling (1997) described the differences between strategic and long-term planning, suggesting that the former assumes:

- dynamism and constant change;
- a changing environment planning is integral to the running of the school;
- the process of planning is important;
- internal and external analysis leads to the development of a shared vision;
- current and future trends are used to make decisions.

Even so there are tensions and, in some ways, it can be argued that the key to being strategic is to *stop being overly rational*. This is not to suggest that the leader-manager should be irrational. However, he or she needs to avoid assuming that the world of educational change is ordered, that change happens in a linear fashion, and that plans get implemented.

These views were well documented by Fullan (1991) who pointed out the messiness of change, warning that it could strike at the core of one's beliefs and conceptions of education, creating doubts about purposes and even competence. If these problems were ignored, he said, only superficial change would occur at best and, at worst, people would retreat into 'a self-protective cocoon, unreflectively rejecting all proposed changes'. Accepting plans and planning, the rational and the ordered as *part* of the process of improvement is a key issue for leaders and managers but so is the ability to respond on the basis of a clear vision and set of values to the unexpected and to understand the subjective and emotional aspects of change. Strategies can emerge as well as be planned. Solutions can come out of creative and emotional inputs as well as from logic and reason.

Becoming transformational: the inspiration of staff

Terrell and Leask (1997) quoted the views of over seventy teachers who listed the characteristics of 'leaders you would die for'. The data is presented here in its raw, unreconstructed form to illustrate the voice of practitioners in its true sense. The teachers looked for leaders who:

> celebrate the achievements of others;
> make you feel valued;
> care for people;
> are charismatic, inspirational and work with you;
> have a vision that can be shared;
> have clear direction;
> respect staff for their knowledge;
> are articulate;
> have strong moral values;
> set clearly defined boundaries;
> have a good memory for details;
> are creative;
> listen to ideas;
> are positive;
> are enthusiastic;
> value people;
> will admit lack of knowledge;
> can do the job;
> welcome constructive criticism;
> praise and thank;
> are empathetic;
> pay attention to detail;
> work as hard as you do;
> are visible;
> earn respect;
> respect others;

support the development and participation of others;
are approachable;
have strength of character;
are dependable, ethical and empowering;
are honest;
will take advice.

According to Beare *et al.* (1993), the term 'transformational leadership' was first developed by Burns in 1978, who described it as a 'relationship of mutual stimulation and elevation that converts followers into leaders and leaders into moral agents'. Foster's (1989) view was:

> Transformational leadership is the ability of an individual to envision a new social condition and to communicate this vision to followers. The leader both inspires and transforms individual followers so that they too develop a new level of concern about their human condition and, sometimes, the condition of humanity at large.

While many of the 24,000 headteachers in the state sector may not aspire to such heights as Martin Luther King, Ghandi and John Kennedy, part of transformational leadership is moving beyond merely adopting the values of the *status quo* but being critical, educative and ethical.

What vision? Whose vision?

For some, the sign of a good headteacher or prospective headteacher is their vision. Hence, candidates are sometimes asked to make presentations at interviews for headships on their vision for the school. Good headteachers should convey a sense of striving for something better, outlining a set of values and inspiring staff by giving some direction or goals. The personal vision of the headteacher is, therefore, clearly important.

Some writers, such as Senge (1990: 9), drew attention to the importance of developing a shared vision with staff, warning against trying to 'dictate a vision'. Indeed building 'the vision' is an unproblematic venture, it is something that should be debated and involves conflict. That is part of the process of vision building. Mere compliance is not enough, commitment and involvement need to be achieved. People have to get on board and take ownership, to become truly collaborative. Fullan and

Hargreaves (1992) noted that collaboration should mean 'creating the vision together, not complying with the head's own'; in fact, 'the articulation of different voices may create initial conflict, but this should be confronted and worked through. It is part of the collaborative process'. It should be remembered that there are different kinds of vision:

- as a personal mission;
- as an expression of a set of values to aspire to hold;
- as private not to be shared because it is too dangerous for some;
- which can be expressed to others;
- as a shining city to work towards;
- in the process of being built with staff.

Vision building is a form of discourse with staff, and a process and not an event, to adapt Fullan's comment. There will be disagreements with staff. Leadership here is surely about listening and responding appropriately to develop the vision that stage further. Valuing the differences because of their contribution to shaping the vision is also important. Providing the context where people can express their views is important because it is a means of finding out where people are coming from.

Developing an agenda for transformation

Given what has been said above about the demands for change in education, two areas might be identified as keys to transformational vision building over the next decade or so. One area is curriculum ideology, the other is the notion of learning and ability.

It is almost a cliché to compare the curriculum of 1998 with the curriculum in 1902 and to note the lack of difference. The next line is inevitably about the *Sabre Tooth Curriculum* the satire published in 1939 (Hooper, 1971). Tensions already exist between the prescribed state curriculum of Britain and what is needed in a modern world. Clearly, at a time of an explosion of knowledge and greater access to that knowledge we ought to be focusing on the skills of acquiring, selecting, evaluating, testing and developing that knowledge; at a time of social, political and economic change we should be exploring an education that promotes social justice and equity; at a time of concern for the environment we should be promoting sustainability.

What seems unhelpful is a curriculum that is heavily content and subject-based. Review of the National Curriculum may well address some of these concerns. Even so, a major issue for the truly transformational leader will be handling the tension between what is prescribed and what the individual school needs.

Another aspect is the difficulty faced in moving from education being seen as a minority pursuit to one where the majority succeeds. The achievement of the majority in secondary education has long been the concern of many, being recorded in many documents including the Newsom Report of 1963 and the National Commission on Education of 1993.

Examination results in Britain in the latter half of the 1990s showed increases in pass rates. SCAA (1996) showed an increase in A* to C grades awarded, from 22.6 per cent in 1975 to 43.5 per cent in 1995. In 1955 Walker showed that only 10 per cent of children were in full time education at the age of seventeen whereas in 1995 the figure was 59 per cent. In 1955 only 4 per cent of 18-year-olds went to university, in the late 1990s 31 per cent did. Walker (1998) alleged that such trends were mirrored in both France and Germany. The leader-manager needs to have a clear understanding of these trends, their causes, the limitations in the present situation and the consequences for future action.

Teachers and the general public have put forward many explanations:

- examinations have become easier;
- all the improvements that could be made have been made; the natural limit for success is reached ('the slack' has been taken up);
- improvements in examination success are explained by good pupils doing better.

The first explanation was rejected by SCAA (1996). The third is often considered to be what is currently happening. The second explanation seems to base itself on the assumption that general intelligence, being the foundation for ability, is normally distributed in the population, that is, that inevitably some have more, some have less and most are average. The work of Gardner (1984; 1993) began to challenge some of these assumptions. The fact that teachers were focused on criterion-referenced assessment and were teaching students to pass should invalidate the notion of norm referencing. Another explanation for the success in education could well be the suggestion that we have begun to adopt different models for understanding the teaching and learning process that accept that all children can achieve the requirements and criteria of public examination.

This perspective would be based on a rejection of the idea of the notion of a single general intelligence and ability and the adoption of a constructivist theory of education: the notion that concepts are built through experience and that a teacher's role is to create the conditions under which development may take place. From this perspective, intelligence is seen as multiple and learning as achieved through a judiciously balanced and customised mix of visual, auditory and kinaesthetic approaches. We may also need to change the view of public examinations as a filtering process through which only a few can achieve success to one where they are about many meeting standards and criteria.

One of the key issues of leadership for the future is how the paradigm of the past can be unlocked and a new paradigm established that builds a system of education which is inclusive.

Ethical and values-led leadership and management

The description, above, of leaders for whom teachers would like to work hard, contains many illustrations of values. Leaders who value people and the contribution they make are inclusive and show a sense of equality. They convey a sense of right and wrong, act with honesty and create a sense of moral leadership. The personal vision embodies a set of values that are held with conviction and illustrated through daily behaviour and decision-making. The culture being created by the transformational leader is a display of those values. Yet, as has been described above, transformational leadership is about working with and developing the values of others.

Foster (1989) debated one further aspect of leadership, that of its ethical position. Three issues were of concern:

(1) The relationship between means and ends
(2) The ethical use of power
(3) The potential for elevating people to new levels of morality

Ethical questions are not easy for headteachers, particularly when faced with the moral dilemmas involved in competition for pupils. As a participant on a course mentioned: 'Should you be developing your school so effectively that you are capturing the intake of the school down the road that is perceived to be less good than you are?' There is a moral and ethical dimension to education that cannot and should not be ignored.

The tension in collegiality, involvement and inclusion

Brundrett (1998) described the spread of the idea of collegiality and whole staff involvement within the United Kingdom and internationally. He raised several philosophical and practical difficulties for achieving collegiality, particularly in larger schools, including the need for consensus, differences in experience and expertise, the danger of micro-political forces and the spread of stakeholder constituencies. He noted the added problems of working in a highly centralised and directed environment. It simply is not good enough, at least for headteachers and managers, as was noted in one school, to say 'We don't believe in the National Curriculum'.

Fullan (1993) further developed these issues, commenting on the value of genuine collaboration and collegiality and on some of the pitfalls:

> Teachers must work in highly interactive and collaborative ways, avoiding the pitfalls of wasted collegiality… Collaboration is one of the most misunderstood concepts in the change business. It is not automatically a good thing. It does not mean consensus.

Hersey and Blanchard (1982) outlined different ways of working with staff dependent upon their level of development. Highly developed staff might be delegated to, because they had the skills and experience to cope. Others required more support and perhaps some coaching. Others, those with commitment but little competence, needed close direction. Their work illustrated the true nature of leadership being supportive according to circumstances and the individual.

Teamwork, collegiality and collaboration have been central tenets of management literature. Whitaker (1993) talked about encouraging collaboration, Hopkins (1994) had two conditions for school improvement: involvement and co-ordination. Fullan (1993) described the power of involvement and teamwork to develop shared understandings, common goals and the culture of the school. Few would say that this is unproblematic and the inclusion of all staff is a key issue for managers and leaders. Inclusion and collaboration are not entirely in the hands of the leader manager, even if it may arguably be largely so. Collaboration and involvement are about including the:

- difficult member of staff;
- wayward member of staff;
- disaffected member of staff;
- the not very competent member of staff.

A major factor arising from IIP work in many schools was the involvement of non-teaching staff in the life and work of the school. Finding appropriate occasions when it was productive and safe for both the staff and the school for this to happen is not an easy task. Nevertheless, the IIP initiative drew attention to the fact that an organisation like a school can only be truly effective if all staff are pulling in the same direction and feel committed to and part of the enterprise.

Involving staff and collaborating with staff, who might have let you down, not be very competent or who are very awkward is challenging for the leader and manager. Building constructive relationships through consultancy skills and conflict management strategies are key aspects of the leader-managers job. In several cases, revealed in IIP work, schools which had difficulties with development had them because of issues of unresolved relationships rather than any difficulty with managing the action planning process. The nature of staff involvement is interesting. Etzioni (1975) talked about:

- **Alienative involvement** where power is used to coerce staff into being involved.
- **Calculative involvement** where staff need to know what is in it for them in terms of relative costs and benefits, rewards and sanctions and where leaders have the power over material rewards.
- **Moral involvement** where there is a commitment to the goals of the institution or towards people. This happens mostly where there is the exercise of power over the giving or withholding of praise or allocation of status which enhances self-esteem. There are connections here it would seem with staff motivation.

Releasing leadership from the middle

Perhaps too often we have relied upon the image of the leader. Bradford and Cohen (1984) adopted the term 'heroic leader' for those who:

- have single handedly turned round an organisation;
- know everything about what is going on;
- have more knowledge and expertise than ordinary folk;
- can solve any problems that arise.

They argued that such leadership often blocked communication, was slow to respond to change, frequently led to poor quality decisions, underestimated the capacity of staff leading to less expectations of them.

Real transformational leadership as expressed above is focused on releasing the leadership of others. In schools it is to be found in the leadership of middle managers and subject co-ordinators, as well as in headteachers, deputy headteachers and other staff. Foster (1989) argued that leadership is communal and shared, that 'leaders exist only because of the relationship with followers, and that this relationship allows followers to assume leadership and leaders, in turn, to become followers'. This is an interesting concept for it sees the function of leadership as one of providing the conditions for other leaders to emerge. A broader illustration can be found in the work of Hopkins *et al.* (1994). The issue for school leaders is then one of how to develop leadership in the school. Leaders may emerge from any number of staff in the school. In larger schools the middle manager, the head of department, the subject leader or the year head may be prime candidates as leaders. Terrell and Leask (1997) described the concept of leadership from the middle. How to develop leadership from middle managers is a key issue for senior management.

Supporting the development of high performing staff

'Challenge' is an interesting word and does not always suggest a notion of confrontation in the sense of conflict, except perhaps a certain amount of confronting in the sense of making clear to all parties. A dictionary definition (found in Terrell and Leask, 1997) may include the following:

- an invitation to do something;
- to call something into question;
- to make demands upon;
- to stimulate;

- to make a formal objection to;
- to engage in a fight, argument or contest;
- to question a fact, statement or act;
- to establish a goal or target.

IIP audits revealed that in some schools teachers rarely felt that they met with senior managers, that it was not known what they did and their contribution to the aims and goals of the school was not clear to them. In effect, they were not being challenged, valued or given recognition.

Clearly, negotiating clear goals, actions, targets and success criteria is an important part of the leader-manager role. In larger schools this may well need to be delegated through a clear line-management structure. It is how the vision turns into plans for departments and actions for individuals. The process is about the negotiation of demands and priorities. For some the demands may need to be specific and constrained. For others the demands could be more open-ended.

Clearly development of standards and success criteria helps to negotiate judgements about effectiveness. The school can negotiate success criteria. The Ofsted framework provided a useful list of criteria for effectiveness, and one that few teachers questioned (as opposed to the process of inspection). Use of the TTA's national standards for newly qualified teachers, for special educational needs co-ordinators (SENCOs), for subject leaders and for headteachers is also helpful as a source of criteria for negotiating judgements concerning effectiveness.

Throughout we have alluded to negotiation, not because we wish to soften the approach to accountability but because we feel there needs to be a genuine two-way approach towards clarifying goals and setting targets, which is challenging to both parties, leader-manager and teacher.

High performance through professional development

High performance levels are best viewed as arising from an appropriate mix of pressure and support. In the area of support come career/staff development interviews, appraisal processes, and mentoring, which have typically focused upon identifying needs and developing individual or career action plans, and all forms of professional development. Table 5.1 is adapted from West-Burnham and O'Sullivan (1998: 6) and shows needs at different stages of a teacher's career.

Table 5.1: Needs at different career stages

Stage	Years	In-service activity
Induction	1st year	Probationer support
Consolidation	4-6 years	Adding to professional knowledge
Orientation	5-8 years	Reflection, refreshment, one-term secondment to a centre for advanced studies and possible career change
Advanced seminars	8-12 years	Part time studies to develop subject expertise and strategic overview of the curriculum
Mid career advanced studies	12-15 years	Leadership and management training on one term to one year secondments
Senior management/ refreshment		Preparation for senior management or refreshment programmes

The assessment of needs is another difficult negotiation, for there are many sources of needs, including those of the government, LEA, school, pupils, parents, and teacher. West-Burnham and O'Sullivan (1998) reminded us that the Advisory Committee on Induction and Training of Teachers, as long ago as 1974, mapped out the principles and framework for in-service development of teachers. The framework bears some resemblance to the work of Dreyfuss in outlining different needs for different stages of professional career.

Some caution is needed when using this type of model to avoid the dangers of assuming that there is only one set career pattern. In effect, there are multiple possibilities, including 'fast-tracking'.

Nevertheless, for many years, professional development has been characterised by its *ad hoc* nature and a lack of certainty about its impact. Matters however have begun to change, particularly with the advent of the Green Paper (DfEE, 1998c). A number of factors have been at work:

- Moves over recent years towards a broad view of what constitutes professional development
- The emergence, under the auspices of the TTA, of a coherent framework of national standards to under-pin all levels of professional development and training
- The implementation of a three level leadership programme for

aspiring headteachers (NPQH), newly appointed headteachers (HEADLAMP) and experienced headteachers (LPSH)
- The concern of a range of parties – Ofsted, the TTA and government with the impact of professional development on practice and school improvement

Beyond the rhetoric of the learning organisation

The concept of the learning organisation has become increasingly popular and implies an organisation that is responsive, developing, able to embrace change, able to adapt and to be flexible. Typically, learning organisations reduce bureaucracy and hierarchy, and encourage collaboration. Individual staff and teams are empowered to act and the organisation forms and reforms around the skills of people rather than around fixed and rigid roles (see Jenkins, 1991). Senge (1991: 141) believed that 'organisations learn through individuals who learn', and he introduced a number of key concepts, the first of which was 'personal mastery':

> 'Personal mastery' is the phrase my colleagues and I use for the discipline of personal growth and learning. People with high levels of personal mastery are continually expanding their ability to create the results they truly seek. From their quest for continual learning comes the spirit of the learning organisation.

He called for a review of the constraints imposed on staff by their own mental models, suggesting that 'the discipline of dialogue also involves learning how to recognise the patterns of interaction that undermine learning'.

Against this background the headteacher can be seen as the lead learner. He or she can also ask themselves where in their learning organisation is the staff debate about pedagogy, curriculum objectives, and the latest research findings on effective teaching. IIP audit data revealed that many school staff associations operated for staff social functions and that staff meetings were often for information giving. In some schools there was opportunity for informal discussions.

The fifth discipline for the learning organisation, according to Senge, is systems thinking which fuses all other strategies and techniques into a coherent body. All staff should learn to see the whole picture.

Building in-school staff development opportunities

The effective leader-manager uses the opportunities for staff development inside the school. These include meetings, inset days, development planning and project activities. Hopkins *et al.* (1989) also illustrated the process of evaluation as development.

Joyce and Showers (1988) outlined the results of their research into effective training. They saw a series of possible training strategies – information giving, outlining of theory, demonstration, practice, coaching and giving feedback. They argued that different strategies had different impacts. For example, a talk or presentation was only likely to raise awareness of an issue. To change practice involved the use of all strategies but especially the use of feedback on practice. Programmes that focus on 'models of learning', such as those outlined by Joyce *et al.* (1997), can be particularly effective, and illustrate the importance of a good grasp and connection with learning theory and what is known about best practice through research. In effect, there needs to be a recognition that people have different preferences as to how they like to learn and these need to be utilised if effective learning is to occur.

Action research

If improvements in schools are to occur, then professional development must be firmly rooted in the real teaching and leadership activities of the school. Examples are to be found in the school improvement projects, many of which form part of NPQH training and development. Another example is to be found in action research. Elliott (1992) defined action research as, 'the study of a social situation with a view to improving the quality of action within it'.

The development of the associated teacher as researcher movement has a long history. Its justification as an important process for improvement and curriculum development has been well established by Elliott and others. The power of action research is that it is a process of collaborative learning through critical reflection on data as evidence and leads to action for improvement.

Terrell (1996) illustrated the need for action researchers to be supported in an ethical way by a facilitator using a model involving the concepts of entry, contracting, collecting data, using theoretical models as tools of analysis, choosing options and implementing them.

The earlier phases of the action research movement merged into calls for teaching to become a research-based profession (see, for instance, TTA, 1996). The encouragement and support of professional research projects forms part of the remit of the TTA whose commitment to this concept may be seen in a variety of documents (see, for instance TTA, 1997, 1998c). There is also a firm foundation, often supported by LEAs and HEIs in this area.

Networking and partnership

Insularity whether within a school or between schools is a barrier to learning. Networking through conferences, courses, visits to schools and businesses are often described by teachers as refreshing, motivational and informative. Many of the outcomes cannot be predicted or planned for, although they may fit within a clear strategic goal, such as the development of middle management. Outcomes that develop may be in the form of confidence, ideas, confirmation of success, motivation, or having a break and a change of pace, which can be energising. Such partnership gained in popularity, as we may see in, for instance, the White Paper, *Excellence in Schools* (DfEE, 1998a), which promoted the idea of partnership strongly.

Activating staff through motivation

Motivating is such a central aspect of working with people it is surprising to see how little it is understood and related to management practice. One may ask the connection between the practice of teacher appraisal or the negotiation of targets, or the practice of development planning with notions of what motivates staff to become high performers. A number of writers saw motivation in terms of *what* motivates an individual and stressed the personal, psychological factors involved. One example of this type of theory is provided by Maslow's (1954) hierarchy of physiological needs and needs for safety, love, esteem and self-actualisation. Another example is from Herzberg (1966), who identified a number of motivators – a sense of achievement, recognition, responsibility, the nature of work and opportunities for personal growth and advancement. He argued that by designing a job to foster these factors, job satisfaction can be increased and that people will work better. On the other hand he identified a series of what he called hygiene factors – salary, job security, working conditions, nature of supervision, policy, administration and interpersonal relationships. He argued that managers must take steps to ensure that dissatisfaction in these areas did not become a problem but that dealing with these factors would not turn them into motivators. Another useful model was provided by McClelland (1963), who identified three types of need – for power, for affiliation and for achievement.

By contrast other theories of motivation focus on the *process* and consider the impact of situational or environmental factors on motivation and performance. Such theories include expectancy theories and goal theories of motivation. Basically, the former are based on the idea that an individual makes a calculation based on the amount of energy and effort they need to expend in order to achieve a desired outcome. The more the outcome is seen as satisfying a need, the more satisfying the need matters, and the greater the perceived probability of achieving it with an acceptable level of effort, the higher the level of motivation. (See, for example, Handy, 1993). Finally, a useful way of thinking about motivation is provided by goal theory. This is essentially based on the idea that having clear and achievable goals is motivating as is the process of setting goals.

The implications of these theories are that leader-managers need to think carefully about individual staff needs and the rewards people value. Jobs need to be designed to allow individuals to fulfil their needs. Reward systems must be seen as fair and equitable. Leader-managers need to create a framework of clear expectations and clarify the links between effort and outcomes. They also need to ensure that desired levels of performance are within people's grasp. Connections here should be made with other sections of this chapter, including the ideas discussed in the areas of developing leadership in others, the inclusion of staff, collaboration, and professional development.

Conclusion: maintaining personal energy

Enthusiasm and energy come with a new position of leadership. Things need to be done and fast. After a while, for some, there may be a period of disillusionment when things are not moving as fast or as well as hoped. Then there may be periods later, when you feel that you have achieved what you set out to achieve initially. Then the passion must be stoked, the energy raised and so on. What is going to happen in the second five-year period? You have been through many strategies before and with a low turnover of staff, they too have been there before.

The answer is perhaps to be found in a number of places, in the approach to transformational leadership outlined above, in getting in tune with your own motivational needs and looking for new ways to fulfil them, through personal and professional development, through the support of colleagues. What is important to hold on to is a belief that the most valuable resource of a school is its staff, and leading and managing them effectively is the best route to school improvement.

6.   The Efficient and Effective Deployment of Staff and Resources

Neil Burton

Introduction

The strength of school lies in the strengths of the teaching and support staff it employs (West-Burnham, 1993; Wye, 1993). Given this assumption, the prime task of management must be to ensure the effective and efficient deployment of staff in terms of:

- recruitment and retention;
- target setting and the monitoring of performance;
- individual expertise in relation to tasks;
- resources and financial management.

Since the availability of finance is frequently the limiting factor in such provision, it has become one of the key educational issues.

The recent historical context

Control over this key educational resource is only possible at the level of the individual school when that school has control over the allocation of funds. Since the 1980s in the United Kingdom and several other countries, most notably Australia, New Zealand and Canada, there have been progressive moves to ensure that the financial decision-making becomes increasingly close to 'shop floor'. In England and Wales the introduction of the 1988 Education Reform Act led to a significant change in the relationship between schools and LEAs. These were now required to devolve funding for the education of children to the schools that they attended, through a published formula, retaining only a small proportion of the educational funding for administration and support services. LMS allowed schools to act with a degree of freedom only previously experienced by independent schools. In order to curtail this freedom, LMS was also accompanied by the introduction of a compulsory National Curriculum, pupil testing and regular inspections to ensure that certain criteria were being met. In effect the power of the LEAs to influence local educational issues was transferred to schools, and to central government.

Some schools were able to opt for even greater financial independence than LMS offered. Benefiting from significant financial incentives in the form of grants, many schools chose to become grant maintained schools (GM), totally independent of their LEA and receiving their budgets direct from central government via the quasi-nongovernmental organisation (quango) the Schools Funding Agency (SFA).

The accountants Coopers and Lybrand (1988), asked to produce a report by the (then) government to identify the potential benefits of devolved financial management, stated:

> Good management requires ... [that] the performance of the (school) is monitored and the (school) is held to account for its performance and its use of funds ... (LMS) will give schools the flexibility to respond directly and promptly to the needs of the school and its pupils in a way which will increase the effectiveness and quality of the services provided. Schools will have more incentive to seek efficiency and economy in their use of resources.

They implied that for schools to manage their finances they must also accept a wider view of the role of managers within education, the control of finance being the enabling force to effect wider educational change to reflect priorities of the school, encapsulated in 'school development plans'.

Prior to the 1988 Education Reform Act, identical schools, in the same area, might receive very different levels of funding from their LEA. School budgets were now to be determined by a formula which would apply to all schools in the LEA, with some transitional allowances in the first years of operation.

In many instances, historical patterns of spending were reproduced, as closely as was possible, through the formulae. The DfEE restricted the LEAs by requiring 80 per cent of the Aggregated Schools Budget (ASB) to be allocated to schools on the basis of pupil numbers (weighted by age) – age-weighted pupil units (AWPU). The conscious decision by the government to use AWPU as the main determinant for school funding ensured that pupil numbers became the key focus for schools and would lead to competition for pupil enrolments. GM schools were also given the funding that would otherwise been retained by the LEA for central services and were also given preferential treatment when making bids for capital projects.

Even with transitional payments to schools there were clearly going to be winners and losers as compared with the previous system. Those schools which benefited most from the formula approach had certain characteristics in common including:

- rising pupil numbers;
- young or inexperienced teaching staff (who tended to be less expensive than more experienced staff);
- little previous benefit, on any regular basis from, 'discretionary' awards from the LEA.

By 1994, it was becoming clear that many schools were being forced to make staff redundant to 'balance the books' on the back of declining pupil numbers and the end of transitional payments. With teacher salaries being such a high proportion of school costs, many schools began to insist on more flexible staffing arrangements which led to an increase in part-time and fixed-term contracts.

As well as responding to the external pressures to instigate formal and effective accounting and budgeting procedures, there was also a clear need to consider the allocation of resources within schools afresh.

Micro-economics of education

According to DeHayes and Lovrinic (1994: 81) 'the term "economics of education" was first used in 1960'. As an area of study it thrived for a short while until, in the 1980s there was 'a loss of interest amongst applied economists in an area in which an ideal measure of output remained elusive' (Throsby, 1986: 175). The intervening years saw the publication of many texts and even more articles on this applied area of study (*cf.* Baxter, 1977; Blaug, 1968 and 1970; Vaizey, 1962; Sheehan, 1973; Mace, 1993) which tended to take a social and economic policy view. The approach has been revisited occasionally since (for example Johnes, 1993), mainly to update and re-examine the same areas: institutional budgeting, sources of educational funding and measures of educational efficiency.

Given that the financial structure of education in England and Wales as a whole has changed so significantly since the 1988 Education Reform Act, which then led to equally significant changes to the funding systems in pre-school, further and higher education, it may appear that the economics of education is ripe for further investigation. Much of the research that has been carried out has focused on funding – the allocation of funds between and within institutions; or the arguments for and against education vouchers, which had been rehearsed for many years prior to their temporary introduction for pre-school education.

It is not difficult to interpret the basic principles of economic theory, as developed in any one of a number of core economic texts (see Baumol and Blinder, 1994; Lipsey and Halsey, 1992; Samuelson, 1995; and Whitehead, 1996) widely available, in the context of the 'market' or at least the supply and demand for education. As with all areas of economic activity in which the state has a significant degree of control, there will be distortions from any simplified model that economic theory might suggest.

The basic assumptions of *classical* market theory hold that as price increases, producers will be willing to sell more and consumers will be willing to purchase less, leading to an equilibrium position (PQ). If the quantity produced exceeds that point there will be excess supply, and below that level, excess demand. In education, the market is far from this classical ideal; both the price (age-weighted pupil funding) and the maximum quantity (enrolment numbers) are set by the funding body, either the LEA or SFA. But, as both Kedney (1991: 4) and Palfreyson (1994: 26) expressed independently, 'costing does not equal pricing'. Also, according to Pettifor (1985: 39), education is not a 'profit maximising sector', the main driving force behind neoclassical economics. Its aims are more to do with 'sales maximisation' (after the work of J.W. Baumol) or 'satisficing', a term coined by the American economist H. Simon. Since both sales, or more accurately enrolment maximisation, and 'satisficing' could be the main driving force; achieving the highest quality possible whilst working within given constraints; a 'goal orientation where funding is an enabler' (Pettifor, 1984: 35) would appear to be a key element.

Funding per pupil is at a rate which is set locally and all schools within that area, LEA or SFA funded, receive the same, with some enhancement for pupils who are identified as having specific special educational needs. At the time of writing it is not possible for a school in one LEA to offer places to pupils living in another LEA which is paying higher fees, though often children living in one LEA area will attend a school in another.

Economic cost

There are several economic definitions of 'cost', all equally valid, but some more appropriate for use in this particular study than others. Pettifor (1984: 63) asserts that 'cost can be assessed in two distinct forms … opportunity cost … and … actual outlay cost'. Opportunity cost is defined by Levin (1975: 98) as the 'set of social sacrifices associated with a particular choice among social-policy alternatives', which makes it very difficult to place a particular monetary value on it. An alternative, more accountable definition, is that opportunity cost is 'concerned with the value of the best alternative use to which the resources can be put' (Kedney and Davies, 1994), for example the income that might be realised by renting out teaching rooms.

Cost, according to Stone (1992: 1) is 'about what is paid to secure or accomplish something of value'. Actual outlay costs would appear to be a much more practical approach, but problems concerning the accounting of these costs and, in particular attributing or apportioning them to specific activities or courses, can also make the costs derived from this source open to interpretation. These issues will be examined further as different cost-accounting approaches are explored in depth.

Cost is generally divided into two categories, 'fixed-cost' and 'variable-cost'. The division between the two is not absolute but a product of sensitivity to change, either over time or as a result of changes to pupil numbers. In the very long run (a time period which is open to debate and dependent upon many factors which vary from industry to industry) all costs will be variable; in the very short run a much greater proportion of the factors which affect costs will be 'fixed'.

Given that all costs can be said to be variable in the long-term, another important expression of cost is 'average cost', defined as the total cost of a given output divided by that output. The constraints placed on the ability to produce a given output by the availability of resources (in the case of education this might be the number of teachers or teaching rooms available) and the associated variable and fixed costs, a long-run average cost curve can be seen to be the summation of several, successive short-run cost curves, the long-run curve being an envelope which contains the short-run curves.

Also demonstrated by such an arrangement is the classical interpretation of 'economies of scale', where long-run average cost is minimised. This is the point of optimal economic efficiency. Two other 'maximum efficiency' definitions are 'price efficiency' – cheap as possible for a given output; and 'technical efficiency' – inputs combined to maximise output (Mace, 1993: 8). Prior to this point, the next short-run average cost curve will provide an increase in output at a lower level of cost than the previous short-run situation. Beyond this point, a situation of decreasing economies of scale, any subsequent short-run average cost curves will only be able to increase output by increasing costs – an upward turn of the long-run average cost curve. It is important that education plans in the long term in order for it to take full advantage of any long-term cost savings that are available from having settled staffing and accommodation.

Long- and short-run average cost functions are more specifically applied to the macro-economics of education (Pettifor, 1984) where optimal institutional sizing and long-term stability are the goals. The micro-economics of costing educational activity has two other cost factors that need to be taken into account: marginal costing and step economies. The definition of marginal cost varies slightly from economist to economist, but to synthesise from the work of Lipsey (1992), Samuelson (1995) and Baumol and Blinder (1994), marginal cost is the additional cost of producing one more unit of output.

One approach to output determination would be to produce up to the point where the extra cost of producing one more unit of output is minimised; beyond that point subsequent units of output would begin to cost more to produce than previous ones. Dunworthy and Bottomley (1973) in stating that 'it is marginal cost, not average cost that is relevant to a decision to expand a level of activity', placed themselves firmly in this camp.

An alternative approach would be to continue to expand production until marginal cost equals average cost, the point at which average cost is minimised and usually the optimum production level. With the addition of a profit multiplier or factor, average and marginal cost pricing can be used to set the price charged for a product in an open market where demand is price flexible and at least in excess of the unit cost. From a costing perspective, as opposed to a strictly economic one, Lucey (1996b) described a means of marginal cost decision-making in terms of break-even or cost-volume-profit (CVP) analysis. This is the point where total sales exceeds total costs plus any required contribution to profits.

Step economies, or step costs, are according to Lucey (1996b), 'costs which remain constant over a range of activity'. Whereas economies of scale intimate that the larger the output the lower the unit cost, step economies acknowledge the realities of cost curves being *stepped* rather than smooth. It also acknowledges that the marginal cost of some units will be significantly in excess of the units both preceding and following it due to production capacities being exceeded. For example, the cost of the fourteenth person going on a journey in a fourteen seat minibus will be relatively small if not almost zero, but a fifteenth person will require the use of an additional minibus – a considerable marginal cost. Subsequent additions to the passenger list will have a very small marginal cost until the twenty-ninth passenger comes along. In education the dividing line is not so absolute, but it is just as dramatic in terms of the implications for costs. There will come a point where the class size has reached a situation where it will need to be divided into two separate classes, doubling room and teaching requirements. If there is unused capacity, a room and teacher being available, then although the costs for the course may be significant, within the institution there will be a more efficient use of resources. If both staff and space utilisation are at capacity, then the costs will be significant, either through room hire and part-time staff payments (a short-term approach) or by building and staff appointments (a long-term approach). In either terms the micro-economics will be the same. For this given total cost curve, once maximum capacity is reached for any range of output, a significant cost outlay is required to increase production further.

It is worth noting that while the marginal cost curves are identical for each level of production the average cost curve is affected less each time a step in costs takes place. At particularly high levels of production, average cost should smooth out to a large extent.

From an examination of past research into the cost of education it will be seen that different researchers have taken up different definitions of what 'educational output' actually is – some have compared the effects of valuing or measuring education by these different outputs. The three main ways in which output has been measured has been in terms of the numbers of pupils, number of examination passes and the number of 'study units' completed. Given that there is significant variation within each of these measures (not all pupils, examination passes and study units are the same), it is necessary to discuss the definitions of 'educational output' within the context of particular studies. It should be noted that the most appropriate definition for the examples given whilst explaining the economics of education above, would be the number of pupils, where the pupils are uniform and on a single course or phase of education.

To bridge the gap between the economics of education and costing educational activity, there is a variety of different types of model to choose from. Lucey (1996a) provided a useful digest of the different forms and their potential applications. To begin with, there are two distinct categories of models; normative and descriptive. Normative models are 'concerned with finding the best, optimum or ideal solution to a problem', whereas descriptive models 'describe the behaviour of a system without attempting to find the best solution'. An example of a descriptive model is a simulation which 'represents the behaviour of a real system'. It is envisaged that this study will lead to the production of normative models: mathematical, 'one which tries to show the workings of the real world by means of mathematical symbols, equations and formulae' and exacting heuristic models which 'use a set of intuitive rules which managers hope will produce at least a workable solution'.

Costing education

Budgeting and costing are two different approaches to determining the necessary funds for educational activities. Budgeting focuses on the allocation of available funds; costing on the funds that are required to allow certain educational activities to take place. Through reference to a variety of sources, further distinctions will be drawn between the two.

The activity of costing is best defined in terms of its purpose or outcomes. Costing systems, according to Hans (1996: 93) can be 'descriptive, telling administrators how much a given activity or process costs, and second they can be predictive, suggesting how resources ought to be combined in the future for cost effective use'. This definition, from the United States education system, demonstrates that the importance currently placed on sound financial management is not restricted to Britain. But, as Lucey (1996b: 6) stated, 'to be of use, costing information must be appropriate, relevant, timely, well presented and sufficiently accurate for the intended purpose'. These two statements provide a focal point of reference on which to base a further examination of the literature.

A significant proportion of the available literature concerned with educational management emanating from Britain has concentrated on the personnel management aspects rather than financial management. This may be understandable for, as Kedney (1991) explained, 'if provision is up and running, the quality is judged to be at least adequate, life is generally thought to be reasonable and will stay that way, so why bother with costing'. By 1994, with changes to the funding of education in Britain, De Hayes and Lovrinic observing trends concluded that 'the importance of cost information increases as resources diminish'.

Even when the control of educational finances are considered, it is frequently in terms of the allocation of devolved funding to particular educational resources (Bush *et al.*, 1994). The overwhelming bulk of the available literature has concentrated on issues of funding. Clearly the question being addressed is 'how do we allocate the funds we have?' rather than 'how much does it cost?'.

This approach, of concentrating on available funds rather than the actual costs, tends to be encouraged by the funding bodies in British education which rely, to a very large extent, on *formula* methods to arrive at allocations for particular institutions. Levacic (1989) derided the formula method used for funding schools, in that each LEA has a different formula, based on historical costings, and these do not relate to educational activity in other than gross terms.

This 'top-down' model has forced educational managers, with ever-decreasing resource allocations (in real terms), to attempt to make savings without any encouragement to discover the actual costs of the various aspects of the course programmes. This has led to short-term cost reduction techniques being employed and a search for 'acceptable ways of saving money' (Kedney and Davies, 1994) with an emphasis on 'cut it out now and put it back later'. But, as Knight (1985) rationalised: 'let no-one deride the word "cheaper". There is no advantage in education being more expensive than it has to be.'

The formula, on which the funding allocation is based, is developed from an incremental budgeting approach to costing; this is the approach that institutions are implicitly encouraged to follow. On incremental budgeting or historical funding Levacic (1990) noted: 'It does not provide a coherent and integrated approach to management planning which links resource allocation to the achievement of institutional aims or purposes.'

In simple terms, the resource or funding allocation of previous years dictates allocation in subsequent years – a steady state or static approach which is rather at odds with the dynamic changes currently facing initial teacher training (ITT). 'The experiential base of managers has, therefore, been one of year-on-year marginal change and specific funding' (Kedney and Davies, 1994) which tends to mitigate against long-term planning.

Dynamic systems are available, most notably the planning, programming, budgeting system (PPBS). This system was developed, within an educational context, for the California State Department of Education and published in the document *Conceptual design for a PPBS for California School Districts* in 1969 and imported into Britain by the accountants Coopers & Lybrand who were developing and writing support documentation for the introduction of LMS. It was described as 'objective budgeting' (Levacic, 1990), where the institution set clear aims and allocates resources accordingly and in so doing identified what expenditure was being incurred for. It does have strong critics though. As far back as 1989 Sharma claimed that 'at best (it) is only superficial, and could ... lead to very erroneous conclusions being drawn'.

Levacic (1989) provided access to a number of authors from the United States, who had significantly more experience at using dynamic, cost-based, budgeting methods that their British counterparts. For example, House (1989) complained that this setting of institutional or course goals with measurable objectives, which were then costed, would lead to a situation where 'the repression and dullness of the classroom will increase and we will have succeeded in crucifying our children on the cross of economic efficiency'.

Brockman (1989) set out the differences between programme and incremental budgeting (PB and IB):

(1) PB reflects an educational plan ...
(2) Planning is holistic rather than incremental ...
(3) Planning by program focuses on the programs that are new as differentiated from those that are continuing. It emphasises the multi-year impact of new programs ...
(4) All programs affect all other programs in the unit ...
(5) IB is eliminated ... *in favour of* ... zero based budgeting (*ZBB*)
(6) Contingency funds will not be available ... [my italics]

Through this process Brockman expected issues of finance to become a more understood aspect of the educational decision-making process at all levels. To define the purpose of courses and identifiable targets, and to consider different ways of approaching problems, was encouraged.

ZBB was, in some ways, a simplified version of PPBS, being according to Levacic (1990) 'a clear attempt to avoid historical budgeting' and was 'less complicated than PPBS because it only requires the budget manager to split up the budget into decision units. A decision unit could be a department, a curriculum area or a service area'. Instead of defining pro-grammes for the PPBS, existing, recognised cost centres could be used.

In comparison with IB, ZBB emphasised taking a fresh look at costs incurred. Incrementalism tends to be based around a fixed core and 'decisions are based upon last year's budget' (Davies, 1994), characterised as 'muddling through'. Area managers, according to Harkley (1989), would be required to justify resource allocations annually, rather than allow them to roll over. Johnes (1993) argued that 'ZBB is costly in terms of administration time' and 'might also frustrate long-term planning by introducing discontinuities', suggesting compromise might be appropriate.

Davies, working on the premise that the 'budgeting process is a dynamic one', offered a compromise, of sorts, between the traditional incremental approach and the more radical ZBB. He developed a 'budget-ary cycle' where, in the review part of the cycle, the current position was explored, then a forecast made using a multi-year time horizon (MYTH), considering alternative changes to the overall resource base; the imple-mentation stage was where the budget was actually allocated; and the evaluation phase examined 'how well the resource allocation decisions have enabled the institution to meet objectives in an effective and efficient way'. As a compromise, this approach does tend to favour the incremental approach by its cyclical nature. There is, perhaps, insufficient investig-ation of the nature of costs in this approach to be able to suggest signifi-cant changes to current funding patterns.

A line can be drawn between budgeting and 'ingredient' forms of costing, budget costs according to Gray (1984) being based on planned expenditure and ingredient approaches on actual expenditure. Moving to-wards an ingredient approach, mathematical models become available.

Starting from 'knowing what something costs is the first stage in weighing of its value against that cost', Fielden and Peason (1989: 97-9) took an alternative approach to educational financial matters, identifying five categories of costs:

- 'direct' (e.g. academic staff)
- 'indirect' (e.g. maintenance of the grounds)
- 'marginal' (e.g. the cost of an extra pupil in a particular class)
- 'total' (e.g. for the class or per pupil)
- 'opportunity' (e.g. the cost of not be able to use the same resources to provide an alternative course)

and identified ways of perceiving any outcomes or benefits:

- 'measurable and realisable outcomes' (e.g. changing the length of the pupil day)
- 'measurable but unrealisable' (e.g. reducing teaching sessions to 55 minutes; although an acknowledgement of reality, to use the 5 minutes 'saved' would be difficult)
- 'immeasurable outcomes'.

This provided a vocabulary and a basic framework to operate within, but practical issues were left unresolved. Jones (1989) brought mathematical formulae to the problem assuming that 'the aim of the operational manager is to reduce unit costs'. Where unit cost is defined as:

$$\frac{\text{course length multiplied by the hours taught per week}}{\text{number presented for assessment multiplied by the pass-rate}}$$

The denominator being an expression of educational output.
The overall cost of a course being given by the expression:

$$[(CHW)/X + M]N$$

where:

C = equipment cost per hour
H = hours taught per week
W = weeks taught per year
X = optimum number of students
M = materials per student
N = actual enrolment

Although designed with further education (FE) in mind, with open enrolment and over-supply of school places it is becoming a progressively more applicable model for mainstream schools.

Birch (1989: 132) defined four steps for programmed budgeting of college based FE courses:

- set admissions policy (target enrolment);
- calculate the total student hours the course will require;
- set SSR (student staff ratio) and average lecturer hours to calculate staff costs to service students;
- calculate departmental (intra-course) costs.

Hans (1996) stated simply that 'costing in HE currently lacks uniformity and precision', rather blandly summing up some of the contributions to costing that have been presented above. She observed, referring to the situation in the United States, that 'college and university costing is undergoing a rapid and extensive change', the evidence base for this assertion being the increasingly systematic use of activity-based costing (ABC) in higher education, on particularly a macro- but also a micro-costing basis. ABC developed from the writing of Professors Kaplan and Cooper working at Harvard University in the mid 1980s. The system was designed to enable economies of scale to be acknowledged within the accounting procedures by apportioning cost more directly in relation to the usage of resources, in particular, realistic costings, where indirect costs formed a large proportion of total costs, and 'the identification of the major activities which cause overhead costs' (Innes and Mitchell, 1991). On the positive side it relied, initially, on 'backflush accounting', starting with the finished product and working backwards, ensuring that all resource costs were justified.

Within the general approach to ABC, as proposed by Hans, it should be recognised that 'full costing of activities and processes is not always necessary or appropriate', in effect the costs of the process of costing must be allowed for. Managers must use their judgement to decide when ABC should be used.

As it reaches the modelling phase it can become very complex, with the potential for subjectiveness as the choice of production activities (cost drivers), and the means by which indirect cost is attributed, is made. According to Horngren *et al.* (1994: 28) indirect costs are those 'costs that are related to the cost object but cannot be traced to it in an economically feasible way'. Three other key pieces of ABC terminology have been defined by Lucey (1996b: 111): a 'cost centre', being an arbitrary gathering together of costs (in schools this will usually be a department, year/subject group or faculty); 'cost allocation', which is the action of charging costs to cost centres; and 'cost apportionment', the splitting of costs over several centres (such as landscaping and security).

ABC has been warmly welcomed by financial managers in many sectors of the general economy as a means of effectively controlling and managing costs of production with much greater precision than was ever possible before. Many costs that were incurred by companies using 'modern production methods' were simply aggregated and assigned to 'fixed cost overheads', their true source not being able to be linked to any particular products. Innes and Mitchell (1991) pointed out that 'ABC highlights the fact that many overheads, conventionally classified as fixed cost are in fact susceptible to variation, not in respect to volume changes, but in respect to changes in activities which cause their occurrence'. Given the high levels of centrally-retained funding income, many educational institutions apply to cover centralised costs which are not normally directly linked to classes or courses, DeHayes and Lovrinic (1994) observed that 'ABC provides a method to trace financial inputs through various production activities ... to a variety of outputs of ... education'.

In this way the 'true, long-term cost of a product or service' (Howson and Mitchell, 1995) can be established and cost allocation can be made as 'a fair distribution of overheads to cost centres', 'allowing policies on top slicing and cost allocation to be devised'.

There is a significant departure in the underlying approach of ABC compared with previous models, at least according to some of its proponents. According to DeHayes and Lovrinic (1994: 83): 'Current budgetary processes portray the cost of inputs such as personnel, rather than the cost of outputs, such as course or class provision or even exam results.'

The emphasis here is clearly on the cost of achieving or producing something tangible. With ABC, all costs must be linked to the end products. To assess and judge fully the value added by various educational processes, DeHayes and Lovrinic claimed that the relevant cost components must be included.

Probably the most damning inadequacy that pre-ABC techniques are accused of, is product cross-subsidization, or, as Horngren *et al.* (1994) described it 'peanut butter costing', where the costs of resources are uniformly assigned to cost objects. Decisions as to which courses, or even schools, are financially viable can only be made where the information regarding the cost of those courses (schools) is accurate and clearly distinguishable from the cost of other courses (schools). It is crucial that positive criteria and unassailable methods are employed in the apportionment of costs.

Alone, ABC is purely an accounting system which is as clear and accurate as the information that is put into it. The choice of cost drivers, those easily measurable indicators (such as staff/student ratio) which are used as a basis for determining the scale of costs to be attributed, is absolutely crucial and, potentially could be manipulated to give a range of different answers to the same question. It is with this point in mind that Hans (1996) suggested that 'university budgets probably represent ... the result of an overwhelmingly political process'.

The true value of ABC is really achieved when the costs, derived from the use of ABC, are applied as constraints to linear and non-linear programming problems. The viability (or non-viability) of courses and the most efficient enrolment numbers can then be identified along with the most efficient mix of resources. It will also be possible to identify the point where, although a course may not be covering the full costs, it will be returning more than the marginal costs and so be making a contribution to the centralised fixed-cost overheads. This will ensure that courses that might otherwise be dropped as uneconomic, continue to a point where they are no longer able to cover the marginal costs. Turney (1996) called this avoiding 'the death spiral', in which, using full costs, uneconomic lines are dropped leading to overheads being spread over a smaller production base, making those products, in turn, uneconomic.

Conclusions: the economic realities of education

The politics within the management of education has always skewed the application of pure economic decisions. Pupils tend to be far from homogeneous units of input and a single (or very limited) level of output would not be deemed desirable – once certain minimum quality thresholds had been achieved. It could be argued that with the introduction of a National Curriculum for compulsory education; baseline assessment on entry to formal education; annual testing of pupils (with set targets for schools to achieve); and regular inspection of schools and prescribed approaches to the teaching of literacy and numeracy – the 'means of production' within education are becoming increasingly uniform; the actual resources available, on a per pupil basis, may vary considerably from school to school.

Small rural schools have been subsidised at the expense of larger, more technically efficient ones because of the perceived central role that village primary schools play in holding small communities together. Understandably politicians behind funding bodies are often unwilling to make their decisions on economics alone, looking beyond the direct, attributable costs of maintaining schools with particularly high staff cost per pupil ratios.

Schools that are doing well according to all available (non-financial) indicators – examination/test results, Ofsted reports – may be doing so through uneconomic means by having a higher proportion of experienced (that is, more highly paid) staff than comparable schools. As the cost of teaching staff can account for 50 to 80 per cent of the school's total costs, expensive staff can soon have a significant effect on the overall finances of the school.

Areas in which schools select, to a greater or lesser degree, the students that they will enrol also have a decided advantage. If a school is able to insist on a higher quality input, then they reduce the average quality of the pupil entering other schools in the locality, with likely variations in the quality (in terms of examination results) of students on exit. For this reason, measures of 'value-added' have been called for since the publication of league table of examination results by school.

The economics of centrally funded public education in the United States is such that more affluent areas are able to afford to spend more on their schools as the taxes collected to fund schools are mainly retained locally. As a result children are only allowed to attend schools in their local tax areas and the resourcing of provision has tended to widen.

Small schools or small classes are often quoted by parents as being the reason why they were attracted to placing their children in a particular primary school, which makes them increasingly popular and leads directly to the destruction of the qualities that first made them attractive. Making such schools larger, unless there are significantly under-utilised resources, will lead to significant costs through step economics.

It is important that all of these political social-engineering aspects of education which impinge directly upon funding are taken into account when any study is made. Measures of input and output need to be clarified; step economies of scale need to be acknowledged; and fixed and variable costs need to be identified along with physical and social external constraints which may be applied to any particular school.

7.   Accountability

Jan Wilson

Introduction

This chapter discusses the concept of accountability, and the role of the headteacher. The intention is to provide practical guidance to help senior managers of schools understand the relationship between direct and functional accountability and leadership.

The debate on accountability has dominated political and public thinking in Britain in recent times. It is based upon questions about why schools outcomes differ from each other. The debate began with examining the effects of individual headteachers, their styles, characteristics and approaches upon the processes and outcomes of schools. But it has also fed the intense political arguments about different types of schools and how well these serve Britain. The accountability debate has led to performance tables, national and local authority based target setting and tighter Ofsted inspection frameworks, leading inexorably to the closure of the 'bad' school whilst the 'good' recruited more pupils. This was based on the assumption that schools would respond to public pressure and to the market choices that parents would make, once they were informed about the outcomes of what schools achieve. However, also emerging from this public and professional discussion has been the professional review of performance evaluation and the development of research and knowledge into how schools can be improved, with its potential for highlighting areas for improvement. In principle this refers to the amount that the individual school (or different classes, phases, departments within a school) contribute to the pupils' educational outcomes – once allowances have been made for the effects of factors not directly controlled by the school.

The assessment of a school's value-added characteristics has developed rapidly and the accountability element is beginning to be taken seriously; and a variety of issues are being addressed related to school improvement, such as the correlation between the quality of teaching and the achievement of pupils, and that between the quality of teaching and leadership.

Definitions of accountability

One of the most common fallacies individuals are guilty of is failing to distinguish between accountability and responsibility. Accountability and responsibility are quite different although they both occur in the daily activities of a school. Accountability can never be delegated. A leader is accountable for everything that goes on within the organisation. However, responsibility can (and perhaps should) be placed on those who actually do the work. The term 'accountability' describes a relationship in which one party has an obligation, contractual or otherwise, to account for his or her performance of certain actions to another.

> Holders of public office are accountable for their decisions and action to the public and must submit themselves to whatever scrutiny is appropriate to their office. (Nolan Committee, 1997)

This is a challenging viewpoint for many senior managers of schools, who can feel overwhelmed by the demands of government, not only in the amount of data being demanded by the centre but also by the legislative drive for schools to be more accountable and to make more information available to parents and governors about the performance of the child and the institution as a whole. Along with greater delegation and increased self-management comes the need for greater accountability, which is translated into the desire to measure progress against a range of performance indicators and to publish results.

Initially, when financial management was introduced, schools were anxious about financial controls, budgetary management and administrative arrangements. Headteachers began to see that they had to develop strategic processes that linked their financial planning to the improvement of teaching and learning in a school through the successful management of innovation and change. Alongside these early developments in self-management or self-governance, changes in the culture of accountability were also occurring, in the form of parental choice, focusing upon the customer, setting benchmarks, defining fitness for purpose and aiming for continuous improvement. The emergence of the National Curriculum, assessment and Ofsted led to a control and accountability culture. The view that the school knew best and parents were kept at arms length has been replaced by a more equal home/school relationship. Selection by open enrolment has meant that parents and students are perceived as customers whose needs must be ascertained and met.

Much of the same applies to the governing body as to the parents; there is a legislative framework, (DfEE, 1995) which sets out the main roles of the governors. Headteachers have a duty to advise and assist the governing body to discharge its function. They are accountable to the governing body for the overall running of the school including carrying out agreed policies.

Direct accountability is the most straightforward type of relationship. Kogan (1986) argued that only this type of relationship could strictly be called an accountability relationship and defined it as 'a condition in which individual role holders are liable to review and the application of sanctions, if their actions fail to satisfy those with whom they are in an accountability relationship'.

Hence a headteacher is directly responsible to the governing body because ultimately it has the power to dismiss him or her. There are, however, a number of groups with which headteachers work, not in a directly accountable role, but in a working partnership or functional role, and these include pupils, parents, staff, local employers such as the LEA, the local community, Ofsted and the DfEE. Before examining these partnership or functional accountabilities further, it will be useful to consider some theoretical perspectives on accountability.

Perspectives on accountability

Conceptualising on accountability has come about with the promotion of the benefits of significantly increased autonomy for schools. The arguments for increased autonomy to schools from the LEA are similar to those directed at organisations in the business sector, that those close to the people/children know best what needs to be done.

Thomas (1987) argued that decentralised unit managers are better able to make choices to maximise efficiency because:

> The unit managers are (i) closer to the clients; and (ii) better able, than more remotely sited managers, to identify the needs of the clients. In addition, unit managers (iii) will give primacy to satisfying the needs and (iv) will also know the best (i.e. the most efficient) way of combining available resources to meet as many of these needs as possible. Finally in making decisions on resource combinations, the unit manager will vary the proportion of different resources as (v) production requires and (vi) relative price changes.

These arguments about the improvements through increased organisational autonomy are part of a similar debate about the benefits of decentralisation in all aspects of education, affecting schools and LEAs. With this greater level of autonomy and decentralisation from the local employers, comes a need for the senior managers to develop requisite leadership and management competencies to act in this new environment. Peters (1992: 568) believed that as organisations take on more autonomy, they also become more accountable. 'Since information is less distorted, feedback loops (positive or negative) are shorter, and there are more tries in a market economy, accountability is automatically maximised.'

It is therefore, interesting to consider the implications of the interaction of models of educational accountability devised by Kogan (1986):

(1) **public or state control** which entails the use of authority by elected representatives, appointed officials and the heads and others who manage schools;

(2) **professional control** that control of education by teachers and professional administrators; with this is associated self-reporting evaluation;

(3) **consumerist control** or influences which might take the form of:
    (a) participatory democracy or partnership in the public sector;
    (b) market mechanisms in the private or partly privatised sector.

More autonomy for senior leaders means more choice, but also paradoxically, more room for error. Handy (1994) saw that there are two types of error:

There is Type 1 error which in simple terms means getting it wrong and a Type 2 error which, in effect means not getting it right, or as right as it could have been. There is an important difference. A Type 2 error means that the full possibilities of the situation have not been exploited and developed; enough was not enough.

Senior managers in schools used to be held responsible for Type 1 errors, but now we have a new accountability, for the things we could have done but did not. The two levels of accountability are a fact of life and are the main focus of a range of both direct and functional accountability relationships.

The management issues caused by the rapidly evolving role and accountabilities of headteachers can be viewed by examining theories of educational management. A large number of schools were and still are organised on hierarchical approaches which stress vertical relationships and the accountability of leaders to external agencies. Packwood (1977: 1) explained this:

> The hierarchy is the general structure in all developed cultures for achieving work objectives that are beyond the control of a single individual. Through a series of manager-subordinate relationships it explicitly locates accountability for work. The manager in the hierarchy is accountable not only for his or her, performance, but also for the work of subordinates.

In this model, authority is delegated from senior to junior roles while accountability for performance passes in the reverse direction:

> Authority and accountability are imposed in that they are attached to roles not the personalities of the individuals who occupy roles. (9-10)

Central to hierarchical models is the concept of accountability. Leaders are responsible to a range of agencies for the performance of subordinates and the activities of the school. However, in many schools the desire to develop staff participation in decision-making; the possible process that leaders could use for conflict resolution, between goals held at individual, departmental and institutional levels; the pace and complexity of change and the emerging findings from school effectiveness and improvement research, which has been supported by Ofsted/DfEE has led to a move towards a form of collegiality model. Collegial models are attractive because they advocate teacher-participation in decision-making and because they assume a common set of values held by members of the school who have subject expertise.

> Collegial models seem to be particularly appropriate for organisations such as schools and colleges that have significant numbers of pro-fessional staff or are small organisations, teachers possess authority arising directly from their knowledge and skill. They have an authority of expertise that contrasts with positional authority, associated with formal models. Professional authority occurs where decisions are made on an individual basis rather than being standard-ised. Education necessarily demands a professional approach because pupils and students need personal attention. Teachers require a measure of autonomy in the classroom but also need to collaborate to ensure a coherent approach to teaching and learning. Collegial models assume that professionals also have a right to share in the wider, decision-making process. (Bush, 1995: 53)

However, the desire to maintain staff participation in decision-making may conflict with the pressure to become increasingly accountable to direct and functional funding and quality control bodies. There is a tension between participation and accountability.

Bush provided conceptual frameworks linking theory to practice on the significance of good management for the effective operation of schools and colleges, in recognition of the trend towards self-management and the understanding of managerial competence for educational leaders. He presented and analysed six perspectives in terms of the assumptions made about the goals of educational institutions, the nature of the organisational structure, relationships with the external environment and the most appropriate modes of leadership. These are models which are:

Formal – with their emphasis on hierarchical structures, rational processes and official authority;

Collegial – with their stresses on the authority of expertise, shared values and objectives of professional staff and decision-making based on consensus;

Political – with their assumptions of conflict between interest groups and of decisions dependent on the relative resources of power deployed by the various factors;

Subjective – with their emphasis on individual interpretation of events and their rejection of the concept of organisational goals;

Ambiguity – stressing the unpredictability of organisations, the lack of clarity about goals and the fluid nature of participation in decision-making;

Cultural – emphasising the values and beliefs in organisations and the symbols, rituals used to reinforce culture.

As Bush said, each model offers valid insights into the nature and management of schools and colleges. Yet all the perspectives are limited, in that they do not give a complete picture of educational institutions. Rather, they turn the spotlight on particular features of the organisation and consequently leave other features blank. Most educational institutions display features from most or all of the models. As Morgan pointed out (1986: 321): 'Any realistic approach to organisational analysis must start from the premise that organisations can be many things at one and the same time.'

It may be possible to conclude that most schools are likely to possess most of the characteristics of the formal hierarchical models combined with the collegial models, most of the time. This, therefore, places head-teachers in a volatile opposition. They are clearly held directly accountable to the governors and will be seen to be accountable for others through their functional accountabilities to Ofsted/OHMCI(Wales), DfEE, local employers, parents and the community, yet at times this may appear to mitigate against team building, constancy, staff participation and their accountability to the staff.

The dilemma of accountability, perceived by many newly appointed headteachers, however, may not be impossible to solve. Although a theoretical model can only give a partial understanding of school reality, it might be possible to obtain a more comprehensive understanding by integrating the models into an overarching framework. Chapman, (1993: 212) stressed the need for heads to develop broader perspectives in order to enhance organisational awareness: 'Visionary and creative leadership and effective management in education require deliberate and conscious attempts at integration, enmeshment and coherence.'

Enderud (1980) and Davies and Morgan (1983) developed integrative models that are reflected by the strategic planning model proposed by Weindling (1997). It appears from their work, that, to move staff from the hierarchical model to a collegial approach or to use a 'top-down/bottom-up' collegial model combined with the clear accountabilities of the hierarchical model, there are three inter-connected levels of planning, which move from agreeing values and goals to strategic planning, through the school development plan to a more detailed action plan. Strategic planning has as its key, the notion of long-term thinking, which considers the vision and values of all of the members (stakeholders or functional accountabilities) of the organisation, as well as the anticipated external forces and trends which affect the school, in order to improve effectiveness. Strategic planning can be seen in some schools to use accountabilities as an individual management tool to assist leaders in maintaining a clear focus and a process to manage the increasingly turbulent environment and the challenges that confront schools. Through this process the members of the organisation envision its future and develop the necessary procedures to achieve that future, (collegial approach) in order to ensure that the school and each individual can meet their accountabilities, (hierarchical approach) through planning, action, monitoring, evaluation and review.

This eclectic approach is supported by Morgan (1986: 32) who argued that organisational analysis based upon the following two multiple perspectives is a key factor for effective headteachers balancing out dilemmas of leadership and accountabilities:

- a diagnostic reading of the situation being investigated, using different metaphors to identify or highlight key aspects of the situation;
- a critical evaluation of the significance of the different interpretations resulting from the diagnosis.

As Bush wrote (1995: 54) these skills are consistent with the concept of the 'reflective practitioner', whose managerial approach incorporates both good experience, a distillation of theoretical models based on wide reading and discussion, and practical, pragmatic training that enables future senior leaders to develop competencies and knowledge. This combination of theory and knowledge balanced against rigorous practice enables the headteacher to acquire the overview required for strategic management.

Therefore, following this brief examination of theoretical perspectives, it would be appropriate to examine the practical issues of accountability and the role of the headteacher.

Governance and accountability

Every governing body operates differently, according to the type of school, what the schools' articles of government say and who is on the governing body. Headteachers are central to the way in which schools are governed.

The governing body is responsible for determining the aims and over-all conduct of the school. This includes deciding, with the headteacher, how the school should develop in order to maintain and improve its standards of education. In discussion with the governing body, the head-teacher is responsible for formulating policies for their eventual approval. The headteacher is also responsible for implementing these policies, managing and administering the school, and organising and operating the school's curriculum. The headteacher provides information, advice and recommendations and the governors should treat this information with respect and use it with discretion.

The governing body has a legitimate role in monitoring the success (or otherwise) of the school's actions. All staff should see the governors as an integral part of the school, whose purpose is to ensure that the best decisions are made in the interests of the children. Below is an example of the division of responsibilities between the governing body and the head-teacher for the curriculum (DfEE, 1996):

The Headteacher:	**The Governing Body:**
draws up the curriculum plan within the overall statutory framework and the policy framework set by the governing body;	determines a policy for delivering a broad and balanced curriculum within the statutory framework in consultation with the headteacher, including a policy on sex education;

ensures its implementation;	satisfies itself that requirements for the delivery and assessment of the National Curriculum are being met and that religious education is being provided;
is responsible for day-to-day decisions on the curriculum.	ensures that appropriate monitoring arrangements are in place and that outcomes are being evaluated through reports from the headteacher.

DfEE and Ofsted (1995) suggested that one of the features of an effective school was where the school regarded itself as a 'learning organisation'. Headteachers could play a special part in ensuring that the governing body was fully integrated into the 'learning organisation' by making demands on governors. Governors and headteachers should develop a shared vision and goals before working together on a strategic plan which will support the school development plan. The work of Downes and Holt (1996) revealed that: 'Many governing bodies focused upon relative trivia; the state of the toilets or the drains. Brains not drains should be the governors first priority.'

However, if this is to happen, the headteachers have to ensure that the governors are fully informed, advised and involved in the life of the school. The working relationship between the headteacher and chairman/woman of governors needs to be characterised by a sense of purpose, mutual respect and willingness to negotiate. For this to be effective the two partners need to share information, responsibility, skills, decision-making and accountability. In many ways, the headteacher is accountable *for* as well as *to* the governing body, in order to support them to meet their accountabilities.

Duties of a governing body

The British Parliament has given the following broad powers and accountabilities to governing bodies:

- deciding (with the headteacher and LEA, if appropriate) the aims and policies of the school and how standards can be improved;
- deciding the conduct of the school;
- helping to draw up the school development plan;
- ensuring that the national curriculum subjects and religious education are taught and reporting national curriculum assessment and examination results;
- selecting the headteacher and appointing, promoting, supporting and disciplining other staff;
- acting as a link between the school and the community;
- drawing up the post-inspection action plan and monitoring how the plan is put into action.

In grant maintained schools, governors also have the duty to

- oversee the management of school land, property and investments.

Accountability to pupils, parents and staff

A headteacher's prime responsibility is for the children and young people in their care, although their accountability may often be exercised through the parents, or other responsible adults, as the legal guardians of the pupils. As pupils mature, accountability may be increasingly given to them directly, particularly in the case after they reach the age of eighteen. Ofsted and OHMCI (Wales) evaluate and report on how well the governors, headteachers and staff, with management responsibilities, contribute to the education provided by the school and the standards achieved by all its pupils by examining the extent to which as Ofsted (1995) explained: 'the leadership and management produce an effective school; one that promotes and sustains improvement in educational standards achieved and the quality of the education provided', and further stated:

> The Headteacher is the professional leader of the school, responsible and accountable for the direction of its work and for its day to day management and organisation. In an effective school the Headteacher has a direct concern for the sustained improvement of quality and standards, for equality of opportunity for all pupils and for the development of policies and use of resources to achieve these ends.

The key objective for senior managers is to make pupils learning the hub of their existence. As Davies and Ellison (1997) wrote on managing teaching and learning:

> For Fullan (1993), the obvious conclusion is that we cannot have students as continuous learners and effective collaborators without teachers sharing these same characteristics. Fullan refers to the four themes which emanate from the research of Nias *et al.* (1992) into successful curriculum development: teachers learning in a climate of support, the time needed for teachers to change their beliefs and practices during which tension and disagreements have to be worked through; shared values and decision-making structures with commitment of time and development of leadership, not just at headteacher level but through the teacher body; and the unpredictable and dynamic nature of the change process as factors beyond the control of the school continually present themselves.

The DfEE (1995) gave the following example of the headteacher's responsibilities and accountabilities to the staff.

The headteacher:

- makes proposals for a staffing structure;
- selects staff within the limits of delegation agreed by the governing body;
- manages and leads the school staff;
- handles discipline, grievance and first line management in the first instance, within the terms statuary requirements, instruments and articles of government and any standing orders where they exist, and the staff discipline and grievance procedure established by the governing body;
- submits reports to the governors or the staff committee, as required;
- manages in the first instance, consultations with the staff and professional associations on behalf of the governing body.

The headteacher is responsible for ensuring that the number, and qualifications and experience of the staff match the demands of the curriculum. They also carry the accountability for the arrangements for the induction, appraisal and professional development of the staff.

The 1981 Education Act first put into statutory form the obligation to diagnose the individual needs of a child or student and to provide a tailor-made educational programme, which was communicated, agreed and discussed with parents. This change in the parental role was to encourage parents to regard themselves more as consumers, able to choose from a range of educational products. Parents have the right to expect a good education for their child, that is broad and balanced and to expect the school to deliver the highest possible standards of teaching.

The headteacher is accountable for this quality of learning, access to the school, providing information on their child's progress and involvement in the process. Parents have the responsibility to ensure that their child attends school between the ages of five and sixteen. The headteacher is accountable for the effectiveness of the school's partnership with parents and the contribution which the school's links with the community make to the pupils' attainment and personal development.

Accountability for effectiveness and efficiency

The most important aspect of school autonomy is the reconsideration of whether nor not the available money is used effectively and efficiently. This is where there is scope for leadership, vision and lateral thinking. (Downes, 1997)

The senior manager's aim must be to get the job done most effectively at the lowest cost. Effective school leaders need to understand the budget cycle and to train their team to understand it as well.

The budget process cannot be seen as something that happens at the end of the school financial year but as a key part of the strategic planning process in order to ensure that the school raises pupil achievement, meets its aims and objectives, and is efficient and effective.

Effectiveness is also about whether the school achieves its aims and objectives for all of its pupils, in order to raise pupil achievement. Characteristics of effective schools identified by Weindling (1997), were that there was an emphasis on learning, classroom management, discipline and school climate, school management, vision and monitoring, staff development, parental involvement, and that the school used the LEA or outside agencies to support improvement, development and change.

Below is an example of the division of responsibilities between governing body and headteacher for the finance and budget (DfEE, 1995):

The Headteacher:	The Governing Body, in consideration of its ultimate responsibility for the budget:
draws up the proposed budget options for – delegated funds; – special purpose grants; – other anticipated income for consideration and approval by the governing body;	discusses and adopts the budget (with any amend-ments which are agreed); agrees limits of delegation and the power to transfer between budget headings (virement);
incurs expenditure within delegated limits, once the budget has been agreed;	monitors expenditure against budget and evaluates the outcome;
submits regular monitoring reports of expenditure against budget to the governing body, or finance committee.	these functions, apart from the approval of the budget, may be delegated to a finance committee where one exists to work with the Headteacher.

The efficient school achieves high outcomes for its pupils at minimum of cost, it wastes none of its financial resources and derives maximum benefit from what it already has, in order to achieve value for money.

Skilful management of the internal and external financial and resource boundaries are key competencies of senior managers and a growing aspect of headteacher accountability. However, it is clear that the two aspects of effectiveness and efficiency cannot be incurred in isolation from each other. It is important for governors and staff to review the data arising from the outcomes of monitoring, and evaluate pupil achievement, to envisage not only how they are meeting the school targets, but also to make realistic judgements about where they see the school developing in three years time. The process of monitoring and evaluating performance of teaching and learning, linked to a review of the efficient use of budgets, staff and resources, enables the school to become a 'learning organisation' (Senge, 1990).

Finally, it is appropriate to consider the *National Standards for Headteachers* (TTA, 1998a):

> Headteachers account for the efficiency and effectiveness of the school to the governors, and others, including pupils, parents, staff, local employers and the local community.

> Headteachers:

> (1) provide information, objective advice and support to the governing body to enable it to meet its responsibilities for securing effective teaching and learning and improved standards of achievement and for achieving efficiency and value for money;

> (2) create and develop an organisation in which all staff recognise that they are accountable, for the success of the school;

> (3) present a coherent and accurate amount of the school's performance in a form appropriate to a range of audiences, including governors, the LEA, the local community, Ofsted/OHMCI (Wales), and others, to enable them to play their part effectively;

> (4) ensure that parents and pupils are well informed about the curriculum, attainment and progress and about the contribution that they can make to achieving the school's targets for improvement.

Headteachers in schools and colleges have the information they need on pupil performance in order to develop plans and strategies to raise pupil achievement and standards. But they do need partners in government – the LEAs, Ofsted/OHMCI (Wales) and the DfEE – to support them in their direct and functional accountabilities.

8. Leadership

Rob Bollington

Introduction

The quality of a school has increasingly been seen to depend in large measure on the quality of its leadership. The following comments typify this belief:

> The quality of leadership makes the difference between the success and failure of a school. That is why headteachers are at the heart of the Government's drive to secure higher standards in all our schools. (Millett, 1998: 1)

> Strong leadership, often from a recently appointed headteacher, is the key feature of all the schools that have made substantial improvement. (Woodhead, 1998)

> Good heads are crucial to the success of schools. The best heads match the best leaders anywhere. We need to develop strong and effective leaders, reward them well and give them the freedom to manage, without losing accountability … We also want to ensure that schools are able to recognise leadership by other teachers who give strategic direction in schools. (DfEE, 1998c: 21)

> Outstanding leadership has invariably emerged as a key characteristic of outstanding schools. There can no longer be doubt that those seeking quality in education must ensure its presence and that the development of potential leaders must be given high priority. (Beare *et al.*, 1989: 89)

From research into school effectiveness, inspection evidence, government and government agencies, the same message has emerged; leadership makes a difference, perhaps *the* difference. This chapter begins by tracing the background to the current emphasis and examines a range of perspectives on leadership. It then considers possible future developments. The perspective taken is that there is no one best way to lead and that leadership, contrary to the emphasis sometimes given, should not be seen as the sole preserve of the headteacher.

Definitions and background

Countless attempts have been made to define leadership. Indeed:

> Decades of academic analysis have given us more than 350 definitions of leadership ... Never have so many labored for so long to say so little. Multiple interpretations of leadership exist, each providing a sliver of insight but each remaining an incomplete and wholly inadequate explanation ... Definitions reflect fads, fashions, political tides and academic trends. (Bennis and Nanus, 1985: 4-5)

Others have echoed this point. For example, Grace (1995: 192) argued that

> Conceptions of educational leadership are dynamic, contested, historically and culturally situated and at the centre of socio-political and ideological struggles about the future of schooling. Conceptions of educational leadership are not simply technical formulations for making schools effective as organisations, they are also fundamental expressions of cultural and political values.

In a world of change, uncertainty and ambiguity, it has become difficult to believe that any one definition of leadership will hold good for all:

> Leadership requires using power to influence the thoughts and actions of other people. (Zalenik, 1992: 126)

> Leadership is the art of influencing others to their maximum performance to accomplish any task, objective or project. (Cohen, 1990: 9)

Leadership is what gives an organization its vision and its ability to translate that vision into reality. (Bennis and Nanus, 1985: 20)

Leadership is concerned with achieving *goals*, working with *people*, in a social *organisation*, being *ethical* and exercising *power* ... leaders know themselves, the colleagues they are working with and understand the school in which they are working. They also use a variety of ways of working in the light of their perceptions of these three sets of variables (self, colleagues and context) and how they interrelate. Leadership is thus not only an active role, it is a dynamic one [original italics]. (Southworth, 1998: 9)

True school leaders enhance learning outcomes for students through influencing others in the school community to take collaborative responsibility and action for their own learning and work. (Donaldson, and Marnik, 1995: 3-4)

A whole range of assumptions and values tends to underpin each definition of leadership. It is possible to analyse definitions in terms of some of the following dimensions, which relate to whether leadership is seen as:

- democratic or authoritarian;
- directive or empowering;
- more or less concerned with individuals' needs, a group's needs or achieving outcomes;
- concerned with bringing about change or maintaining the *status quo*;
- focusing on the leader or the followers or the interaction between them;
- getting people to question critically or accept established values and beliefs.

The same can be said about the many attempts made to distinguish between leadership and management. Often management is seen as concerned with getting things done, with operational matters and with issues of implementing policies and procedures. By contrast, leadership is often seen as concerned with doing the right things, with strategic matters and providing direction and a sense of purpose. Bennis (1989: 45) argued that:

- The manager administers; the leader innovates.
- The manager is a copy; the leader is an original.
- The manager maintains; the leader develops.
- The manager focuses on systems and structure; the leader focuses on people.
- The manager relies on control; the leader inspires trust.
- The manager has a short-range view; the leader has a long-range perspective.
- The manager asks how and when; the leader asks what and why.
- The manager has his eye always on the bottom line; the leader has his eye on the horizon.
- The manager imitates; the leader originates.
- The manager accepts the *status quo*; the leader challenges it.
- The manager is the classic good soldier; the leader is his own person.
- The manager does things right; the leader does the right thing.

A similar attempt to differentiate between leadership and management was provided by West-Burnham (1997: 117) who suggested that 'leading' is concerned with 'vision', 'strategic issues', 'transformation', 'ends', 'people' and 'doing the right thing'; whereas 'managing' is concerned with 'implementation', 'operational issues', 'transaction', 'means', 'systems' and 'doing things right'.

Another perspective was provided by distinguishing between the 'leading professional' and 'chief executive' sub-roles of headship (Hughes, 1988). This approach drew attention to the range of responsibilities that a headteacher has to balance and the possibility for varying types of emphasis in how the role is carried out. It is possible to analyse an individual's approach to school leadership in terms of whether he or she places more or less emphasis on the chief executive or leading professional dimensions. Of course, the world has moved on since this model (opposite) was first devised and although the different dimensions still make sense, the elements within each cell can be updated. Over time, first local management of schools and possibilities for changing status and then the advent of fair funding encouraged the development of headteachers as chief executives. However, emphasis on school improvement and raising standards provided a countervailing influence that placed the emphasis on the headteacher as leading professional. It may be as some argue that 'future models may well require a radical re-definition or even separation

Leading professional sub-role	**Chief executive sub-role**
Internal	*Internal*

Leading professional		Chief executive
1. Professional guidance of staff 2. Personal teaching 3. Counselling of pupils and parents etc.	⇆	Allocative and co-ordinating functions within the school

External ↕		*External* ↕
1. Acting as spokes-person for the school in educational matters 2. Involvement in external professional activities (the cosmo-politan role)	⇆	Relationships with the governing body, and with the LEA as employing authority (Hughes, 1988: 15)

of the managerial or administrative functions from the pedagogical and moral leadership of learning communities' (Collarbone and Shaw, 1998). Arguably, the key to success is to place the emphasis on actions that improve the quality of teaching and learning and to see those administrative tasks that cannot be delegated as an opportunity to exercise professional leadership. In the end, a renewed emphasis on the leading professional sub-role is vital if there is to be a sharp focus in schools on their core purpose of improving the quality of teaching and learning. The same tensions between leadership and management functions and between the executive and professional sub-roles also apply at other levels of leadership. For example, does a head of department or curriculum co-ordinator give more weight to administrative tasks or to leading developments in teaching and learning? The increased role envisaged by the British Government for non-teaching staff in future schools might make a difference to this tension over time.

The distinctions between leadership and management and between the leading professional and chief executive sub-roles can be useful in that they provide a checklist; but in practice leadership and management are best seen as closely linked and as two sides of the same coin. To function effectively in a role carrying responsibility in a school, both its leadership and management dimensions need attending. In doing so, however, it is as well to bear in mind that 'the problem with many organisations, and especially the ones that are failing, is that they tend to be overmanaged and underled' (Bennis and Nanus, 1985: 21). The shift in emphasis from management to leadership has been accompanied by an increasing emphasis on the need to handle rapid and multiple change with all the attendant uncertainties. In such circumstances, an increasing focus on *leadership* dimensions such as vision, transformation, people and doing the right things is not surprising. This emphasis appears set to continue. Implementing or *managing* traditional procedures and systems without questioning their continued suitability risks failing to keep up or get ahead of events. Such an approach can also fail to take account of global trends and of how well an organisation is doing in comparison with local and international parallels in terms of standards achieved. Preoccupation with leadership reflects this situation. Leaders are needed who look ahead and look around and ask the necessary questions. Such leaders are crucial to raising standards and to school improvement. In the current context, leadership is often viewed as about working with people to create and move towards a shared vision of what an organisation might become. Such an approach implies that all involved are open to learning and engaged upon a journey in which they and their organisation change and develop.

Leadership qualities

Some writers on leadership have attempted to identify the critical traits or qualities that make people effective as leaders. Such an approach was initially linked with a belief that good leaders or 'great men' are born, not made. In other words, it was linked with a belief that, according to an unnamed lecturer in 1934 at St Andrews University (Adair, 1988: 1)

> it is a fact that some men possess an inbred superiority which gives them a dominating influence over their contemporaries, and marks them out unmistakably for leadership … [and that] there are those who, with an assured and unquestioned title, take the leading place, and shape the general conduct.

In more recent times, although there has understandably been less emphasis on 'inbred superiority' and 'great men', the focus has switched to attempts to identify general leadership traits. The approach comes across particularly in the areas of recruitment, selection and training. Those who have tried to identify key characteristics of leaders have emphasised the difference made by the particular qualities of an individual.

The lists produced have often been long and certainly have been varied. In terms of common ground, Handy (1993: 98) pointed out that most studies of leadership traits single out the following:

Intelligence should be above average but not of genius level. Particularly good in solving complex and abstract problems.

Initiative. Independence and inventiveness, the capacity to perceive a need for action and the urge to do it. Appears to correlate quite well with age, i.e. drops off after 40;

Self assurance. Implies self-confidence, reasonably high self-ratings on competence and aspiration levels, and on perceived ultimate occupational level in society [original italics].

He went on to refer to recent studies that added

The helicopter factor. The ability to rise above the particulars of a situation and perceive it in its overall relations to the environment.

and continued:

In addition most successful leaders appear to:

Have good health;
Be above average height or well below it;
Come from the upper socio-economic levels in society.

Adair (1988: 13) concluded his discussion of leadership qualities with the comment that 'most people accept that leadership implies *personality*. Enthusiasm and warmth are often deemed to be especially important. There is also an impressive testimony in history that *character*, incorporating moral courage and integrity, matters enormously' [original italics].

More recently the TTA's (1998) national standards for headteachers, subject leaders and special educational needs co-ordinators included a list of leadership attributes. These form part of a complex set of leadership qualities and are set alongside knowledge, understanding, skills and areas of capability. In other words, personal qualities are seen as part of the leadership equation. The attributes included are as follows:

- personal impact and presence;
- adaptability to changing circumstances and new ideas;
- energy, vigour and perseverance;
- self-confidence;
- enthusiasm;
- intellectual ability;
- reliability and integrity;
- commitment.

It is interesting to stand this approach on its head and to think about in-effective leaders. Bolam *et al.* (1993: 31-2) listed qualities to be found in ineffective leaders. They included

- lacking dynamism and failing to inspire;
- being insufficiently forceful;
- failing to be at ease with others and to enable them to feel at ease, particularly in difficult and demanding situations;
- inability to accept any form of questioning or perceived criticism.

There are a number of difficulties with the attempts to distinguish the critical qualities or traits of leadership. People accepted as effective leaders often vary considerably in qualities they possess. It is also possible to see leaders depending on differing qualities according to the situation they are in. A leader effective in one situation can be ineffective or less effective in another. It can be argued, for example, that the qualities needed by head-teachers tasked with turning round failing schools are different from the ones needed by headteachers in other situations. The possession of certain traits or qualities does not appear to guarantee success in practice or in all situations. Other factors, such as the nature of the other people involved and the circumstances, come into play. Nevertheless, the attempt to identify leadership traits has had a particular influence on recruitment and selection and in the areas of assessment, self-evaluation, training and development. What appears most helpful is for leaders to be aware of how their qualities enable them to be effective. Sometimes this can best be achieved by focusing on the behaviours linked to a particular quality. This can in turn lead to the increased self-awareness that can enable a leader to use his or her strengths to greater effect. Bennis (1989), while noting the wide differences between leaders, pointed out some common character-istics, not dissimilar in tenor from the ones noted above – a guiding vision, a passion, integrity (based on self-knowledge, candour and maturity), trust, curiosity and daring. He pointed to the importance of such qualities, arguing that 'leadership is first being, then doing. Everything the leader does reflects what he or she is'. However, this is only part of the picture.

Competence and competency

'Competence' and 'competencies' are terms used for the skills, abilities and characteristics that people bring to their work. They are terms that cover a broader area than an individual's character and personal qualities. The word 'competence' tends to be preferred in Britain whereas the word 'competency' tends to be used in the United States. In effect, 'competence' is used to refer to the ability to perform to a minimum specified standard. On the other hand, 'competency' refers to the characteristics and abilities that enable some people to excel and perform at a superior level. A com-petence approach can be found in both the generic MCI and the school focused derivative, developed by School Management South (Earley, 1992). In the MCI approach, jobs are defined in terms of key purposes, key roles, units, elements and performance criteria. The framework can be used for training and assessment purposes. At the heart of this approach is a logical and systematic analysis of work carried out. The competency approach, by contrast, is based on observing the character-istics and behaviours of people who excel at their job. The focus is on what enables them to perform at a higher level than others. Examples of this approach can be found in the work of the National Education Assessment Centre (NEAC), which for a number of years has assessed the competency of senior staff in schools. It is also evident in the work of Hay McBer Ltd, most recently for the LPSH. They identified a set of fifteen characteristics of effective headteachers through in-depth interviews with a group of highly effective headteachers, (House of Commons Select Committee on Education and Employment, 1998, B 18):

Personal values and passionate conviction

- Respect for others
- Challenge and support
- Personal conviction

Creating the vision

- Strategic thinking
- Drive for improvement

Planning, delivering, monitoring, evaluating and improving

- Analytical thinking
- Initiative
- Transformational leadership
- Teamworking
- Understanding others
- Developing potential

Building commitment and support

- Impact and influence
- Holding people accountable

Gathering information and gaining understanding

- Social awareness
- Scanning the environment

With the aid of a framework such as this, it is possible to collect evidence of someone's behaviour to illustrate the degree to which they demonstrate a particular competency. It is then possible to identify areas of weakness and to devise an action plan for personal development. The work on competence and competency is useful in focusing on what an individual can bring to his or her leadership role. Both approaches provide systematic frameworks for personal development. There are some limitations, however. The competence approach can be limiting with its focus on minimum standards and can be criticised for being too detailed in the way it breaks jobs down into smaller and smaller parts. The competency approach avoids the first criticism by focusing on what enables people to perform well but once again it dissects a complex whole.

This discussion of competence and competency provides an appropriate context for discussing the TTA's (1998a) national professional development framework of standards. The rationale for the approach taken is as follows:

(1) The key to unlocking the full potential of pupils in our schools lies in the expertise of teachers and headteachers. Research and inspection evidence demonstrate the close correlation between the quality of teaching and the achievement of pupils and between the quality of leadership and the quality of teaching. It is these links which lie at the heart of the Government's drive for school improvement.

(2) A principal aim of the TTA is to promote effective and efficient professional development for teachers and headteachers, targeted on improvements in the quality of teaching and leadership which will have the maximum impact on pupils' learning. The cornerstone of this work is the development of national standards for the teaching profession to define expertise in key roles.

(3) National standards have been developed for:

- the award of Qualified Teacher Status (QTS);
- Special Educational Needs Co-ordinators (SENCOs);
- subject leaders;
- headteachers.

(4) The main aims of the national standards are to:

(a) set out clear expectations for teachers at key points in the profession;
(b) help teachers at different points in the profession to plan and monitor their development, training and performance effectively, and to set clear, relevant targets for improving their effectiveness;

(c) ensure that the focus at every point is on improving the achievement of pupils and the quality of their education;

(d) provide a basis for the professional recognition of teachers' expertise and achievements; and

(e) help providers of professional development to plan and provide high quality, relevant training which meets the needs of individual teachers and headteachers, makes good use of their time and has the maximum benefit for pupils.

(5) The national standards set out the professional knowledge, understanding, skills and attributes necessary to carry out effectively the key tasks of that role. It is the sum of these aspects which defines the expertise demanded of the role, in order to achieve the outcomes set out in the standards.

Additionally, the standards reflect national educational priorities and are based on wide consultation. They are designed to provide a structure for professional development and appraisal. The national standards provide a description for each role they cover that specifies what an individual needs to perform the tasks set out for the role. The emphasis is on the professional knowledge and understanding, skills and attributes necessary to the range of tasks covered by the role. Some people find this approach rather mechanistic and reductionist and feel that by breaking a role down to this extent its holistic nature is lost. Others worry that such an approach is designed to produce 'clones' and will discourage creativity and flair. These criticisms miss the point. These standards provide a common language for discussing a role, giving a starting point for professional dialogue, and are best viewed as a platform from which to take off rather than as a straitjacket designed to constrain. They leave open the question of style and method. For example, the *National Standards for Headteachers* (TTA, 1998a) stated that headteachers 'ensure that the management, finance, organisation and administration of the school support its vision and aims; and ensure that policies and practices take account of national, local and school data, and inspection and research findings'. How this is done is left open. This brings us to the issue of leadership style.

Leadership style

A dominant theme in much that has been written and said about leadership is the issue of leadership style. This is perhaps best defined as how a leader's typical way or manner of doing things is perceived by those around him or her. At the heart of the various attempts to categorise leadership style are distinctions on the one hand between democratic and authoritarian approaches, and on the other between a concern for people and relationships, and a concern for tasks or results.

The many models and theories of leadership and management that have been produced over the years tend to be contested and are often criticised on empirical grounds, particularly where they originate in one type of organisation or culture and are then applied uncritically to different contexts. They do, however, provide a starting point for personal reflection. They are perhaps best approached as lenses through which to view our individual approaches to leadership and management or as hypotheses to test against our experience.

Two early pieces of research underpin a good deal of more recent work on leadership style. Research by White and Lippitt in 1939 and 1940 distinguished between three styles of leadership – autocratic, democratic and *laissez-faire*. Research at the Ohio State University in the 1940s identified two major dimensions of leadership behaviour – 'consideration' and 'initiating structure'. ('Consideration' refers to concern for how people feel and involves being supportive, friendly and open, giving recognition and inviting participation and two-way communication. 'Initiating structure' involves specifying expectations for how tasks are to be carried out. In practice many leaders operate somewhere between the extremes. Leadership behaviour, Tannenbaum and Schmidt (1958) suggested, varies along a continuum from low subordinate participation in decision-making to high subordinate decision-making varying from the former position, where the leader takes decisions and tells the group about them, to the latter where the leader delegates and allows decisions to be taken within defined limits through group discussion. Further insight into the matter of management and leadership style can be gained from the work of Blake and Mouton (1964) in which they constructed a grid based on the idea that leaders vary along a scale in both their concern for people and their concern for getting the job done. Each of the two axes of the grid is a nine-point scale producing key styles as follows:

'Country club management'	Low concern for results High concern for relationships	Importance attached to lack of conflict and good relationships. Keeping people happy is more important than achieving results.
'Impoverished management'	Low concern for results Low concern for relationships	Passive approach. Lack of energy and effort.
'Middle of the road management'	Moderate concern for results and relationships	Compromise struck between achieving results and maintaining good relationships.
'Task oriented management'	High concern for results Low concern for relationships	Task oriented approach. Results put before people.
'Team management'	High concern for results High concern for relationships	Strong emphasis on achieving results through a concern for the welfare of staff, high morale and effective teamwork.

This model has been very influential, highlighting the central issue for leaders of balancing a concern for efficiency and getting the job done with satisfying staff needs and maintaining morale. On the face of it the 'team management' style appears to be the ideal and has often been advocated because it is associated with participation, involvement, trust and mutual support and respect. Handy (1993: 100) noted that there is:

evidence that supportive styles of leadership:

- are related to subordinate satisfaction;
- are related to lower turnover and grievance rates;
- result in less inter-group conflict;
- are often the preferred styles of subordinates.

There are also many instances where supportive styles of leadership were found to be associated with higher-producing work groups.

Nevertheless, the evidence does not appear to hold good in all situations and a particular style of leadership may not be equally appropriate with all staff in all circumstances or at all times. In an urgent situation where failure to take decisive action could be damaging or even dangerous, it is probable that a concern for getting results would outweigh a concern for morale. Similarly when a member of staff has significant personal problems, it is likely that, unless some care is shown for the individual person, efficiency and results will not be achieved.

Contingency theories of leadership attempt to account for the range of factors involved in leadership, such as the nature of the task and the group and the leader's position. Fiedler (1969) argued that the effectiveness of a particular leadership style depends on the situation. For him, it did not make sense to speak of a leader as effective or ineffective in general terms, but rather to see a leader as effective in one situation and ineffective in another. He analysed the situation in terms of three sets of variables:

- the position power of the leader i.e. the amount of power the leader has;
- the structure of the task i.e. the extent to which the task is well-defined and has clear outcomes;
- the personal relationship between the leader and the members of the group i.e. the degree to which the leader is liked and accepted.

For Fiedler, the most favourable situations were ones where the relationships between the leader and the group were good and the task well defined; the least favourable situations were ones where relationships were poor and tasks ill-defined and unstructured. He argued that task-oriented leaders tend to be most effective in either favourable or unfavourable situations. They also do well when the task is unstructured but position power is strong. When the situation is neither especially favourable nor unfavourable, then a people-oriented leader is more effective. For example, where the task is ill-defined but the leader has a good relationship with the group, then a supportive, non-directive approach by the leader will get the best from people.

Fiedler's work moves us away from any notion that there is one best all-purpose leadership style for all occasions and makes us focus on the context as well as upon the leader. A particular style of leadership will work best in a particular situation. It points to the issue of selecting an appropriate leader for a particular context and opens the possibility of tackling problems by modifying the situation to suit the leader as well as by training the leader to change. Nevertheless his work has been criticised in terms of its empirical basis and on the grounds that he 'makes things too simple by restricting the problem to the nature of the task and the relationship between the leader and his subordinates' (Handy, 1993).

Hersey and Blanchard (1988) developed a form of contingency theory referred to as 'situational leadership'. In their model of leadership, the appropriate style varies according to a range of factors, notably the competence and commitment of the group or individual being led or managed. Where the leader is dealing with someone lacking in competence, then a directive, telling style of leadership is appropriate. However, as confidence, commitment and competence increase, the leader must move progressively from directing to coaching to supporting to delegating.

Style (1): Directing

When people take on a new task, they tend to need direction, structure, supervision and feedback. They can become difficult if the direction and feedback are not provided.

Style (2): Coaching

As people gain some competence in the task, they reach the second stage in the model and need to be sold on an idea, supported with feedback and provided with fresh ideas and coaching. They need both direction and support.

Style (3): Supporting	People at this stage are more confident in their ability to decide on what tasks need to be done and to plan ahead. But they also need to participate in decision-making with the leader of the group. At this stage, they need praise and to be listened to. They benefit from a facilitative style of leadership.
Style (4): Delegating	The leader sets out the broad parameters for the task, knowing that people can get on with their work without close supervision or constant feedback. People's experience means they need little direction and their commitment means they need little support.

People vary in terms of the speed and degree to which they are able to progress through the four stages. In judging an appropriate style, the leader needs to give weight to both the competence and commitment of the group or individual. In other words, just because someone is well motivated and committed does not mean they are capable of doing a job. This model provides a useful basis for analysing leadership and is a helpful starting point in raising self-awareness about how effectively a leader is performing. People appear to see themselves as operating more in supporting or coaching styles than in directing or delegating styles. The model can, therefore, raise the question for an individual headteacher or teacher as to whether there are situations in which they could usefully vary their style. It can be a useful means of analysing the best approach to take in situations involving giving feedback on performance such as appraisal or mentoring. The clear message is that 'there are four leadership styles: *Directing, Coaching, Supporting and Delegating*. But ... There is no one best leadership style' [original italics] (Blanchard *et al.*, 1994: 46).

Handy (1993) described a model of leadership that he sees as an extension of contingency theories of leadership. He called this model the 'best fit' approach. For him, there were four sets of factors to consider –

the leader, the subordinates, the task and the environment. He argued that the best style of leadership for any given situation is achieved when there is a best fit between the leader, the task and the group. He went on to say that the freedom to achieve such a fit is affected by environmental factors, such as the norms of the organisation, the power of the leader, relation-ships, the variety of tasks and changes in personnel.

For Handy, the 'best fit' approach maintained that there is no such thing as the 'right' style of leadership, but that leadership will be most effective when the requirements of the *leader*, the *subordinates* and the *task* fit together. This fit can be measured on a scale that runs from 'tight' to 'flexible' and, Handy stated: 'Confronted with a lack of fit the leader must consider which of the three factors to adjust in order to achieve a fit.'

The models of leadership discussed so far provide a useful starting point for self-evaluation. They suggest that teachers and headteachers need to consider not only their own preferred style, but also the nature of the task, the people involved and the circumstances in deciding on how to handle a situation. They provide a means of reflecting upon experience and give rise to insights into practice. Another perspective is provided by the concepts of transactional and transformational leadership (McGregor Burns, 1978). *Transformational leadership* refers to an approach to leader-ship, which places an emphasis on engaging people in a shared vision for the organisation. On the other hand, *transactional leadership* refers to an approach where leaders offer some kind of reward or incentive in return for the achievement of goals. In other words it is about an exchange of one thing for another. In many ways, the distinction is similar to that drawn earlier between leadership and management. Collarbone and Billingham, (1998: 3) summarised the key differences. They suggested that transform-ational leadership builds on the need for meaning; is pre-occupied with purposes, values, morals and ethics; transcends daily affairs; is oriented to-wards long-term goals without compromising human values; separates causes and symptoms and works at prevention; focuses more on missions and strategies for achieving them; makes full use of human resources; designs and re-designs jobs to make them meaningful and challenging; realises human potential; and aligns internal structures and systems to reinforce overarching values and goals. On the other hand, they surmised, transational leadership builds on the need to do the job and make a living; is pre-occupied with power and position, politics and perks; is swamped in daily affairs; is oriented to short-term goals and hard data; confuses causes and symptoms and is concerned with treatment; focuses on tactical issues; relies on human relations to oil human interactions; follows and fulfils role expectations by striving to work effectively within the current system; and supports structures and systems that reinforce the bottom line, maximise efficiency and guarantee short-term gains.

It can be argued that transformational leadership is especially appropriate at a time of change. The importance of vision in leadership was developed by Bennis and Nanus (1985) for example, who argued that 'leadership is what gives an organisation its vision and its ability to translate that vision into reality'. They developed the case for a style of leadership that is about transformation by pointing to a leader's need to:

- create a new and compelling vision capable of bringing the work force to a new place;
- develop commitment for the new vision;
- institutionalise the new vision.

To do this they argued, a leader must have a vision or 'mental image of a possible and desirable future state of the organisation'. Furthermore this vision must be a 'realistic, credible, attractive future for the organisation, a condition that is better in some important ways than what now exists' (89). Nanus (1992: 3) returned to this theme later saying that 'there is no more powerful engine driving an organisation towards excellence and long-range success than an attractive, worthwhile and achievable vision of the future, widely shared'. He argued (16) that 'selecting and articulating the right vision … is the toughest task and the truest test of great leadership'. Such a vision is seen as crucial to gaining commitment and enthusiasm and to empowering people to act in the knowledge of direction they need to go in. It will reflect underlying values and in practice, often contains an ethical stance. As Holmes (1993: 16) wrote:

> For the school leader, vision is, at its simplest, the mental image of the kind of school you are trying to build for the future. That vision includes the aspirations you have for the present and future pupils in the school, the quality of teaching and learning which you think is attainable and the values which should influence everything which happens in the school.

Put another way (Nanus, 1992: 156):

Vision + Commitment = Shared Purpose

Shared Purpose + Empowered People +Appropriate Organisational Changes + Strategic Thinking = Successful Visionary Leadership

Southworth (1998: 43-55) provided a useful discussion of the place of transactional and transformational leadership in schools, seeing the two approaches as 'complementary and supplementary'. For him transactional leadership primarily focused on the maintenance functions of a school. Transformational leadership is concerned with school's development needs and goals. It is leadership that contributes to school improvement. He argued that transformational leadership is about:

- empowerment;
- team leadership;
- development;
- learning;
- vision.

From this perspective, transformational leadership is seen as having the potential to change a school's culture and create the conditions for improvement. It can, the argument goes, unleash the combined power of a group of individuals pulling in the same direction with commitment, energy and focus towards a vision that is both compelling and clear. Of course, it is possible to place an emphasis on the role of vision while operating in a more or less democratic or authoritarian manner. A vision can involve genuine collaboration, based on a shared view of the future, or be basically the headteacher's vision that is imposed on the group. It might be argued, however, that real commitment is only achieved when people are helped to develop the competence and commitment to become involved in the development of the vision. The process of involvement gives people a chance to articulate and test their underlying values and enables a negotiated common vision to emerge to which there is an emotional as well as an intellectual commitment. It can also be seen as the embodiment of professionalism. The evidence presented to the Select Committee on Education and Employment (1998, B 19) about headship echoed these points about the importance of vision:

Mr Dyson, of Hay McBer, told us: Excelling heads … create a vision, a very vivid vision, of what it is they want to do. They then move on to actually building commitment around that vision by involving people, the other teachers in the school, the parents, the governors, in actually planning for the delivery of that vision. Then the whole process is one of monitoring and evaluating of progress and then modification of the vision if necessary.

An interesting description of a transformational style of leadership and the contrast with what came before is provided from a Total Quality Management (TQM) perspective by Murgatroyd and Morgan (1993) who suggested that traditional forms of leadership in schools have often been characterised by solving problems quickly; the assumption that change is modest and should not affect the basic work of the school; waiting for something to occur before we take action; being rational; leaving those in charge to worry about the big picture; and by the acceptance that there is little we can do to shape our own strategy.

According to Murgatroyd and Morgan (1993) TQM leadership requires a very different set of assumptions about management and the work of managers. They proposed that such leadership is, by contrast, about imagination and empowerment and that the role of the TQM leader is to activate, coach, educate and assist colleagues so that they focus on a shared vision and strategy. They identified what they saw as the five key features of a successful TQM organisation including alignment within the organisation (where everyone pulls together towards the same strategic ends); an understanding of the customer-driven basis of quality; an organisation designed around teams; the setting of challenging goals; and the systematic daily management of the organisation where all of these factors have been put in place. Murgatroyd and Morgan argued that TQM has been remarkably effective but without them it is likely to be ineffective.

These are useful checklists for school leaders to use to review how the school is operating. In particular, they draw attention to some of the actions which transformational leaders need to take – coaching, guiding, mentoring, educating, assisting, supporting, painting the big picture and attending to detail. The five critical features of a TQM organisation can also be seen as a potentially powerful combination of ingredients that have a synergy and force that can take a school or other organisation forward. The emphasis on teamwork fits in well with the idea that leadership is most effective when exercised at a number of points in a school.

The role of vision in schools can be seen in the experience of practitioners including the experience of a number of the witnesses called by the Select Committee referred to earlier. For example (paragraph 19):

> Ms Mary Marsh, the headteacher of Holland Park School, argued that the key to improving performance was the headteacher's success in building a team of people who share 'the same vision, values and objectives'.

Another example comes in the following comment from a North American school principal which illustrates the value of a clear set of guiding principles:

> I now visualize the course of a school as a river with smooth currents and pounding, steep rapids. My school sits upon this river, moving with the flow. Empowered by my 'guiding principles', there are rapids that I choose to run and those that are best to circumvent. There are smooth waters that are comfortable, but when the calm continues too long, I can lift my oar, stir the current, and challenge the crew to explore new territory. Most important, I must keep us all flowing toward our main goal – discovering what is in the best interest of our children. (VanderMolen, 1995: 3)

The use of metaphors of leadership is an interesting topic. 'Navigating a river' sits alongside others that are commonly heard:

- the captain of the ship steering a steady course;
- the helicopter pilot hovering above the terrain, sometimes going ahead to look over the horizon, sometimes landing at a particular point where action is needed;
- the juggler trying to keep all the balls in the air for as long as possible;
- the conductor of the orchestra controlling rhythm and pace, interpreting the score, bringing people in when necessary and ensuring the orchestra completes its task successfully;
- the tightrope walker trying to retain a difficult balance and move forward.

There are many more. The point is that by reflecting on our own metaphors of leadership, we can gain insights into our motivation and style. We can ask whether our actions, our beliefs and our intentions are in line with what circumstances call for. VanderMolen's metaphor appears particularly appropriate in times of change and uncertainty.

Returning to the issue of vision in leadership, there is one final perspective to discuss. Vision can be seen as an essential foundation of strategic planning. 'Leaders create vision (a realistic and appealing picture of the future) and strategies (a logic for how the vision can be achieved). Leadership is transformational. Future leaders will need to be skilled at turning visions into reality' (Collarbone and Shaw, 1998). A clear vision of the school in the future can serve to 'inspire' and to 'act as a corner-stone for decision-making'. It can 'enable all in the school to find common points for focusing energy to achieve sustainable steep-slope quality improvements, i.e. vision is the primary vehicle for creating alignment of energies within an organisation' (Murgatroyd and Morgan, 1993). To have this impact a vision needs to be compelling, to be communicated and to be lived. A more detailed discussion of strategic leadership is provided in Chapter 3. All that is attempted here is to summarise some key points:

- you stand more chance of getting to where you want to be if you know where you are going;
- in a world of rapid change there are limitations to strategic planning; some plans will be realised, others will need to be modi-fied or get blown off course by unpredictable events; strategies can emerge as well as being deliberately planned;
- having a vision provides a yardstick against which to judge strategic plans; it also gives people a yardstick by which to judge strategies that emerge and a secure base to act from when faced with the unexpected;
- if people are clear about the overall aims of the school, they can better select an appropriate course of action in any given situation; strategic intent is as important as strategic planning.

Strategic planning typically involves a series of steps, (see for example, Weindling, 1997). In essence, a school clarifies its vision and checks that this meets the needs of its stakeholders – parents, pupils, staff, governors etc. It then carries out an analysis of its internal strengths and weaknesses and external opportunities and threats before identifying the gaps between where it is now and where it wants to be in the future. Out of this analysis

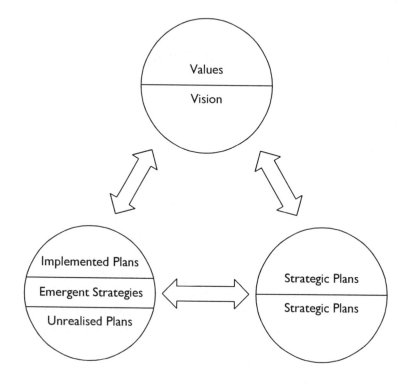

Figure 8.1:   Strategic planning

of the internal and external environments, priorities are established and long-term and short-term plans are produced. As the process takes place, what is done is monitored and evaluated to allow for adjustments. The strength of such an approach lies in the way it roots strategic analysis and planning in vision. In thinking about strategy, however, it is important to allow for unpredicted events and to recognise that strategies can also emerge over time. There are limits to the effectiveness of logic and rational planning in a changing world. Providing people have a clear and shared vision, they are more likely to be able to seize unexpected opportunities that arise and use these. Figure 8.1 above illustrates the processes involved.

To this point a number of ways of thinking about leadership have been considered and importance has been attached to a number of issues:

- the need for teachers and headteachers to identify their own strengths and weaknesses and to attend to their own personal and professional development;

- the need for those in positions of leadership to become more aware of their own strengths and how to use these effectively;
- the idea that there is a range of appropriate styles of leadership and the most appropriate style depends on the people involved, the nature of the task and the circumstances;
- the importance, in the current context of rapid change, of providing a school with a clear and compelling vision so that it has some guiding principles to help it develop;
- the need to root both deliberate, rational planning in this vision, when dealing with predictable matters, and to use it to determine how to respond to unexpected change or external demands.

There are, of course, other ways of thinking about leadership, for example:

Description	Example	Key messages
Leader as steward	Block, 1993	Empowerment, placing control close to where the work is done, accountability dispersed through organisation.
The servant leader	Greenleaf, 1970	Leaders should see themselves as serving others. Involves listening, empathy, sensitivity, foresight and creating a sense of community in the organisation.
Leadership in learning organisations	Senge, 1992	Leader is a designer, steward and teacher.

| Invitational leadership | Stoll and Fink, 1996 | Involves communicating to people that they are valued, trusted and responsible. Involves developing a shared vision and sharing leadership. |
| Leader as educator | Heifetz, 1994 | Get people to face up to problems and work out solutions, even if this involves conflict. |

These views of leadership reflect a world of uncertainty and change. They try to establish an appropriate approach to leadership and separate leadership from traditional constraints of status, hierarchy and power. At a time of rapid change and a knowledge revolution, it has become hard to see one person, however gifted, as having all the necessary expertise and knowledge to take an organisation forward. These ideas rather than emphasising the leadership of a key individual, rest upon a belief in the potential of everyone in an organisation. Essentially, they place the leader in the position of creating the conditions that empower others to take a share in leadership. They contain a strong moral element and rest on a belief in human potential and creativity. They involve integrity on the part of the leader and a climate of trust and respect. Southworth (1998) made this point as follows:

Leadership is not the prerogative of one person, it is a collaborative and corporate act. At any one time, one or more individuals will be leading aspects of the school's work and development and others will be following. At a later time others will be leading and those who formerly led will now be followers. Such an interactive approach to leadership moves staff closer to becoming a 'community of learners' (Sergiovanni, 1994) where staff each play a part in leading aspects of the school. Such leadership is less to do with independence and much more to do with developing interdependent leaders. This interdependence avoids the problems which often occur when there is just one leader. It is not uncommon when a person has a monopoly on leadership for the group to become too reliant on them, for a culture of dependency to form and, sometimes, for a personality cult to develop. Shared leadership strives to unlock the potential colleagues possess. By encouraging leadership at all levels there is a sense of staff participation, engagement and empowerment. The leaders do not 'give away' their power; they encourage others to use their own powers. When this happens the school has much greater power than when a single person is viewed as the powerful one because everyone is literally empowered.

In other words, the emphasis now in schools needs to be on what Naisbitt and Aburdene (1990) referred to as a 'democratic yet demanding leadership that respects people and encourages self-management, autonomous teams, and entrepreneurial units'.

Future trends

These comments about the importance of shared or dispersed leadership take us to the final part of this chapter, which takes the form of a discussion of future trends in education and their possible impact on school leadership.

A good deal of attention has been focused on what education will be like in the future. That the *status quo* is no longer an option is widely acknowledged. For example Collarbone and Shaw (1998) have argued that

> ... there is a fundamental need to reinvent our education system. Over the past few years a growing number of pundits have begun to argue that despite decades of reform there has been little evidence of real change or measurable improvement in school standards.

The education system has to respond to rapid and continuous change and a range of factors in the new century, such as:

- the increasingly radical impact of developments in information and communication technology, providing alternative means of access to information from all over the world;

- a concern for higher standards of achievement, especially in core skills;
- the importance of lifelong learning and continuous updating, re-skilling and personal development;
- the need to operate in a global rather than a local or national context;
- the importance of addressing higher customer expectations and the needs of the community;
- the need to make optimum use of resources;
- the overarching importance of rooting developments in concerns for the quality of life and the protection of the environment.

As the Select Committee noted (1998, para 55):

> Schools will continue to face changing expectations, including the need to ensure higher standards of achievement, collect and analyse more data about children's achievement, offer a wider range of services, adapt educational provision to the needs of the local community and provide education in a range of settings. The rapidly-growing use of information and communications technology (ICT) is also creating new challenges for schools. It follows from all this that the future task of the headteacher is perhaps even more challenging than it is at present.

For school leaders, it is important to engage in thinking about possible future scenarios – futures thinking – in order to develop a vision for the school and to exercise strategic leadership. Help can be gained from a range of authors, (for example, Davies and Ellison, 1997 and 1999), who analyse trends and developments. Among them, Caldwell and Haywood (1998: 118) have provided an interesting analysis of trends that will have an impact on the twenty-first century, arguing that because of the explosion of knowledge and the pervasive and penetrating influence of information technology, the world in the twenty-first century will be fundamentally different from the past. Central to their arguments was the concept that most opportunities for young people will be in knowledge-based work and that, therefore, the key economic resources for developed nations will be the knowledge and intellect of their young people. Thus the most important capacity will be for what has come to be known as 'lifelong learning'.

These trends point to the need to respond to the knowledge revolution and move to a 'learning society'. As Barber (1996: 304) said, we are

> fumbling painfully – to create a learning society from the ashes of industrialism. The policy agenda of the learning society is beginning to form: standards must rise, schools must improve, lifelong learning must become more than an aspiration; and increased investment in education from government, business and individuals is becoming essential.

Barber went on to make the point that the language we use can have a powerful effect on the transition needed. We need to move from asking people, 'what do you do?' to 'what did you learn today?' For Barber, the move to a learning society involved not just improved learning in school, but also an increased emphasis on learning in organised out-of-school locations and learning at home. We can anticipate changes to the way schools are used and organised. As Collarbone and Shaw (1998) argued:

> As information and communications technologies develop, there will be dramatic changes to learning and teaching. The school day will be transformed as will human resource management. There will be re-examination of the type and use of the school buildings and resources. A wide range of professionals and para-professionals will support learning with access to the world's 'great teachers'. There will be team learning and the development of equity and access policies to ensure all benefit from available learning resources.

For the next generation of school children, the school year and the school day are likely to look different. To quote Barber (1996: 259) again, 'we should be aiming to shorten the formal school day and lengthen the learning day'. Schools are likely to be just one means of learning and one source of guidance for people of all ages; to be reference points for the community rather than a workplace for the under eighteen-year-olds.

Clearly these possible changes to schools have implications for school leaders. In this context, headteachers will need to develop, articulate and live a vision for the school, based on an understanding of current and future trends. They will also need to create conditions in which the leadership of a wide range of staff is fostered. The role will involve striking a balance between providing direction and sharing leadership throughout the school community. Who leads and who follows will depend on expertise and the nature of the process being undertaken rather than on formal position. In other words:

> Whatever the future holds in store, the journey to the learning society will require the effective school to encourage self-management of learning and raise insightful views about current reality. It will contain effective leaders who feel empowered to learn and are able to empower others to learn. Effective schools will promote a learning culture, not only for their pupils, but also for their staff and for the communities of which they are a part. The headteacher, as lead learner and teacher, will invite pupils, staff, parents, governors and others in the development of a learning and an achievement culture in the school. (Collarbone and Billingham, 1998: 5-6)

Put another way, unless the headteacher attends to school improvement, it is unlikely to happen. However, unless the headteacher empowers and encourages others and creates conditions in which all can learn and develop, then the degree of improvement will be far less than necessary.

Professional and personal learning for all is very much a part of the learning society. The lifelong learning envisaged for teachers and head-teachers will need to be achieved through a variety of means. A major opportunity is available through developments in information and communication technology, as the development of the National Grid for Learning is beginning to illustrate. Teachers and headteachers are going to be able increasingly to access expertise, information and resources through the Internet. What will be important will be the availability of learning opportunities within and outside the workplace. The concept of high quality training opportunities tailored to meet individual needs and based on a clear analysis of what a job involves is an important one to develop. We are beginning to see how this can be done with the TTA's professional development framework and the development of programmes relevant to different career stages. Fullan (1991: 160-1) referred to a piece of research by Leithwood and Jantzi into the success of school principals in achieving school improvement. He reported that they found the successful principals used six broad strategies in which they:

- strengthened the school's (improvement) culture;

- used a variety of bureaucratic mechanisms to stimulate and reinforce cultural change;
- fostered staff development;
- engaged in direct and frequent communication about cultural norms, values and belief;
- shared power and responsibility with others; and
- used symbols to express cultural values.

Style can vary but what matters is the creation of learning communities that use imaginative and creative ways of continually responding to the rapid pace of change. Leadership in such communities is likely to be shared and dispersed. The Green Paper, (DfEE, 1998c: 25), made this point as follows: 'While heads are of crucial importance, leadership in schools is often shared and studies show that this shared leadership responsibility is a characteristic of successful heads.'

Some of the words of the Select Committee (1998, paragraph 194, 6) provide an appropriate conclusion pointing to the opportunities for choice and diversity:

> There is no single ideal model of school leadership: it will vary according to the needs of a particular school at a given time. Good headteachers clearly share common values and skills and the relative importance of different attributes will vary according to the circumstances of individual schools. The important point is that schools should have the freedom and the capability to choose the right solutions, in terms of people and structures, to allow them to develop all their pupils' potential to the full. This is particularly the case in the light of ongoing changes to the nature of schools ...

Contributors

Mark Brundrett has taught in secondary, middle, and primary schools and was, for five years, the headteacher of a primary school. He was senior lecturer in education at Nene University College, Northampton, where he was Programme Leader for the MA in Education Studies. He has published on a wide range of issues in education including information and communication technology, English, and the sociology of teacher training, as well as education management. He is a highly experienced NPQH trainer and is currently Programme Leader for the MA in Education Management at De Montfort University, School of Education.

Dianne Duncan is a Senior Lecturer in education and teaches English in teacher education programmes at the University of Hertfordshire. In addition to working in two other institutions of higher education, she has been a primary school teacher, headteacher and an Ofsted Inspector. She is author of *Becoming a Primary School Teacher: a study of mature women,* (Trentham Books, 1999).

Dominic Elliott holds the degrees of BA, MBA, and PhD. He has published a number of articles and books in the fields of strategic and crisis management; he is a founder member of the Centre for Business Continuity Planning and is Reviews Editor for *Risk Management: an international journal*. Dominic's keen interest in education is closely linked to his experience as a father of four children and work as a school governor.

Peter Silcock has been involved in teacher education for many years including periods at the University of Hertfordshire and Nene University

College, Northampton. He is Chairman of the Association for the Study of Primary Education (ASPE). He has published widely in the field of education and his latest book is entitled *New Progressivism*.

Ian and Kath Terrell are both highly experienced teachers. Ian Terrell has taught in a number of secondary schools. He was a lecturer at Anglia Polytechnic University and De Montfort University before returning to Anglia Polytechnic University as principal lecturer in charge of continuing professional development. He has published a number of books and articles on education management. Kath Terrell has extensive experience as a primary teacher and she is currently the headteacher of a primary school.

Neil Burton has taught as a maths, science and technology teacher in both secondary and primary schools, and was an adviser for science education, publishing a wide range of books, materials and articles on science and mathematics as well as on education management. He has acted as consultant to a number of publishers. He is currently lecturer in education management at Leicester University Education Management Development Unit where he contributes to the Master of Business Administration programme.

Jan Wilson has been the headteacher of a small rural primary school, an infant and nursery school and a large inner-city primary school. She was principal lecturer at Bishop Grosseteste University College, Lincoln, where she was responsible for continuing and in-service education, and where she continues to lead the MA in Primary Education. She has also been a Primary Inspector in Northamptonshire. Currently she is working with primary and secondary schools in the maintained and independent sectors in both the United Kingdom and overseas; she is a trainer and moderator for the National Professional Qualification for Headship in the East Midlands, an assessor for the Advanced Skills Teacher Qualification, and she is carrying out research into how schools and headteachers manage change effectively.

Rob Bollington spent the first fifteen years of his career in a variety of teaching and management roles in secondary schools. He has subsequently carried out a range of other roles in education. He was a member of the evaluation team for the 1987/9 School Teacher Appraisal

Pilot Study and was responsible for the co-ordination of appraisal for Bedfordshire LEA. More recent work has included overall responsibility for management and professional development in Bedfordshire and being Head of Maryland College, a centre for personal and professional education for adults. He is currently Centre Manager of the East Midlands Training and Development Centre for the National Professional Qualification for Headship. He has published in the areas of appraisal, evaluation and professional development.

References

Adair, J. (1988) *Effective Leadership*. London: Pan Books.

Adams, K. (1996) "Competency's American origins and the conflicting approaches in use today", *Competency*, 3, 2, 44-8.

Adey, P. and Shayer, M. (1994) *Really Raising Standards*. London: Routledge.

Alexander, R. (1998) "Basics, cores and choices: towards a new primary curriculum", *Education 3-13*, 26, 2, 60-9.

Alexander, R. (1992) *Policy and Practice in Primary Education*. London: Routledge.

Ansoff, I. (1991) "Critique of Henry Mintzberg's 'The Design School': reconsidering the basic premises of strategic management", *Strategic Management Journal*, 12, 449-61.

Atkinson, R.L., Atkinson, R.C., Smith, E.E., Bem D.J. and Hilgard, E.R. (1990) *Introduction to Psychology* (10th edn). London: Harcourt, Brace, Jovanovich.

Bagley, C., Woods, P. and Glatter, R. (1997) "Scanning the market: school strategies for discovering parental preferences" in M. Preedy, R. Glatter, and L. Levacic (1997) *Educational Management: strategy quality and resources*. Buckingham: Open University Press.

Bailey, A. and Johnson, G. (1997) "How strategies develop in organisations" in M. Preedy, R. Glatter, and L. Levacic (1997) *Educational Management: strategy quality and resources*. Buckingham: Open University Press.

Bailey, T. (1986) "Recent trends in management training for headteachers: a European perspective" in E. Hoyle (ed.) *World Yearbook of Education 1986: the Management of Schools*. London: Kogan Page.

Ballinger, E.A. (1985) *An Interim Analysis of Available Evaluation Reports on Basic and OTTO Programmes*. National Development Centre for School Management Training, Bristol: University of Bristol School of Education.

Barber, M. (1996) *The Learning Game*. London: Victor Gollancz.

Barnes, C. (1993) *Practical Marketing for Schools*. Oxford: Blackwell.

Barnett, R.A. (1994) *The Limits of Competence*. Buckingham: SRHE and Open University Press.

Barnett, R.A. (1987) "Part-time degree courses: institutional provision in the UK", *Higher Education Review*, 20, 1, 7-25.

Barth, R. (1986) "On sheep and goats and educational reform", *Phi Delta Kappan*, 4, 293-6.

Baumol, W. and Blinder, A. (1994) *Economics: principles and policy* (6th edn). London: Dryden Press.

Baxter, C. (ed.) (1977) *Economics and Education Policy: a reader*. Harlow: Longman.

Bazalgette, J. (1996) "Greater than a mere sum of skills", *Times Educational Supplement*, 31 May, 17.

Beare, H., Caldwell, B.J. and Millikan, R.H. (1992) *Creating an Excellent School*. London: Routledge.

Bell, L. (1988) *Management Skills in Primary Schools*. London: Routledge.

Bell, J. and Harrison, B. (1995) *Vision and Values in Managing Education*. London: Fulton.

Bennett, N. (1976) *Teaching Styles and Pupil Progress*. London: Open Books.

Bennett, S.N. (1992) *Managing Learning in the Primary Classroom*. Stoke on Trent: ASPE/Trentham Books.

Bennett, S.N. (1987) "Changing perspectives on teaching and learning processes in the post-Plowden era", *Educational Psychology*, 13, 1, 67-79.

Bennis, W. (1989) *On Becoming a Leader*. Massachusetts: Addison and Wesley.

Bennis, W. and Nanus, B. (1985) *Leaders: The strategies for taking charge*. New York: Harper and Row.

Birch, D. (1989) "Program budgeting for colleges" in R. Levacic (ed.) *Financial Management in Education*. Buckingham: Open University Press.

Blake, R. and Mouton, S. (1964) *The Managerial Grid*. Houston, Texas: Gulf Publishing.

Blanchard, K, Zigarmi, P. and Zigarmi, D. (1994) *Leadership and the One Minute Manager*. London: Harper Collins.

Blaug, M. (1970) *An Introduction to the Economics of Education*. London: Allen Lane.

Blaug, M. (1968) *Economics of Education: Selected Readings*. London: Penguin.

Blyth, H.A.L. (1984) *Development, Experience and Curriculum in Primary Education*. London: Croom Helm.

Bolam, R. (1997) "Management development for headteachers", *Educational Management and Administration*, 25, 3, 265-83.

Bolam, R. (1984) *First Year of the NDCSMT: a progress report*. Bristol: University of Bristol.

Bolam, R., McMahon, A., Pocklington, K. and Weindling, D. (1993) *Effective managers in schools – a report for the Department for Education via the School Management Task Force Professional Working Party*. London: HMSO.

Bowles, G. (1992) *Education Management Development Project: Final Report*. CEMD: North West Region.

Bowman, C., Asch, D. (1996) *Managing Strategy*. London: Macmillan.

Bradford, S. and Cohen, M. (1984) *Managing for Excellence: a guide to developing high performance in company organizations*. New York: Wiley.

Brimblecombe, N., Ormston, M. and Shaw, M. (1996) "Gender differences in teacher response to school inspections", *Educational Studies*, 22, 1, 27-9.

Brockman, F. (1989) "Program budgeting: implications for secondary principals" in R. Brookman, K. and Anderson, K. (eds.) (1992) *Educational Administration*. Harlow: Longman.

Brundrett, M. (1998) "What lies behind collegiality, legitimation or control?", *Educational Management and Administration*, 26, 3, 10-27.

Buckley, J. (1985) *The Training of Secondary School Heads*. Windsor: NFER Nelson.

Burchell, H. (1995) "A useful role for competence statements in post-compulsory teacher education?", *Assessment and Evaluation in Higher Education*, 20, 3, 252-9.

Burns, J.M. (1978) *Leadership*. New York: Harper and Row.

Bush, T. (1986) *Theories of Educational Management*. London: Harper and Row.

Bush, T. (ed.) (1989) *Management of Education: theory and practice*. Milton Keynes: Open University Press.

Bush, T. (1998) "Organisational culture and strategic management" in D. Middlewood and J. Lumby (1998) *Strategic Management in Schools and Colleges*. London: Paul Chapman Publishers.

Bush, T. and West-Burnham, J. (eds.) (1994) *The Principles of Educational Management*. Harlow: Longman.

Bush, T., Glatter, R., Goodey, J. and Riches, C. (eds.) (1980) *Approaches to School Management*. London: Harper.

Busher, H. and Paxton, L. (1997) "HEADLAMP – a local experience in partnership" in H. Tomlinson (ed.) (1997) *Managing Continuing Professional Development in Schools and Colleges*. London: Paul Chapman.

Caldwell, B.J. and Haywood, D.K. (1998) *The Future of Schools: lessons from the reform of public education*. London: Falmer Press.

Caldwell, B.J. and Spinks, J. (1992) *Leading the Self-Managing School*. London: Falmer Press.

Carr, W. (1995) *For Education: towards a critical educational enquiry*. Buckingham: Open University Press.

Cave, E. and Wilkinson, C. (1992) "Developing managerial capabilities in education" in M. Bennett, M. Crawford and C. Riches (eds.) *Managing Change in Education*. London: Paul Chapman.

Chapman, J. (1993) "Leadership, school-based decision-making and school effectiveness", in C. Dimmock (ed.) *School-based Management and School Effectiveness*. London: Routledge.

Cheong Cheng, Y. (1996) "Effectiveness of curriculum change in school", *International Journal of Educational Management*, 8, 3.

Chomsky, N. (1959) "Review of 'Verbal Behaviour' by B.F. Skinner", *Language*, 35, 226

Chown, A. (1994) "Beyond competence", *British Journal of In-service Education*, 20, 2, 161-80.

Clerkin, C. (1985) "What do primary heads actually do all day?", *School Organization*, 15, 4, 63-84.

Cohen, W.A. ((1990) *The Art of a Leader*. Englewood Cliffs, New Jersey: Prentice Hall.

Cole, M. and Wertsch, S.V. (1996) "Beyond the individual and social antimony in discussions of Piaget and Vygotsky", *Human Development*, 39.

Coleman, J.S., Campbell, E., Hobson, C., McPartland, J., Mood, A., Weinfield, F. and York, R. (1996) *Equality of Educational Opportunity*. Washington: National Centre for Educational Statistics.

Collarbone, P. and Billingham, M. (1998) *Leadership and Our Schools*. London: Institute of Education.

Collarbone, P. and Shaw, R. (1998) "Learning how to lead", *Times Educational Supplement*, 4 December.

Coombs, P. and Hallak, J. (1987) *Cost Analysis in Education*. Boston: John Hopkins University Press.

Coopers and Lybrand (1988) *Local Management of Schools*. London: HMSO.

Crawford, M., Kydd, L. and Parker, S. (eds.) (1994) *Educational Management in Action: a collection of case studies*. London: Paul Chapman.

Crawford, M., Kydd, L. and Riches C. (1997) *Leadership and Teams in Educational Management*. Buckingham: Open University Press.

Cullen, E. (1992) "A vital way to manage change", *Education*, 13, November, 3-17.

Davies, B. and Ellison, L. (1999) *Strategic Direction and Development of the School*. London: Routledge.

Davies, B and Ellison, L. (1997) *School Leadership for the 21st Century: a competency and knowledge approach*. London: Routledge.

Davies, L. (1987) "The role of the primary school head", *Educational Management and Administration*, 15, 1.

Davies, B. (1994) "Models of decision making in resource allocation" in T. Bush and J. West-Burnham (eds.) *The Principles of Educational Management*. Harlow: Longman.

Davies, J.L. and Morgan, A.W. (1983) "Management of higher education in a period of contraction and uncertainty", in O. Body-Barrett, T. Bush, J. Goodey, J. McNay and M. Preedy (eds.) *Approaches to Post School Managemement*. London: Harper and Row.

Day, C. (1988) "In-service as consultancy: the evaluation of a management programme for primary school curriculum leaders" in C. Aubrey (ed.) *Consultancy in the U.K., its Role and Contribution to Educational Change*. Sussex: Falmer Press.

Day, M. (1990) "Management competences come out", *Competence and Assessment*, 13, 3-5.

Deal, T.E. and Kennedy, A. (1983) "Culture and school performance", *Educational Leadership*, 40, 5, 140-1.

Deal, T.E. and Kennedy, A. (1982) *Corporate Cultures*. London: Penguin Business.

DeHayes, D. and Lovrinic, J. (1994) "ABC model for assessing economic performance", *New Directions for Institutional Research*, 82, 81-93.

Dennison, W.F. (1985) "Research report: training headteachers as managers: current trends and developments", *Durham and Newcastle Research Review*, 2, 221-4.

DES (1985) *Effect of Local Authority Expenditure Policies on Education Provision in England*. London: HMSO.

DES (1983) *The In-Service Teacher Training Grants Scheme* (Circular 3/83). London: HMSO.

Desforges, C. (1997) "Children's application of knowledge". Paper delivered to the tenth ASPE (Association for the Study of Primary Education) annual conference, Dartington Hall, Devon.

Desforges, C. (1993) "Children's learning: has it improved?", *Education 3-13*, 213, 3-10.

DfEE (1998a) *Excellence in Schools*. London: HMSO.

DfEE (1998b) *Governors Guide to Law*. London: HMSO.

DfEE (1998c) *Teachers: meeting the challenge of change*. London: The Stationery Office.

DfEE (1997) *From Targets to Action – guidance to support effective target setting in schools*. London: HMSO.

DfEE (1996a) *Teamwork and School Improvement*. London: HMSO.

DfEE (1996b) *Guidance on Good Governance*. London: HMSO.

DfEE, Ofsted, BIS (1995) *Governing Bodies and Effective Schools*. London: Ofsted.

Donaldson, A.G. and Marnik, G.F. (1995) *Becoming Better Leaders*. California: Corwin Press.

Downes, P (1997) "Managing school finance" in B. Davies and L. Ellison (eds.) *School Leadership for the 21st Century: a competency and knowledge approach*. London: Routledge.

Downes, P. and Holt, A. (1996) *Working Together – Great Expectations – Getting the Head/Governor Relationship Right in Improving Schools*. London: DfEE.

Driver, R. (1989) "Students' conceptions and the learning of science", *International Journal of Science Education*, 11 (special issue), 481-90.

Driver, R. and Bell, B. (1986) "Students' thinking and the learning of science: a constructivist view", *School Science Review*, 67, 443-56.

Dudley, J. (1992) *Profiling and Competences: Final Report*. West Midlands Regional Collaborative Project: University of Wolverhampton.

Duignan, P. (1989) "Reflective management, the key to quality leadership" in C. Riches and C. Morgan *Human Resource Management in Education*. Buckingham: Open University Press.

Duignan, P. (1988) "Reflective management: the key to quality leadership", *International Journal of Education Management*, 2, 2, 11-23.

Duignan, P.A. and Macpherson, R.J.S. (1992) *Effective Leadership: a practical theory for new educational managers*. London: Falmer Press.

Dunworthy, J. and Bottomly, P. (1973) "Economics in academe", *Higher Education Review*, 3, 25-34.

Earley, P. (1992) *The School Management Competences Project*. Crawley: School Management South.

Earley, P. (1991) "Defining and assessing school management competences", *Management in Education*, 5, 4, 31-4.

Earley, P. (1993) "Developing competence in schools: a critique of standards-based approaches to management development", *Educational Management and Administration*, 21, 4, 233-44.

Ecclestone, K. (1994) "Democratic values and purposes: the overlooked challenge of competence", *Educational Studies*, 20, 2, 155-66.

Edwards, R. (1993) "A spanner in the works: Luddism and competence", *Adults Learning*, 4, 5, 124-5.

Egan, C. (1995) *Creating Competitive Advantage*. London: Butterworth Heinemann.

Eisner, E. (1993) "Objectivity in educational research" in M. Hammersley (ed.) *Educational Research, vol I*. Milton Keynes: Open University Press.

Elliott, D. and Smith, D. (1993) "Learning from tragedy: sports stadia disasters in the U.K.", *Industrial and Environmental Crisis Quarterly*, 7, 3, 205-30.

Elliott, J. (1991) *Action Research for Educational Change*. Buckingham: Open University Press.

Enderud, J. (1980) "Administrative leadership in organised anarchy", *International Journal of Institutional Management in Higher Education*, 4, 3, 235-53.

Eraut, M. (1994) *Developing Professional Knowledge and Competence*. London: Falmer Press.

Etzioni, A. (1975) *A Comparative Analysis of Complex Organisations*. New York: Free Press.

Evans, K. (1986) "Creating a climate for school leadership", *School Organisation*, 6, 1, 56-78.

Everard, K. (1986) *Developing Management in Schools*. Oxford: Blackwell.

Everard, B. and Morris, G. (1990) *Effective School Management*. London: Paul Chapman.

Fenstermacher, G. (1986) "Philosophy of research on teaching: three aspects" in M.C. Witrock (ed.) *Handbook of Research on Teaching* (3rd edn). New York: MacMillan.

Fielden, J. and Pearson, P. (1989) "Costing education practice" in R. Levacic (ed.) *Financial Management in Education*. Buckingham: Open University Press.

Fiedler, F. (1969) "Leadership: a new model" in C.A. Gibb (ed.) *Leadership*. Harmondsworth: Penguin.

Fielding, M. (1984) "Asking different questions and pursuing different views" in J. Maw *Education plc?* London Institute of Education and Heinemann: London.

Firestone, W.A. (1991) "Introduction" in J.R. Bliss, W.A. Firestone and C.E. Richards (eds.) *Rethinking Effective Schools: Research and Practice.* Englewood Cliffs, New Jersey: Prentice Hall.

Fitz-Gibbon, C. (1995) *The Value Added National Project: Issues to be considered in the Design of a National Value Added System.* London: School Curriculum and Assessment Authority.

Foster, W. (1989) "Towards a critical practice of leadership" in W.J. Smyth (ed.) *Educating Teachers: changing the nature of pedagogical knowledge.* Lewes: Falmer Press.

Fullan, M.G. (1993) *Change Force: probing the depths of educational reform.* London: Falmer.

Fullan, M.G. (1992) *What's Worth Fighting for in Headship?* Milton Keynes: Open University Press.

Fullan, M.G. (1991) *The New Meaning of Educational Change.* London: Cassell.

Fullan, M.G. and Hargreaves, A. (1992) *What's Worth Fighting for in Your School?* Buckingham: Open University Press.

Galton, M. (1998) "Back to consulting the ORACLE", *Times Educational Supplement, Briefing, Research Focus,* 3 July, 24.

Galton, M. (1989) *Teaching in the Primary School.* London: David Fulton.

Galton, M. and Simon, B. (1980) *Progress and Performance in the Primary Classroom.* London: Routledge & Kegan Paul.

Gardner, H. (1993) *Multiple Intelligences: the Theory in Practice.* New York: Basic Books.

Gardner, H. (1985) *The Mind's New Science: a history of the cognitive revolution.* New York: Basic Books.

Gardner, H. (1984) *Frames of Mind.* London: Fontana.

Giles, C. (1995) "School based planning: are UK schools grasping the strategic initiative", *International Journal of Educational Management,* 9, 4.

Glatter, R. (1997) "Context and capability in educational management", *Educational Management and Administration,* 25, 2, 181-92.

Goddard, D., Leask, M. (1992) *The Search for Quality. Planning for Improvement and Managing Change.* London: Paul Chapman.

Goldstein, H. (1996) "Relegate the leagues", *New Economy,* 2, 3, 199-203.

Goldstein, H. (1995) *Multilevel Statistical Models* (2nd edn). London and New York:

Gorringe, R. (1994) *Changing the Culture of a College.* Blagdon: Coombe Lodge Reports. Edward Arnold and Halstead Press.

Grace, G. (1995) *School Leadership: beyond education management.* London: Falmer Press.

Gray, L. (1991) *Marketing in Education.* Buckingham: Open University Press.

Gray, H.L. (1982) *The Management of Educational Change.* Sussex: Falmer Press.

Gray, J. (1990) "The quality of schooling: frameworks for judgements", *British Journal of Educational Studies,* 38, 3, 204-33.

Gray, J. and Wilcox, B. (1996) "The challenge of turning around ineffective schools" in P. Woods (ed.) *Contemporary Issues in Teaching and Learning.* London and New York: Routledge in association with the Open University.

Gray, J. and Wilcox, B. (1995) "In the aftermath of an inspection: the nature and fate of inspection report recommendations", *Research papers in education,* 10, 1-18.

Gray, P. (1984) *Method Assistance Report, Program Paper and Report* (Series no. 104). Portland, Oregon: NW Regional Educational Lab.

Griffiths, M. and Tann, S. (1992) "Using reflective practice to link personal and public theories", *Journal of Education for Teaching*, 18, 1, 69-84.

Gross, R.D. (1992) *Psychology: the science of mind and behaviour* (2nd edn). London: Hodder and Stoughton.

Hager, P. (1995) "Competency standards – help or a hindrance? An Australian perspective", *The Vocational Aspect of Education*, 47, 2, 141-51.

Hall, V., Mackay, H. and Morgan, C. (1986) *Headteachers at Work*. Milton Keynes: Open University Press.

Halford, G.S. (1995) "Learning processes in cognitive development: a reassessment with some unexpected implications", *Human Development*, 38, 295-301.

Halsey, A.H. and da Silva, K. (1987) "Plowden: history and prospect", *Oxford Review of Education*, 13, 1, 3-23.

Handy, C. (1994) *The Empty Raincoat: making sense of the future*. London: Hutchinson.

Handy, C. (1993) *Understanding Organizations*. London: Penguin.

Hans, J. (1996) *Cost Accounting in Higher Education: simple macro- and micro costing techniques*. London: NACUBO.

Hargreaves, A. (1994) *Changing Teachers, Changing Times: Teachers' Work and Culture in the Postmodern Age*. London: Cassell.

Harkley, H. (1989) "Zero based budgeting for schools" in R. Levacic (ed.) *Financial Management in Education*. Buckingham: Open University Press.

Heifetz, R.A. (1994) *Leadership Without Easy Answers*. Cambridge, Massachusetts: Harvard University Press.

Hellawell, D. (1988) "OTTO revisited: training and management performance: some perceptions of headteachers by subordinates", *Journal of Educational Studies*, 14, 2.

Hersey, P. and Blanchard, K. (1982) *Management of Organizational Behavior: utilizing human resources* (4th edn). Englewood Cliffs: Prentice-Hall.

Herzberg, F. (1966) *Motivation to Work*. New York: Wiley.

Hofstede, E. (1991) "Measuring organisational cultures: a qualitative and quantitative study across twenty cases", *Administrative Science Quarterly*, June, 286-316.

Holmes, G. (1993) *Essential School Leadership*. London: Kogan Page.

Hooper, R. (1971) *The Curriculum: context, design and development*. Milton Keynes: Open University Press.

Hopkins, D. (1989) *Evaluation for School Development*. Buckingham: Open University Press.

Hopkins, D., Ainscow, M. and West, M. (1994) *School Improvement in an Era of Change*. London: Cassell.

Hornby, D. and Thomas, R. (1989) "Towards a better standard of management", *Personnel Management*, 21,1, 52-5.

Horngren, C., Foster, G. and Datar, S. (1994) *Cost Accounting: a management emphasis*. London: Prentice Hall.

House, E. (1989) "The dominance of economic accountability" in R. Levacic (ed.) *Financial Management in Education*. Buckingham: Open University Press.

Howson, J. and Mitchell, M. (1995) "Course costing in devolved institutions: perspectives from an academic department", *Higher Education Review*, 25, 3, 7-35.

Hoyle, E. (1986) *World Yearbook of Education: the Management of Schools*. London: Kogan Page.

Hughes, M (1988) "Leadership in professionally staffed organisations" in R. Glatter, *et al.* *Understanding School Management*. Milton Keynes: Open University Press.

Hyland, T. (1993a) "Training, competence and expertise in teacher education", *Teacher Development*, 2, 7, 117-22.

Hyland, T. (1993b) "Professional development and competence-based education", *Educational Studies*, 19, 1, 123-32.

Hyland, T. (1993c) "Competence, knowledge and Education", *Journal of Philosophy of Education*, 27, 1, 57-68.

Innes, J. and Mitchell, F. (1991) *ABC – A Review With Case Studies*. London: CIMA

James, C. and Phillips P. (1997) "The practice of educational marketing in schools" in M. Preedy, R. Glatter and L. Levacic (1997) *Educational Management*. Buckingham: Open University Press.

Jencks, C.S., Smith, M., Ackland, H., Bane, M.J., Cohen, D., Gintis, H., Heyns, B. and Micholson, S. (1972) *Inequality: A Reassessment of the Effect of of Family and Schooling in America*. New York: Rinehart & Winston.

Jenkins, H.O. (1991) *Getting It Right: a handbook for successful school leadership*. Oxford: Blackwell.

Jirasinghe, D. and Lyons, G. (1996) *The Competent Head: a job analysis of heads' tasks and personality factors*. London: Falmer Press.

Jirasinghe, D. and Lyons, G. (1995) "Management competencies in action: a practical framework", *School Organisation*, 15, 3, 267-82.

John, D. (1980) *Leadership in Schools*. London: Heinemann.

Johnes, G. (1993) *The Economics of Education*. London: Macmillian.

Johnson, G. and Scholes, K. (1997) *Exploring Corporate Strategy: Text and Cases* (3rd edn). London: Prentice Hall.

Jones, A. (1987) *Leadership for Tomorrow's Schools*. London: Heinemann.

Jones, D. (1989) "A practical cost approach to budgeting and accountability in colleges" in R. Levacic (ed.) *Financial Management in Education*. Buckingham: Open University Press.

Joyce, B., Calhoun, E., Hopkins, D. (1997) *Models of Learning. Tools of Teaching*. Buckingham: Open University Press.

Joyce, B. and Showers, B. (1988) *Student Achievement Through Staff Development*. New York: Longman.

Kandola, B. (1996) "Putting competency into perspective", *Competency*, 4, 1, 31-4.

Kedney, R. (1991) "Costing open and flexible learning", *OLS News*, 30, 1-14.

Kedney, R. and Davies, T. (1994) "Cost reduction and value for money", *Coombe Lodge Report*, 24, 441-524.

Kitchener, R.F. (1996) "The nature of the social for Piaget and Vygotsky", *Human Development*, 39, 243-9.

Knight, B. (1983) *Managing School Finance*. London: Heinmann.

Kogan, M. (1986) *Education Accountability: an analytic overview*. London: Hutchinson.

Kotter, J. and Schlesinger, L.A. (1979) *Organisation: text cases and readings on the management of organisational design and change*. Homewood, Ill.: Irwin.

Leat, D.K. (1993) "Competence, Teaching, Thinking and Feeling", *Oxford Review of Education*, 19, 4, 499-510.

Leithwood, K.A. (1987) *Preparing School Leaders for Educational Improvement*. Kent: Croom Helm.

Leithwood, K.A., Begley, P.T. and Cousins, J.B. (1992) *Developing Expert Leadership for Future Schools*. London: Falmer Press.

Leithwood, K.A., Cousins, B. and Smith, M. (1989) "A description of the principal's world from a problem solving perspective", *Canadian School Executive*, 9, 9-12.

Leithwood, K.A. and Stager, M. (1989) "Expertise in principals' problem solving", *Educational Administration Quarterly*, 25, 126-61.

Levacic, R. (ed.) (1990) *Financial and Resource Management in Schools*. Buckingham: Open University Press.

Levacic, R. (ed.) (1989) *Financial Management in Education*. Buckingham: Open University Press.

Levin, H. (1975) "Cost-effectiveness analysis in evaluation research" in M. Guttentag and E. Struening (eds.) (1975) *Handbook of Evaluation Research*. London: Sage

Lipsey, R. (1992) *Positive Economics*. London: Weidenfeld and Nicholson.

Lipsey, R. and Halsey, R. (1992) *First Principles of Economics*. London: Weidenfeld and Nicholson.

Liverta-Sempio, O. and Marchetti, A. (1997) "Cognitive development and theories of mind: towards a contextual approach", *European Journal of Psychology of Education*, XII, 1, 3-21.

Lloyd, K. (1981) *Primary School Headship Types – A Study of the Primary Head's Leadership Role Perceptions* (M.Ed Thesis). University of Birmingham.

Louis, K.S. and Miles, M.B. (1990) *Improving the Urban High School: What Works and Why*. London: Cassell.

Luban, L. (1989) "Neoprogressive visions and organisational realities", *Harvard Educational Review*, 59, 217-22.

Lucariello, J. (1995) "Mind, culture, person: elements in a cultural psychology", *Human Development*, 38, 2-8.

Lucey, T. (1996a) *Quantitative Techniques* (5th edn). London: DP Publications.

Lucey, T. (1996b) *Costing* (5th edn). London: DP Publications.

Lumby, J. (1995) "Concepts or competence", *Education*, November 17.

Lund, G. (1990) *Educational Management: Research to identify the Educational Management Development and Training Needs of Primary Headteachers and Deputy Headteachers* (M.Phil Thesis). University of Nottingham.

Lyons, G. (1976) *Heads Tasks: A Handbook of Secondary School Administration*. Windsor: NFER.

Mace, J. (1993) "University funding and university efficiency", *Higher Education Review*, 25/2, 7-22.

MacGilchrist, B., Myers, K. and Read, J. (1997) *The Intelligent School*. London: Paul Chapman.

Management Charter Initiative (MCI) (1990) *Occupational Standards for Managers*. London: Department of Employment and NFMED.

Maslow, A. (1954) *Motivation and Learning*. New York: Harper and Row.

Maw, J. (1984) *Education plc? Headteachers and the new training initiative*. London: University of London.

McClelland (1963) "The achievement motive in economic growth" in B.F. Hoselitz and I. Moore (eds.) *Industrialisation and Society*. The Hague: UNESCO.

McGill, E. and Hendrey, L.B. (1989) "Primary headteachers' perceptions of their management roles and training requirements", *Scottish Educational Review*, 21, 1, 14-25.

McGregor Burns, J. (1978) *Leadership*. New York: Harper and Row.

Mercer, N. (1991) "Accounting for what goes on in classrooms, what have Neo-Vygotskians got to offer?", *Journal of the British Psychological Society*, 15, 1, 61-7.

Middlewood, D. and Lumby, J. (1998) *Strategic Management in Schools and Colleges*. London: Paul Chapman.

Millar, R. (1989) "Constructive criticism", *International Journal of Science Education*, 11 (special issue), 587-96.

Millett, A. (1998) *New Leadership Programme Takes Shape* (http://www. coi.gov.uk/coi/depts/GTT/coi353le.ok).

Mintzberg, H. (1991) "Learning 1 Planning 0. Reply to Igor Ansoff", *Strategic Management Journal*, 12, 463-6.

Mintzberg, H. (1990) "The design school reconsidering the basic premises of strategic management", *Strategic Management Journal*, 11, 171-95.

Mintzberg, H. (1983) *The Structuring of Organisations*. London: Prentice Hall.

Mintzberg, H. (1973) *The Nature of Managerial Work*. New York: Harper and Row.

Mintzberg, H. and Waters, J.A. (1985) "Of Strategies Deliberate or Emergent", *Strategic Management Journal*, July/September, 257-72.

Mitroff, I. and Pauchant, T.C. (1988) "Crisis prone versus crisis avoiding organisations: is your company's culture its own worst enemy in creating crises?", *Industrial Crisis Quarterly*, 2, 53-63.

Morgan C., Hall, V. and Mackay, H. (1983) *The Selection of Secondary School Headteachers*. Milton Keynes: Open University Press.

Morgan, M. (1986) *Images of Organisation*. Newbury Park, California: Sage.

Morris, G. and Murgatroyd, S. (1986) "Management for diverse futures: the task of school management in an uncertain future", *School Organisation*, 6, 2, 46-63.

Mortimore, P. (1991) "The nature and findings of school effectiveness research in the primary sector" in S.Riddell and S.Brown (eds.) *School Effectiveness Research: Its Messages for School Improvement*. London: HMSO.

Mortimore, P. and Whitty, G. (1997) "Can school improvement overcome the effects of disadvantage?" in B. MacGilchrist, B. Myers and J. Read *The Intelligent School*. London: Paul Chapman.

Mortimore, P., Sammons, S., Stoll, L., Lewis, D. and Ecob, R. (1988) *School Matters: the Junior Years*. London: Paul Chapman.

Murgatroyd, S. and Morgan, C. (1993) *Total Quality Management and the School*. Buckingham: Open University Press.

NAHT (1988) *School Management*. Sussex: National Association of Headteachers.

Naisbitt, J. and Aburdene, P. (1990) *Megatrends 2000*. London: Pan.

Nanus, B. (1992) *Visionary Leadership: creating a compelling sense of direction for your organization*. San Francisco: Jossey Bass Publishers.

Nelson, K., Plesa, D., Henseler, S. (1998) "Children's theory of mind: an experiential interpretation", *Human Development*, 41, 7-29.

Nias, J., Southworth, G. and Campbell, P. (1992) *Whole School Curriculum Development in the Primary School*. London: Falmer.

Nias, J. (1980) "Leadership styles and job satisfaction in primary schools" in T. Bush, R. Glatter, J. Goodey and C. Riches (eds.) *Approaches to School Management*. London: Harper and Row.

Ofsted (1995) *Guidance on Inspection*. London: H.M.S.O.

Packwood, T. (1989) "Return to the hierarchy", *Educational Management and Administration,* 17, 1, 9-15.

Packwood, T. (1977) "The school as a hierarchy", *Educational Administration,* 5, 2, 1-6.

Paisey, A. (1981) *Organisation and Management in Schools.* New York: Longman.

Palfreyman, D. (1991) "The art of costing and the politics of pricing" in *Promoting Education,* Part 2, 26-7.

Parkay, F.W. and Hall, G.E. (eds.) (1992) *Becoming a Principal: the challenge of beginning leadership.* London: Allyn and Bacon.

Pauchant, T. and Mitroff, I. (1989) "Do (some) organisations cause their own crises? The cultural profiles of crisis-prone vs. crisis-prepared organisations", *Industrial Crisis Quarterly,* 3, 269-83.

Peters, T. (1987) *Thriving on Chaos.* New York: Knopf.

Peters, T. and Waterman, R. (1982) *In Search of Excellence.* New York: Harper and Row.

Pettifor, J. (1984) *The Economics of the Polytechnic Sector of Higher Education: a study of the determinants of unit cost variations in polytechnics* (Thesis). Trent Polytechnic.

Pickering, J. (1997) "Involving pupils", *Research Matters,* 6.

Plowden Report (1967) *Children and their Primary Schools vol. I & II* (Report of the Central Advisory Council for Education in England). London: HMSO.

Pollard, A. and Tann, S. (1992) *The Reflective Practitioner in the Primary School: a handbook for the classroom* (2nd edn). London: Cassell.

Pollard, A. (1990) *Learning in Primary Schools.* London: Cassell.

Pope, M. (1993) "Anticipating teacher thinking" in C. Day, J. Calderhead and P. Denicolo *Research in Teacher Thinking: understanding professional development.* London: Falmer Press.

Porter, M. (1985) *Competitve Advantage.* New York: Free Press.

Poster, C. and Day, C. (1988) *Partnership in Education Management.* London: Routledge.

Powell, D. (1992) *The Development of Self-Support Groups.* Leeds: University of Leeds/CCDU.

Preedy, M., Glatter, R. and Levacic, L. (1997) *Educational Management.* Buckingham: Open University Press.

Preedy, M. (1993) *Managing the Effective School.* Buckingham: Open University Press.

Purkey, W.W. and Novak, J. (1990) *Inviting School Success* (3rd edn). Belmont, CA: Wadsworth.

Purkey, S.C. and Smith, M.S. (1983) "Effective Schools: A Review", *Elementary School Journal,* 83, 4, 427-52.

Resnick, C.B., Bill, V. and Lesgold, S. (1992) "Developing thinking abilities in arithmetic classs" in A. Demitriou, M. Shayer, A. Efklides *Neo-Piagetian Theories of Cognitive Development, Implications and Applications for Education.* London: International Library of Psychology.

Reynolds, D. and Farrell, S. (1996) *Worlds Apart? A Review of International Surveys of Educational Achievement Involving England.* London: Ofsted.

Reynolds, D. (1992) "School effectiveness and school improvement in the 1990s" in D. Reynolds and P. Cuttance (eds.) *School Effectiveness Research: Policy and Practice.* London: Cassell.

Reynolds, D. (1991) "Changing ineffective schools" in M. Ainscow (ed.) *Effective Schools For All.* London: David Fulton.

Reynolds, D. (1982) "The search for effective schools", *School Organisation*, 2, 3, 215-37.

Riches, C. and Morgan, C. (1989) *Human Resource Management in Education*. Buckingham: Open University Press.

Rosenholtz, S. (1989) *Teachers' Workplace: The Social Organisation of Schools*. New York: Longmans.

Rudduck, J., Chaplain, R. and Wallace, G. (eds.) (1996) *School Improvement – What pupils can tell us*. London: David Fulton.

Rutter, M., Maughan, B., Mortimore, P. and Ouston, J. (1979) *Fifteen Thousand Hours: Secondary Schools and their Effects on Children*. Shepton Mallet: Open Books.

Salomon, G. and Gibberson, T. (1987) "Skills may not be enough: the role of mindfulness in learning transfer", *International Journal of Educational Research*, 11, 6, 623-37.

Sammons, P., Thomas, S. Mortimore, P. (1997) *Forging Links. Effective Schools and Effective Departments*. London: Paul Chapman.

Sammons, P., Hillman, J. and Mortimore, P. (1995) *Key Characteristics of Effective Schools: a Review of School Effectiveness Research* (Report Commissioned by the Office for Standards in Education). London: Institute of Education and Office for Standards in Education.

Samuelson, P. (1995) *Economics*. London: McGraw-Hill.

SCAA (1996) *An Analysis of the 1995 GCSE Results and Trends Over Time*. Middlesex: SCAA.

Scheerens, J. (1992) *Effective Schooling: research, theory and practice*. London: Cassell.

Schein, E. (1985)*Organisation, Culture and Leadership: A Dynamic View*. San Francisco: Jossey-Bass.

Schon, D.A. (1987) *Educating the Reflective Practitioner: Towards a New Design for Teaching and Learning in the Professions*. London: Jossey Bass.

Schon, D.A. (1983) *The Reflective Practitioner*. San Francisco: Jossey-Bass.

Select Committee on Education and Employment (1998) *Ninth Report* (http://www.parliament.the-stationery-off...9798/cmselect/ cmeduemp/725/72511.htm#a54).

Senge, P. (1992) *The Fifth Discipline: the art and practice of the learning organisation*. New York: Century Business.

Sergiovanni, T. (1994) *Building Community in Schools*. San Francisco: Jossey Bass.

Shama, R. (1986) "Course cost modelling in Australian tertiary education", *Journal of Tertiary Educational Administration*, 8, 1, 87-92.

Sheehan, J. (1973) *The Economics of Education*. London: Allen and Unwin.

Silcock, P.J. (1999) *New Progressivism*. London: Falmer Press.

Silver, P. (1983) *Education Administration: theoretical perspective on practice and research*. New York: Harper and Row.

Smith, L. (1996) "With knowledge in mind: novel transformation of the learner or transformation of novel knowledge?", *Human Development*, 30, 257-63.

Smyth, J. (1989) *Critical Perspectives on Educational Leadership*. Lewes: Falmer Press.

Southworth,G. (1998) *Leading Improving Primary Schools*. London: Falmer Press.

Southworth, G. (1988) "Looking at leadership: English primary school headteachers at work", *Education 3-13*, 2, 53-6.

Squire, W. (1987) *Education Management in the United Kingdom*. Aldershot: Gower.

Stacey, R. (1997) *Strategic Management and Organisational Dynamics* (2nd edn). London: Pitman.

Stephenson, J. (1994) "Capability and competence", *Capability*, 1, 1, 3-4.

Stewart, R. (1983) *Choices for Managers*. Maidenhead: McGraw-Hill.

Stoll, L. (ed.) (1996) "Assessing school effectiveness in school improvement network", *Research Matters*.

Stoll, L. and Fink, D. (1996) *Changing Our Schools: linking school effectiveness and school improvement*. Buckingham: Open University Press.

Stone, M. ((1992) "Cost analysis in an educational setting", *Studies in Educational Administration*, 57, 1-11.

Sutherland, P. (1992) *Cognitive Development Today: Piaget and his critics*. London: Paul Chapman.

Tannenbaum, R. and Schmidt, W.H. (1958) "How to choose a leadership pattern", *Harvard Business Review*, 36, 95-101.

Terrell, I., Leask, M. (1997) *Development Planning and School Improvement for Middle Managers*. London: Kogan Page.

Terrell, I. (1992) "Distant and deep: A report on the collaborative research and development of a distant and deep learning project" (Research Paper no. 1). Middlesex University.

Thomas, G. (1997) "School inspection and school improvement". Paper given to the 1997 British Educational Research Association annual conference, University of York.

Thomas, H. (1987) "Efficiency and opportunity in school finance autonomy" in H. Thomas and T. Simpkins (eds.) *Economics and the Management of Education: emerging themes*. London: Falmer.

Thomas, S. and Mortimer, P. (1996) "Comparison of value added models for secondary school effectiveness", *Research Papers in Education*, 11, 1, 5-33.

Throsby, C. (1986) "Cost functions for Australian universities", *Australian Economic Papers*, 25, 47, 175-92.

Torrington, D. and Weightman, J. (1993) *Managing Human Resources* (2nd edn). London: Institute of Personnel Management.

TTA (1998a) *National Standards for Headteachers*. London: Teacher Training Agency.

TTA (1998b) *National Standards for Qualified Teacher Status; Subject Leaders; Special Educational Needs; Headteachers*. London: Teacher Training Agency.

TTA (1998c) *The Teacher Training Agency Corporate Plan 1998–2001*. London: Teacher Training Agency.

TTA (1997) *Teacher Training Agency: annual rview 1997*. London: Teacher Training Agency.

TTA (1996) *Teaching as a Research-based Profession*. London: Teacher Training Agency.

TTA (1995) *HEADLAMP 3/95* (HEADLAMP Programme Document Appendix 2). London: Teacher Training Agency.

Tuckwell, T., Billingham, M. (1997) "Managing Learning and Teaching" in B. Davies, L. Ellison (1997) *School Leadership for the 21st Century*. London: Routledge.

Turner, C. (1990) *Organisational Culture*. Blagdon: Mendip Papers.

Turney, P. (1996) *ABC – The Performance Breakthrough*. London: Kogan Page.

Tysome, T. (1996) "Cushions to soften the heavy blows", *Times Higher Educational Supplement*, 1 March, 10-11.

Vaill, P.B. (1991) *Managing as a Performing Art: new ideas for a world of chaotic change*. San Francisco: Jossey-Bass.

Vaizey, P. (1973) *The Economics of Education*. London: Macmillan.

Valsiner, J. (1992) "Internalization and externalization of constraint systems" in A. Demitriou, M. Shayer, A. Efklides *Neo-Piagetian Theories of Cognitive Development, Implications and Applications for Education*. London: International Library of Psychology.

VanderMolen, J.A. (1995) "Then and now: lessons of a new principal" in R. Thorpe (ed.) *The First Year as Principal*. New Hampshire: Heinemann.

van Velzen, W., Miles, M., Ekholm, M., Hameyer, U. and Robin, D. (1985) *Making School Improvement Work: A Conceptual Guide to Practice*. Lerven, Belgium: Acco.

Verba, M. (1994) "The beginnings of collaboration in peer interaction", *Human Development* 37, 125-39.

Voss, J.F. (1987) "Learning transfer in subject-matter learning: a problem-solving model", *International Journal of Educational Research* 11, 6.

Vygotsky, L.S. (1978) *Mind in Society: the development of higher psychological processes*. Cambridge, Massachussets: Harvard University Press.

Vygotsky, L.S. (1962) *Thought and Language*. Cambridge, Massachussets: M.I.T. Press.

Walker, D. (1998) "Time is the great leveller", *The Guardian*, 18 August.

Walker, J.T. (1996) *The Psychology of Learning*. New Jersey: Prentice-Hall.

Wallace, G. (1996) "Engaging with learning" in J. Rudduck, R. Chaplain and G. Wallace (eds.) *School Improvement: What Can Pupils Tell us?* London: David Fulton.

Wallace, M. (1988a) *Action Learning: practice and potential in school management development*. Bristol: NDC.

Wallace, M. (1988b) *Improving School Management Training: Towards a New Partnership*. Bristol: NDC.

Wallace, M. (1988c) "Innovation for all: management development in small primary schools", *Educational Management and Administration*, 16, 1.

Wallace, M. and Hall, V. (1994) *Teamwork in Secondary School Management*. London: Paul Chapman.

Webb, R. and Vulliamy, G. (1995) "The changing role of the primary deputy headteacher", *School Organisation*, 15, 1, 53-63.

Weindling, D. (1997) "Strategic planning in schools: some practical techniques" in M. Preedy, R. Glatter and R. Levacic *Educational Management: Strategy, Quality and Resources*. Buckingham: Open University Press.

Weir, S. (1989) "The computer in schools: machine as humanizer", *Harvard Educational Review*, 59, 1, 61-73.

West-Burnham, J. (1997) *Managing Quality in Schools* (2nd edn). London: Pitman Publishing.

West-Burnham, J. and O'Sullivan, F. (1998) *Leadership and Professional Development in Schools*. London: Pitman.

Wertsch, J.V. (1991) *Voices of the Mind*. Hemel Hempstead: Harvester-Wheatsheaf.

White, P. (1987) "Self respect, self esteem and the management of educational institutions", *Educational Management and Administration*, 15, 2, 87-98.

White, R. and Lippitt, R. (1959) "Leader behaviour and member reaction in three social climates" in D. Cartwright and A. Zander (eds.) *Group Dynamics, Research and Theory*. London: Tavistock.

Whitehead, G. (1996) *Economics* (15th edn). Oxford: Oxford University Press.

Whitaker, P. (1993) *Managing Change in Schools*. Buckingham: Open University Press.

Whittington, R. (1993) *What is Strategy – and does it matter*. London: Routledge.

Williams, A., Dobson, P. and Walters, M. (1989) *Changing Culture* (2nd edn). London: Institute of Personnel Management.

Wilkinson, M. and Howarth, S. (1996) "What are they looking for and how do we know?", *Education 3-13*, June, 32-6.

Winkley, D. (1983) "An analytical view of primary school leadership", *School Organisation*, 3, 1.

Wood, A.D. (1982) "A training college for headteachers of secondary schools; some thoughts and consideration", *School Organization*, 3, 3, 287-96.

Woods, P.A. (1993) "Responding to the consumer: parental choice and school effectiveness", *School Effectiveness and School Improvement*, 4, 3, 205-9.

Woodhead, C. (1997) *Ofsted Report – Standards and Quality in Education 1996/97* (http://www.official-documents.co.uk/document/Ofsted/ciar/comment.htm).

Wye, R. (1993) "Quality through investors in people". Speech at Institute of Quality Assurance Conference. PLACE?

Young, P. (1984) "The headteacher as manager" in J. Maw *Education plc?* London: University of London.

Zalenik, A. (1992) "Managers and leaders: are they different?", *Harvard Business Review*, March/April, 126.

Index

A

accountability, xiii, 15, 138, 139, 148, 150, 193, 194
Accreditation of Prior Learning, xii
action research, 78, 89, 118, 119
activity based costing, 134
Adair, 159, 187
Adey and Shayer, 73, 75, 77-9
adhocracy, 67
ambiguity models, 144
assessment centres, xii

B

Barber, 181, 187
behaviourism, 73
Bennis and Nanus, 154, 158, 171
Blake and Mouton, 165
Blanchard, 112, 168, 169, 188, 193
budgetary cycle, 132
Bush, 10, 64, 68, 130, 143-5, 189, 190, 196

C

Caldwell and Spinks, 97
Carr, 89, 189
character, 159
Chomsky, 73, 189
Circular 3/83, 2, 3
classical market theory, 125
classical model of strategy, 47
cognitive psychologists, 75
cognitive revolution, 73, 192
collaborative planning, 101

Collarbone and Billingham, 170, 182
collegial models, 143
collegiality, 35, 112, 143
competence movement, 1, 11, 13, 14
complexities of school management, 102
constructivist theory of education, 111
contingency theories, 167
contingency theory, 62
Coopers & Lybrand, 131
corporate planning, 45
costing, 125, 127-30, 132, 134, 135, 193
costing education, 129
cost volume profit, 128
cultural models, 144
culture, 18, 22, 31-3, 36, 38, 39, 43, 46, 52, 61, 63, 64, 68, 81, 84, 100, 101, 104, 105, 111, 112, 140, 144, 165, 172, 179, 182, 189, 190, 193, 195, 198

D

DeHayes and Lovrinic, 124, 135
DES, 2-4, 6, 96, 103, 190
Desforges, 75, 190
disinvitation, 40
Donaldson and Marnik, 155
Driver, 82
duties of a governing body, 147

E

Earley, 12, 13, 16, 161, 191
economic cost, 126
Education Act (1944), 99

Education Reform Act, 123, 125
effective learning, 24, 71, 118
  schools, 23, 30, 182
  teaching, 71
efficient and effective deployment of staff
  and resources, xiii, 122
emergent strategy, 47
environmental analysis, 51
ethical intelligences, 41
Etzioni, 113, 191
excellence in schools, 119, 190

F
Fiedler, 167, 168, 191
fixed cost, 126
From targets to action, 103, 190
Fullan, 35, 36, 104, 106, 108, 109, 112,
  149, 182, 183, 192

G
Galton, 25, 76, 79, 93, 192
generating and selecting options, 60
governance, 146, 151, 190
governing bodies and effective schools,
  147
governing body, 140, 146, 147, 149, 151,
  152, 157
Grace, 154, 192, 196
Grant Maintained Schools, 123, 148

H
Handy, 120, 141, 142, 159, 166, 168-70,
  193, 201
HayMcBer, 11, 15
HEADLAMP, xi, 1, 14, 117, 189, 199
Headteachers' Leadership and Manage-
  ment Programme, see HEADLAMP
hierarchical models, 142, 144
high performing staff, 114
HMI, 6, 7
Hopkins, Ainscow and West, 1, 36
hypothesis testing, 84

I
IIP, 103, 113, 115, 117
improving quality of education for all, 36

intelligent school, 40, 41
internal analysis, 56
Invitational leadership, 40

J
Johnson & Scholes, 64

L
LEA, 2, 4, 7, 9, 34, 51, 116, 123-6, 130,
  140, 141, 148, 150, 152, 157, 186
leadership, xi, xiii, 1, 5, 6, 8, 11, 12, 14-16,
  18, 22, 24, 26, 31, 32, 38, 40, 46, 61-3,
  68, 70, 88, 99, 101-6, 108, 109, 111-14,
  116-18, 120, 121, 138, 139, 141, 143-5,
  148-50, 153-65, 167-81, 183, 187-99,
  201
leadership programme for serving headteachers, see LPSH
leadership style, 165, 167, 168
leading and managing staff, xiii, 96
league tables, 28, 29
learning new ideas, 83
learning society, 181, 182
learning style, 83
Leithwood, 8-10, 12, 182, 183, 194, 195
Levacic, 47, 130-2, 187, 188, 191, 193-5,
  200, 201
LMS, 18, 102, 123, 131, 189
Local Management of Schools, see LMS
local reputation, 53
LPSH, xi, xii, 1, 15, 117, 161

M
Management Charter Initiative, see MCI
management of learning, 72, 182
management of teaching, 86
marketing, 51, 53-5, 194
Maslow's hierarchy of physiological
  needs, 119
maximum efficiency, 127
MCI, 11, 12, 13, 161, 195
megatrends, 97
metanarratives, 72
micropolitical forces, 112
micro-economics, 127, 128
  of education, 124

Millett, 153, 196
Mintzberg, 6, 44, 45, 48, 66, 67, 69, 196
moral involvement, 113
Mortimore, 1, 8, 17, 19, 20, 22-7, 29, 41,
    196, 198, 201
Murgatroyd and Morgan, 173, 175

N
Nanus, 155, 171, 172, 188, 196
National Association of Head Teachers,
    6, 11
National Commission on Education, 110
National Curriculum, 18, 23, 25, 29, 75,
    76, 92, 93, 110, 112, 123, 136, 140, 147,
    148
    Tests, 18
national development centre, 2, 187
National Education Assessment Centre,
    161
National Professional Qualification for
    Headship, see NPQH
National Standards for Headteachers, xiii, 15,
    152, 160, 201
need for more systematic training, 6
Nolan Committee, 139
NPQH, xi-xiii, 1, 15, 117, 118, 184

O
Ofsted, 23, 27, 33, 65, 69, 71, 77, 86, 87,
    89, 92, 96, 103, 115, 117, 137, 184, 201
One Term Training Opportunities, see
    OTTO(s)
OTTO(s), xi, 1-5, 7, 15, 16, 187, 193

P
physical infrastructure, 53
Piaget, 73, 77, 189, 194, 199
PLESCT, 51
Plowden Report, 1, 17, 76, 197, 201
Pollard, 76, 89, 197
problems of conceptual confusion, 10
processual school, 46, 61
professional development, 1, 14, 43, 90,
    96, 97, 115-18, 120, 121, 150, 163, 164,
    177, 182, 186
program and incremental budgeting, 131

psychological theories of learning, 74

R
readiness, 83
reflective practice, 87, 89, 90
reflective practitioners, 88, 89
relevance of structure to strategy, 67
Resnick, 79
Reynolds, 17, 33, 76, 113, 118, 197, 198
Rutter, 1, 17, 18, 21-3, 25, 29, 198, 201

S
Sammons, 19, 24-32, 35, 87, 196, 198
SCAA, 29, 110, 198
Schein, 38, 39, 63, 198
Schon, 16, 87, 89, 90, 198
School Curriculum and Assessment
    Authority, see SCAA
school and departmental outcomes, 32
    development planning, 102, 103
    effectiveness, xi, xii, 1, 8, 16, 18, 21-5,
    27-9, 31-3, 35, 36, 38, 39, 142, 154, 189,
    196, 201
    effectiveness and improvement, xiii, 17
School Management South, 12, 13, 161,
    191
School Management Task Force, 12, 13,
    188
School Teachers Pay and Conditions of
    Employment, 8
Select Committee, 161, 172, 174, 180,
    183, 198
Senge, 48, 108, 117, 152, 177, 198, 201
Senior Management Team, see SMT
sharing meanings, 85
skilled teaching, 82, 87
SMT, 32
Southworth, 5, 9, 155, 172, 178, 198
stakeholder groups, 47, 49, 50, 55, 60, 70
stakeholders, 45, 49-51, 53, 55, 62, 70, 99,
    145, 175
strategic leadership, xiii, 42
    management, 42-7, 60, 68, 70, 146, 189
strategic planning, 42, 145, 175
strategy process, 43, 45-8, 55, 60, 62, 64,
    70

T

Tannenbaum and Schmidt, 165
task engagement, 76
Teacher Training Agency, see TTA
teaching and learning, xiii, 15, 71, 188,
    192, 198
team approach, 103, 104
Total Quality Management, see TQM
TQM, 173, 196
transformational, 107, 108, 162, 170, 172
TTA, xi-xiii, 1, 14-16, 96, 97, 105, 115-
    19, 160, 161, 163, 182, 199, 201

U

unit cost, 128, 133
United States Department of Education,
    24

V

value added, 18, 28-31, 135
    chain for a school, 57
values, 19, 21, 25, 38, 42, 48-50, 63, 64,
    91, 93, 94, 104, 105, 107-9, 111, 143-5,
    149, 154, 155, 162, 171, 172, 174, 183,
    191
variable cost, 126
vision, 9, 26, 31, 35, 42-4, 47-50, 60-2, 64,
    68-70, 84, 103-9, 111, 115, 145, 147,
    150, 155, 158, 161, 162, 164, 170-5, 177,
    178, 180, 181

W

Wallace, 2, 7, 9, 11, 68, 81, 200
Weindling, 45, 50, 106, 145, 150, 175,
    188, 200, 201
West-Burnham, 97, 105, 116, 122, 130,
    156, 189, 190, 200, 201
Woodhead, 153, 201

Z

Zalenik, 154, 201
zero-based budgeting, 131